Battles and Battlefields of the Peninsular War

Charles J. Esdaile

Helion & Company

In memory of my dear friend Jesus Maroto de las Heras to whose kindness and generosity this book owes more than I can possibly say.

Helion & Company Limited
Unit 8 Amherst Business Centre
Budbrooke Road
Warwick
CV34 5WE
England
Tel. 01926 499619
Email: info@helion.co.uk
Website: www.helion.co.uk
X (formerly Twitter): @Helionbooks
Facebook: @HelionBooks
Visit our blog at helionbooks.wordpress.com

Published by Helion & Company 2024
Designed and typeset by Mach 3 Solutions (www.mach3solutions.co.uk)
Cover designed by Paul Hewitt, Battlefield Design (www.battlefield-design.co.uk)

Text © Charles J. Esdaile 2024
Maps by George Anderson © Helion & Company 2024
Illustrations © as individually credited
Cover: The battlefield of Salamanca, author's photo

ISBN 978-1-804515-45-7

British Library Cataloguing-in-Publication Data.
A catalogue record for this book is available from the British Library.

For details of other military history titles published by Helion & Company Limited, contact the above address, or visit our website: http://www.helion.co.uk

We always welcome receiving book proposals from prospective authors.

Contents

Preface

The Peninsular War of 1808–1814 is a subject that is much beloved by history buffs and wargamers: as the perusal of the following pages will show, the literature it has generated is enormous, while it continues to grow, sometimes almost by the day. Yet, for all that, there is one aspect of the subject that has been explored rather less than might have been expected, and that is the terrain over which the war was fought, this being something that is all the more strange in view of the increasing number of visitors who descend on the sites concerned, not to mention the ever greater interest in the wider area of heritage tourism. To the best of my knowledge, then, there is only one guidebook to the battlefields, viz. A. Rawson, *The Peninsular War: a Battlefield Guide* (Pen and Sword, 2009). To Rawson's work may be added a book of colour photographs edited by Ian Fletcher, viz. *The Peninsular War: Wellington's Battlefields Revisited* (Pen and Sword, 2012), but the focus of both works is very much the operations of the Anglo-Portuguese army, a problem that is thrown into high relief by the fact that careful analysis of the lists of French officer casualties elaborated a century or more ago by the historian, Aristide Martinien, shows that only 31 percent of the 38,000 Frenchmen who fell in battle in the struggle lost their lives in combats involving British troops. It is therefore scarcely unreasonable to suggest that there might be room for a further title, and all the more so if it is one that offers an approach that is rather more inclusive. However, it is not just a matter of extending battlefield tourism to sites that would otherwise get few visitors. The photographs in this work were, for the most part, taken during the bicentenary of the conflict – a period which saw the author travel extensively in Spain, Portugal and south-west France as Academic Vice-President of Peninsular War 200, the Ministry of Defence commission charged with over-seeing Britain's participation in the commemorations. With battlefields tending to be situated on important axes of communi-cation or the outskirts of major cities, it is hoped that the images will not just make it easier to visualise the fighting but also be important as a record of the sites. Even as it is, many have been completely lost, while others are currently being threatened by development, as, for example, at Albuera where the famous 'Bloody Hill' has recently been put forward as a possible site of a solar-power farm. With very few Peninsular battlefields covered by protec-tive legislation, the author therefore cannot but hope that this slim work will do something to assist those working to ensure their survival.

As ever, my debts are many. First and foremost, perhaps, should come the man to whom this work is dedicated, namely my good friend, Jesus Maroto de las Heras. An official of the Spanish Ministry of Agriculture who had risen high in the regulation of the olive industry, Jesus was a rather reserved individual, and yet he befriended me at an early date and never ceased to be a ready source of wisdom and advice, while he showed immense generosity in showing me around the sites of the Peninsular War. Without him, this book would be much the poorer, while his death from a rare form of cancer early in 2021 remains a source of immense grief. Next to Jesus must come Nicholas Lipscombe, my military counterpart in Peninsular War 200, a great friend whose companionship sustained me immensely in the often hectic days of 2008–2014. Third of all, of course, is Andrew Bamford of Helion Books, without whom this book would never have taken wing. Fourth, there are other Spanish friends like Leopoldo Stampa, Francisco Luis Díaz Torrejón, Carlos Rilova and Gonzalo Serrats who accompanied me on visits to such battlefields as Talavera, Sagunto, San Marcial and the Nive. And, last but not least, there is my beautiful Sinéad in regard to whom nothing I write will ever do justice.

Charles J. Esdaile
Douglas, Isle of Man, 19 July 2023

Introduction: The Peninsular War, 1808–1814

A bloodbath that may have cost the lives of 500,000 people, the Peninsular War was the fruit of over-confidence, *folie de grandeur* and miscalculation. In October 1807 with the permission and assistance of the Spanish government, French troops were sent by Napoleon to occupy Portugal in order to close it off to British trade. The royal family escaped to Brazil, but resistance was non-existent, and there seems little reason to believe that the French would have experienced more than minor local difficulties in the ordinary course of events. However, impelled by little more than opportunism, as autumn turned to winter Napoleon resolved on intervention in the complicated politics of the Spanish court, his aim being to make Spain a more effective ally. This proved a disastrous mistake. In March 1808 a palace coup had replaced King Charles IV with the heir to the throne, Ferdinand VII. Thanks to the propaganda of powerful elements of the Catholic Church and an aristocracy bent on opposing Bourbon reformism who had seized on the vacuous and malleable Ferdinand as a 'trojan horse', the new king had come to be seen as a 'Prince Charming' who would put all Spain's many ills to rights. French intervention, and, more specifically, the occupation of the capital by a large army commanded by *maréchal* Joachim Murat followed by the invitation of the entire royal family to a 'conference' with Napoleon in Bayonne, therefore provoked unrest: there was, for example, a serious riot in Madrid on 2 May. In consequence, news that Ferdinand had been forced to abdicate in favour of Napoleon's brother, Joseph, was the catalyst for a series of revolts in the many parts of the country that had remained unoccupied by the French, a similar wave of rebellion soon gripping Portugal.

The nature of this revolt has been widely misunderstood. The subject is a complex one, but in short it was not the unanimous uprising for God, king and fatherland of legend. Popular concern was not for the Bourbons or the Braganças, but rather land, bread and revenge on the propertied classes, whilst the leaders of the insurrection entertained a variety of conflicting interests which they sought to pursue at the same time as channelling the people's energies into fighting the French. In consequence, the political history of the war is one of great complexity – its chief feature is the elaboration of a liberal constitution in Spain in 1812 – whilst the background to the struggle was everywhere one of desertion, banditry, agrarian unrest, and resistance to conscription. In those areas actually occupied by the French, true, the invaders were inconvenienced by much irregular resistance, but close analysis of this phenomenon has suggested that in most cases it bore little resemblance to the legend so beloved of the traditional historiography. On close inspection, indeed, much of the 'little war' proves to have been the work of forces of regular troops or local militias raised and controlled by representatives of the Patriot state. At the same time, such irregular bands as were formed were drawn in large part from men who had either already been bandits in

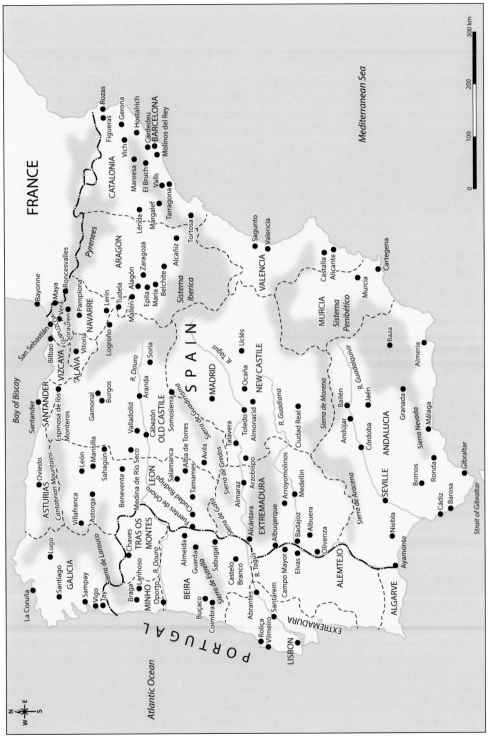

The Iberian Peninsula.

1808 or been drawn into banditry since the start of the war. A prime example here is constituted by the many men who fled to the hills to avoid conscription to the Spanish army, or
who had deserted after being called up. With other men brought in by impressment of one
sort or another, it is in consequence hard to see how the Spanish struggle against Napoleon
can really merit the description of a 'people's war'. All the more is this the case given the fact
that those guerrilla bands which were not militarised in the style of such forces commanded
by the erstwhile peasants, Juan Martín Díez and Francisco Espoz y Mina, did not follow
the French as they evacuated their areas of operation in the latter part of the war, but rather
battened upon the civilian inhabitants and the baggage trains of the Allied armies.

The Militarily speaking, the history of the war is much simpler. Initially, the French armies
were roughly handled, the forces sent to Portugal being expelled by a British expeditionary
force under Lieutenant General Sir Arthur Wellesley (later Duke of Wellington) after a
battle at Vimeiro (21 August 1808) and another contingent forced to surrender at Bailén by
the Spaniards. Other forces, meanwhile, were repulsed from Valencia and Gerona, whilst
Zaragoza not only beat off an initial assault, but also withstood a full-scale siege despite the
fact that it was devoid of regular fortifications. Forced to draw back beyond the River Ebro,
the invaders then received major reinforcements, whilst Napoleon himself came to Spain to
take charge of operations. There followed a whirlwind campaign which saw the Spaniards
suffer major defeats at Espinosa de los Monteros, Gamonal, Tudela and Somosierra. With
the Spanish armies in tatters, on 4 December the Emperor therefore recaptured Madrid.
Meanwhile, the position had also been restored in Catalonia, where the French army of
occupation had for the last few months been bottled up in Barcelona, the Spaniards having
been routed by fresh forces dispatched from France at Cardedeu and Molins de Rei. With
matters in this situation, it seemed entirely possible that the French would go on to overrun the entire Peninsula and end the war at a stroke. All possibility of this, however, was
precluded by a last-minute intervention in the campaign on the part of the British. Having
cleared the French from Portugal, the British expeditionary force had advanced into Spain
under the command of Lieutenant General Sir John Moore. For various reasons it had taken
a long time for it to get ready for action, and for a while it looked as if the British commander
would have no option but to withdraw into Portugal. Eventually, however, Moore resolved
on an offensive against the French communications in Old Castile. As this brought the full
weight of the French armies in northern Spain against his 20,000 men, he was soon forced
to retreat to the coast of Galicia in search of rescue by the Royal Navy, but so many troops
were pulled after him that the French had effectively to abandon their plans for the immediate conquest of Portugal and southern Spain. As for Moore and his army, almost all the
troops were rescued after a rearguard action at La Coruña on 16 January 1809, but their
commander was mortally wounded by a cannon ball at the moment of victory.

The campaign of November 1808–January 1809 set the pattern of operations for the whole
of the next year. In brief, the French controlled most of central and northern Spain, together
with a separate area around Barcelona, whilst Spanish armies held southern Catalonia, the
Levante, Andalucía and Extremadura. As for Portugal, it, too, was in Allied hands with a
British garrison in Lisbon and such few troops as the Portuguese themselves could muster
deployed to protect Elvas, Almeida and Oporto. Called away from Spain by growing fears
of a new war with Austria, Napoleon had left instructions for the various commanders he
had left in Spain – most notably, *maréchaux* Jean de Dieu Soult, Michel Ney and Claude

Perrin (better known by his sobriquet of 'Victor') to crush Allied resistance by a series of powerful offensives, but this plan quickly foundered. The Spanish armies defending Andalucía proved unexpectedly aggressive while the British reinforced their presence in Portugal and, now commanded once again by Sir Arthur Wellesley, repelled a French invasion. Notwithstanding the evacuation of Moore's army, the province of Galicia rose in revolt, and the cities of Zaragoza and Gerona both put up desperate resistance in the face of renewed French attacks (in the case of Gerona, indeed, it did not fall until December). By the summer, then, the initiative had passed to the Allies, the rest of the year being dominated by two major attempts to recover Madrid. Of these, the first – an Anglo-Spanish offensive from the west and south – led merely to stalemate. Thus, a major tactical triumph at Talavera gained almost entirely by the British was deprived of all effect, first, by the arrival of massive French reinforcements released by the fortuitous evacuation of Galicia one month earlier, and, second, serious divisions in the Allied command. The second offensive, however, was a far more serious affair. In the wake of Talavera, Wellesley – now Lord Wellington – refused to engage in any further operations with the Spaniards, and pulled his men back to the Portuguese frontier. In consequence, the offensive was the work of the Spaniards alone. Operating on exterior lines from the north-west, the west and the south in terrain that greatly favoured the vastly superior French cavalry, however, they had no chance and were routed at the battles of Ocaña and Alba de Tormes with terrible losses.

The defeat of the main Spanish field armies and the British decision to concentrate on the defence of Portugal opened a new phase in the conflict. So serious had been the Spanish losses in the campaigns of 1809 that there was little left to put into the line. Nor could these losses be made up: though generous, British supplies of arms and uniforms were insufficient to the task of equipping whole new armies from scratch, whilst resistance to conscription amongst the populace was greater than ever. Meanwhile, with the new Austrian war fought and won, Napoleon was pouring large numbers of fresh troops into Spain, the result being that the initiative passed back to the French. With the Spaniards further emasculated by the outbreak of revolution in Latin America – by now their chief source of revenue – for the next two years the picture is one of constant French advances. City after city fell into the invaders' hands whilst the Spaniards lost more and more of such troops and sinews of war as remained to them. First to fall were Seville, Granada, Córdoba, Málaga and Jaén, all of which were overrun by a massive French offensive in January 1810, whilst these were followed by Oviedo, Astorga, Ciudad Rodrigo, Lérida, Tortosa, Badajoz and Tarragona. By late 1811 all that was left of Patriot Spain was Galicia, the Levante, and the blockaded island city of Cádiz, which had in 1810 become the new capital. Penned up inside Portugal, the British, meanwhile, could do nothing to arrest the march of French conquest, whilst much the same is true of the Spanish guerrillas, who at the same time were coming under more and more pressure. In the end, indeed, it is clear that Napoleon's commanders could have crushed resistance in Spain and then marched against Portugal in such overwhelming force that even Wellington could not have overcome them. All that was needed was for the French armies in the Peninsula to receive a constant stream of replacements and reinforcements. Thanks to the impending invasion of Russia, however, in 1812 the supply of men dried up, the Armée d'Espagne even being stripped of a number of troops. As was only to be expected, the result was that the French forces suddenly found themselves badly over-extended, and all the more so as Napoleon insisted that they continue with the offensive against Valencia which they had begun in the autumn of 1811.

What saved the Allied cause in the Peninsula was therefore not Wellington's genius but rather Napoleon's errors. This, however, is not to decry the British commander's very real contribution to the Allied cause. Particular attention should be paid here to his defence of Portugal in 1810–1811. In accordance with France's resumption of the offensive in the Peninsula in 1810, the summer of that year saw some 68,000 men under *maréchal* André Masséna move across the Portuguese frontier and besiege the fortress of Almeida. This fell very rapidly thanks to the chance explosion of its main powder magazine and the consequent destruction of much of the town, and the French moved on towards Lisbon. Wellington, however, had anticipated such a move and put together a comprehensive plan for the defence of Portugal. From the beginning the countryside in the path of the invaders would be devastated and the French forces harassed by the irregular home guard known as the *ordenança*. If possible, the French would then be brought to battle and forced to retreat, to which end the Portuguese army had been completely rebuilt under the direction of *Marechal do Exército* William Beresford and the main routes toward Lisbon blocked by field works at a number of obvious defensive positions. Failing that, however, the countryside would continue to be devastated, whilst the Anglo-Portuguese army would continue to fall back on Lisbon, along, or so it was hoped, with the bulk of the civilian population. Waiting for them would be probably the greatest single engineering feat in the entire Napoleonic era in the form of the so-called Lines of Torres Vedras, this being an impenetrable belt of fortifications stretching from one side of the peninsula on which Lisbon was built to the other. Whether this plan would have sufficed to hold off the French had they ever unleashed the sort of massive offensive that would have followed the final conquest of Spain is unclear – Wellington, for one, certainly had his doubts – but against the 65,000 men eventually brought against them by Masséna, it was more than adequate. Despite achieving complete success on the battlefield itself, an attempt to turn the French back at Buçaco failed due to Masséna's discovery of an unguarded track round Wellington's northern front, but when the French reached the Lines of Torres Vedras they found that they could go no further. In this situation Masséna did his best, but, deprived of adequate supplies, he could not continue to blockade the lines forever, and in March 1811 he abandoned his headquarters at Santarem and fell back on the Spanish frontier.

However, clearing Masséna from Portugal was one thing, and invading Spain quite another. For the whole of 1811, indeed, the situation on the Portuguese frontier was a stalemate. Authorised by the British government to enter Spain once more, Wellington soon found that this was easier said than done. The crucial border fortresses of Ciudad Rodrigo and Badajoz had been greatly strengthened by the French whilst every attempt to besiege them was met by massive French counter-offensives, as at Albuera and Fuentes de Oñoro. Repelled though these last were, they cost Wellington heavy losses and dissuaded him from marching too far into Spain, whilst progress was in any case rendered still more difficult by the fact that the Anglo-Portuguese army lacked an adequate siege train. Of course, the French were in no better state: twice, indeed, they refused battle rather than attack the British commander in powerful defensive positions inside Portugal, whilst an attempt on Elvas or Almeida (now back in Allied hands again) would have been out of the question. But that is not the point, what matters being rather the simple fact that for the whole of 1811 the British remained able to exert only the most marginal influence on the situation in Spain.

In the autumn of 1811, however, the situation changed dramatically. In the first place, Wellington took delivery of a powerful siege train of a sort he had been completely lacking, and in the second the effect of Napoleon insisting that the French commanders in Spain should continue to expand the territory under their control and, in particular, to continue with the offensive they had launched against Valencia, at the very time that he was pulling men out of Spain and cutting the supply of reinforcements completely destabilised the position on the Portuguese frontier: in brief, the French no longer had the men they needed to contain Wellington. What followed was all too predictable. Seeing his chance, the Anglo-Portuguese commander struck across the border and was quickly able to capture the fortresses of Ciudad Rodrigo and Badajoz, win a major victory at Salamanca and liberate Madrid. Thanks to a variety of problems, of which by far the greatest were the *de facto* collapse of government and society in Spain, and his failure to take the citadel the French had constructed to overawe the city of Burgos, in November 1812 Wellington was again forced to retreat to Portugal, but the French were never fully able to recover and were further weakened by the withdrawal of still more troops in the early months of 1813. Aided by the continued attempts of the French to hold more territory than they could garrison, in May 1813 Wellington was therefore able to launch a fresh offensive that led to the defeat of King Joseph's main field forces at Vitoria on 21 June, after which, Catalonia and a few scattered garrisons aside, most of what remained of his domains had to be evacuated. Bitter fighting continued in the Pyrenees, with the French vainly trying to relieve the besieged fortresses of San Sebastián and Pamplona, but they were repelled at Sorauren and San Marcial, whilst in October 1813 Wellington invaded France and, after several fierce battles, established himself in an unassailable position south of Bayonne. Though French troops stayed in part of Catalonia until the end of hostilities in April of the following year, to all intents and purposes the Peninsular War was over, the battles that Wellington went on to fight at Orthez and Toulouse really belonging more to the campaign of 1814: not for nothing did Sir William Napier call his famous narrative *A History of the War in the Peninsula and the South of France*.

The significance of the Peninsular War was considerable. British historians have, for obvious reasons, been inclined to emphasise the part that it played in the downfall of Napoleon, whilst the Emperor also assigned it much importance, famously calling it his Spanish ulcer. But in this respect its effects have probably been exaggerated. Whilst it gripped the imaginations of many German nationalists, for example, it did not persuade the people of Germany to heed the various attempts to get them to rise against Napoleon that were made in the course of 1809. Nor did it do much to erode the Emperor's war-making capacity: it is hard, for instance, to see how the forces caught up in the Peninsular War would have made much difference in Russia in 1812. Nevertheless, the continued struggle in the Peninsula undoubtedly strengthened the credibility of British diplomacy in the period 1812–1814 whilst the heavy losses suffered in Spain and Portugal certainly played their part in eroding support for the French ruler in the final crisis of the empire. In Spain and Portugal, by contrast, no-one can doubt its importance. In both states it was the key to liberal revolution, loss of empire and a series of civil wars, whilst in Spain in particular it gave birth to a long tradition of military intervention in politics that culminated in the bloody conflict of 1936–1939 and the subsequent dictatorship of General Franco.

Key to the Maps

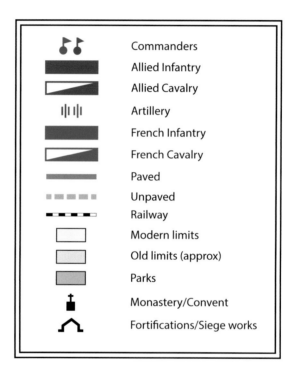

Commanders

Allied Infantry

Allied Cavalry

Artillery

French Infantry

French Cavalry

Paved

Unpaved

Railway

Modern limits

Old limits (approx)

Parks

Monastery/Convent

Fortifications/Siege works

1

The Dos de Mayo
2 May 1808

Ever afterwards known as the Dos de Mayo, the uprising that convulsed Madrid on 2 May 1808 was a key moment in the history of the Napoleonic empire. However, whilst the course of events is clear enough, their nature and significance are open to debate. According to the traditional view, the revolt was sparked off by the tension caused by Napoleon's decision to summon the entire Spanish royal family to Bayonne. With the capital both alarmed and excited, in the early morning of 2 May news spread that the Bourbons' last remaining representatives were about to be sent off to France. Immediately a crowd gathered before the royal palace. Growing more and more excited, and much moved by rumours that Charles IV's youngest son, Francisco de Paula, had burst into tears at the idea of leaving his home, it fell into a frenzy and attacked an aide-de-camp of *maréchal* Joachim Murat who had appeared to supervise the prince's departure, the unfortunate man – one *lieutenant* Auguste Lagrange, who thereby became the first victim of the Peninsular War – being pulled from his horse and hacked to pieces. Nothing loath, Murat, whose headquarters was only a few hundred yards away, immediately sent a squad of troops to restore order. Opening fire, the latter quickly cleared the area around the palace, but the sound of their volleys acted as a dramatic call to arms, the whole city immediately rising in rebellion.

So much for the traditional view. In reality, the situation was much more complex, so much so, indeed, that one can almost go so far as to say that there was no revolt at all. At this point, it should be remembered, there was little or no understanding of Napoleon's intentions with regard to the future of the Spanish monarchy, and it was generally supposed that the only issue on the table was whether the deposed Charles IV should be restored to the throne, or whether, as was the general hope of the populace, that the latter should rather go to his eldest son, Ferdinand, the so-called 'desired one', who had been brought to power by the *de facto* military coup that had taken place at Aranjuez back in March. Popular though Ferdinand was, however, it was not the power of the streets that formed the mainstay of his cause but rather that of a number of interest groups – the Royal Guard, the titled nobility, and elements of the Church. Desperate to prevent the return of Charles IV, these groups hit on the plan of staging a series of demonstrations designed to persuade Napoleon that Ferdinand was too popular to cast aside. One such *démarche* had already been organised in the northern city of León, and the growing turmoil in Madrid, where tensions were already high because of the presence of large numbers of French troops and

The modern-day esplanade in front of the royal palace in Madrid, showing, on the right, the gate through which the carriage bearing the Infante Francisco de Paula should have emerged on the morning of 2 May 1808. Meanwhile, the murder of Auguste Lagrange probably took place in the area occupied by the three men centre-left. (Author's collection)

the threat that this necessarily posed to bread prices, was simply too good an opportunity to miss. Many of the villages round the capital being fiefs of noblemen who had been prominent supporters of Ferdinand, it was very easy to flood the streets of the capital with angry countrymen primed to follow the lead of their social superiors, it being in large part such individuals who formed the crowd that gathered before the palace. As to said lead, this was soon provided. In brief, at around 10:00 a.m., his other relatives having already departed, Francisco de Paula was brought out into the courtyard of the palace to board the coach that was take him to France, and was observed to be in tears. Why this was the case, history does not relate – it may be for no more complicated reason than that the prince was terrified at the sight of so large and angry a crowd – but, be that as it may, a master-locksmith named José Molina y Soriano and a court functionary named Rodrigo López de Ayala immediately started shouting that the prince was being taken and, further, that he did not want to go. Whether the two individuals concerned genuinely wanted a riot is a moot point – it is far more likely that they wanted nothing more than a vocal demonstration of popular support for Fernando – but they were playing with fire, it wanting only the arrival of the unfortunate Lagrange to unleash a torrent of violence.

If there is much uncertainty as to the events that precipitated the Dos de Mayo, we are much clearer as to the course that it took. Madrid being the relatively small place that it was, the

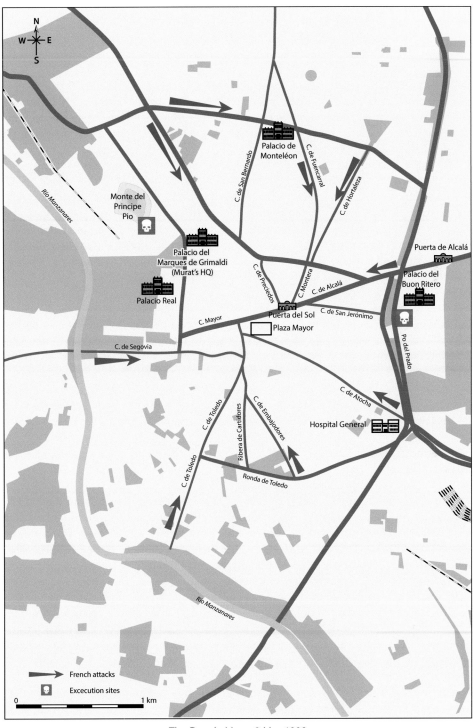

The Dos de Mayo, 2 May 1808.

sound of the volleys fired by the troops sent by Murat to quell the crowd that had assembled at the palace resounded from one end of the city to the other, while hundreds of fugitives fled into the narrow streets leading to the heart of the city screaming that the French were upon them. Needless to say, the result was a general panic, hundreds of the city's inhabitants snatching up whatever weapons came to hand and rushing from their homes in the belief that they were about to be massacred. The few Frenchmen caught on the streets were quickly killed, whilst a cavalry patrol sent to reconnoitre the city centre was cut to pieces in the Puerta del Sol. But French control was barely shaken. Most of Murat's forces were encamped outside Madrid in such places as the royal hunting park known as the Casa de Campo, and columns of the invaders were soon pouring into the city from all sides and battling along the main arteries that converged on the Puerta del Sol, among them the Calle de Alcalá, the Calle de Toledo, the Calle de Segovia, and the Calle de Fuencarral. Faced by overwhelming odds, most resistance quickly came to an end. Indeed, only at the army's chief artillery depot did the French face serious opposition. Here a small group of officers headed by *Capitán* Luis Daoíz and *Capitán* Pedro Velarde took over the cannon and beat off a number of French attacks, but in the end they, too, were overrun. In all perhaps 500 Spaniards were killed or wounded, including 113 prisoners who were executed by firing squad. French casualties, meanwhile, numbered a mere 145. In the wake of these events Spain rose in revolt, the populace being gripped by the belief, first, that the French were bent on their massacre, and second, that the authorities (who had counselled obedience and done their best to get the people of Madrid off the streets) intended to betray them to the invaders. So much for the actual fighting, and its effects. However, to repeat, what is less clear is the nature of the rising. For some historians, it was a spontaneous nationalist revolt, whilst for others it was a premeditated attempt to precipitate rebellion. Such views, however, are difficult to sustain. In fact, the revolt was little more than a mass panic, although it is true that it was both joined by a handful of army officers and later made much use of as a symbol of resistance both by genuine patriots and by ambitious factions eager to secure their own ends.

Madrid Today

The bustling metropolis that is Madrid today is, of course, very different from the Madrid of 1808. That said, notwithstanding the construction of the great east-west thoroughfare known as the Gran Vía in the early twentieth century and, indeed, the attempt of the régime of Joseph Bonaparte to create better civic amenities in the form of a number of new squares (not for nothing was the *rey intruso* nicknamed, amongst other things, the *rey de las plazuelas*), in plan at least, the heart of the old city remains largely unchanged. To attempt a route around the city that would take in each and every one of the sites involved in the fighting, would not be practical, but the visitor should preferably begin their visit on the esplanade in front of the royal palace and end it at the dramatic monument to Daoiz and Velarde in the Plaza del Dos de Mayo (the site of the Palacio de Monteleon, though all that is left of the latter is the gateway before which the defenders met their end). Also worth visiting, meanwhile, are the Conde-Duque barracks in the Calle Conde-Duque (in 1808 the headquarters of the Guardias de Corps) from whence patrols sallied forth in an attempt to reassure the populace once the fighting had subsided; the Puerta del Sol (the site of the clash with the French cavalry immortalised by Francisco de Goya in the first of the two great canvasses he dedicated to the revolt);

and the monument to the victims of Murat's firing squads just off the Plaza de España on the Paseo de Rosales (the spot which formed the scene of the second of Goya's famous canvasses). Finally, it is also worth walking the length of the Calle de Fuencarral or the Calle de Toledo, both of them, as noted, routes by which the French fought their way into the heart of the city.

Of course, it was not just on 2 May 1808 that Madrid was directly caught up in the events of the war. Thus, in December of that same year, it was the chief target of the great counter-offensive that Napoleon launched in a bid to recover from the catastrophe of Bailén (see Chapter 3). As the French closed in on the capital in the wake of the Battle of Somosierra (see Chapter 4), the population of Madrid became increasingly agitated and started to build barricades at most of the important entrances into the city. When the invaders arrived before the city on 2 December, they found themselves confronted by an angry mob armed with everything from blunderbusses and fowling pieces to cleavers and kitchen knives. Even now violence might have been averted: eager not to compromise the return of Joseph Bonaparte, Napoleon repeatedly offered the authorities reasonable terms, but they were so terrified of the crowd that the junta of defence which had been formed to take control of the situation did not dare accept them. On 3 December, then, the Emperor launched a demon-stration against the city, sending his troops across the heights occupied by the gardens of the old royal palace from where they advanced on the barricades that the populace had built on the far side of the north-south carriage-ride known as the Paseo de la Castellana. The result was only too predictable: ill-armed and lacking proper arms, most of the defenders fled at once, only a small handful standing their ground to go down fighting. Only the fact that Napoleon did not press the attack saved Madrid from being overrun at once, while the surrender was not postponed for more than 24 hours, the junta of defence sending plenipo-tentiaries to Napoleon to offer the city's submission the very next morning.

As with the places which witnessed the events of the revolt of 2 May, those affected by the fighting of 3 December are much changed, indeed so much so as to be almost unrec-ognisable: the spots where the clashes were fiercest – the intersections on the Paseo de la Castellana known as Cibeles and Neptuno – are both perpetually swamped by heavy traffic, even if the fountains with which they were beautified in the eighteenth century have both survived intact, while almost none of the buildings that surround them date from the era. One exception, however, is the renowned Thyssen-Bornemisza Museum. Situated on the corner of the Carrera de San Jeronimo, this occupies what was in 1808 the palace of the Duques de Medinacelí and, according to tradition, witnessed the massacre of a group of defenders who took refuge within its walls. Be sure, too, to visit the Puerta de Alcala and inspect the impact of round shot fired by Napoleon's guns during the fighting.

Following the events of December 1808, Madrid remained in French hands until the first week of August 1812 when it was evacuated by King Joseph in the face of Wellington's advance on the capital following the Battle of Salamanca. When the Anglo-Portuguese forces entered the city on 12 August (the author's birthday, no less!), they were famously mobbed by cheering crowds so dense that they would scarcely have had more difficulty making their way had they been opposed by the French. For those interested in following the route taken by the liberators, this last can be done by starting at the Puente de Segovia and heading up towards the city centre by the street of the same name and then turning into the Calle Mayor, though the most evocative place to visit is beyond doubt the Plaza de la Villa, which saw Wellington receive the acclamation of an ecstatic crowd from the balcony of the then city hall.

Right: Situated in the eastern fringes of the Casa de Campo near the railway viaduct known as the Puente de los Franceses, this pleasant walk is a fragment of the highway used by Wellington's army to enter Madrid on 12 August 1812. (Author's collection)

Below: The Plaza de la Villa. Having entered Madrid, Wellington received the acclaim of the crowd from the balconies of the building on the right (the town hall). Meanwhile, the other buildings in the photograph, some of the oldest structures in the capital, are all largely unchanged since the Peninsular War. (Author's collection)

2

Medina de Río Seco

14 July 1808

A considerable French victory and the only one ever to be gained by *maréchal* Jean-Baptiste Bessières on his own account, the Battle of Medina de Río Seco set a pattern that was to be followed by many other clashes between the French and Spanish armies in the first years of the Peninsular War. Thus, an ill-considered and poorly co-ordinated Spanish thrust at the French forces in central Spain led to an action fought at a hopeless disadvantage on the high plains of the *meseta,* and heavy Spanish losses. Chief responsibility for the campaign lay with the Captain General of Old Castile, *Teniente-General* Gregorio García de la Cuesta, a tough and determined soldier with an excellent record from the so-called War of the Convention of 1793–1795. Driven from his capital of Valladolid by a heavy defeat at Cabezón on 12 June, Cuesta, as he is customarily called, retired to the western part of his dominions with his few regular troops, most of them troopers of the royal bodyguard known as the Guardias de Corps, and built up a new army of volunteers and conscripts raised from the area around León. Eager to recover Valladolid, he demanded the support of the patriotic junta that had been established in neighbouring Galicia. Eager to boost its reputation, this last decided that it ought to heed these calls – aside from anything else, it possessed a large army of regular troops – but at the same time it instructed the commander of its forces, the newly-promoted *Teniente-General* Joaquín Blake y Joyes, the grandson of a Scottish Jacobite who had taken service with Spain, to continue to protect Galicia. Blake being a cautious figure who was new to independent command, the result was disaster. Whereas the only hope of victory was to strike hard and fast with all the resources at his disposal, he moved forward across the plains of, first, León, and then Castilla la Vieja, very slowly and dropped off two of his four infantry divisions to guard his communications with his home province. Eventually, however, he joined Cuesta at Medina de Río Seco, a small town a few miles to the north-west of Valladolid, with 15,000 men and 20 guns. Together the two Spanish commanders had some 22,000 men, but there were only 600 cavalry, whilst almost all Cuesta's men were raw levies. Still worse, perhaps, from the very beginning the two commanders appear to have loathed one another, with Blake regarding Cuesta as an aging 'dug-out' and Cuesta regarding Blake as a revolutionary upstart, the latter having been appointed to the command of the Galician forces after their original commander, *Teniente-General* Antonio Filanghieri, had been murdered by rioters in the course of the uprising, matters not being helped by the fact that the two generals, both of whom believed, of course, that they should take command of

The Paramo de Valdecuevas viewed from the Tesón de Moclín. Merle's division attacked uphill from beyond the line of trees. (Author's collection)

the united Spanish forces, were men of diametrically opposed temperaments (if Cuesta was notoriously bold and fiery, Blake verged on the downright timorous).

Given time, some of the problems in the Spanish camp might have been ironed out, but time was something that the rival commanders did not have. On the contrary, scarcely had Blake arrived in Medina de Río Seco around midday on 13 July than news arrived that a large French force was in Valladolid. Amidst scenes of great confusion, the Spaniards therefore rushed to take up positions screening the town from an attack in that direction. In this respect, they were quite fortunate, for a mile or more in the direction of Valladolid was a long ridge known as the Paramo de Valdecuevas the slopes of which facing the presumed direction of the enemy attack were in places extremely steep. Before long, then, the 1st Division of Blake's Army of Galicia headed by *Mariscal de Campo* Felipe Jado Cagigal, together with an independent brigade-strength formation known as the Vanguard commanded by *Brigadier* Juan Caamaño y Pardo, Conde de Maceda, were drawn up on the section of the ridge directly overlooking the road from Valladolid, with the 4th Division of the same force stationed on a lower ridge a few hundred yards to the north under its commander, *Mariscal de Campo* Francisco de Paula Gómez de Terán, Marqués de Portazgo, and Cuesta's Army of Castile positioned well to the left rear in the valley of the rivulet, from which Medina de Río Seco took its name, as a reserve. As for the two squadrons of cavalry that was all the mounted force that Blake had with him, these were stationed on the extreme right at the spot where the Valladolid road rounded the southern end of the Paramo de Valdecuevas.

Had the French acted in the manner that Blake and Cuesta expected, these dispositions would have made some sense for the combined Spanish forces were in effect arrayed in

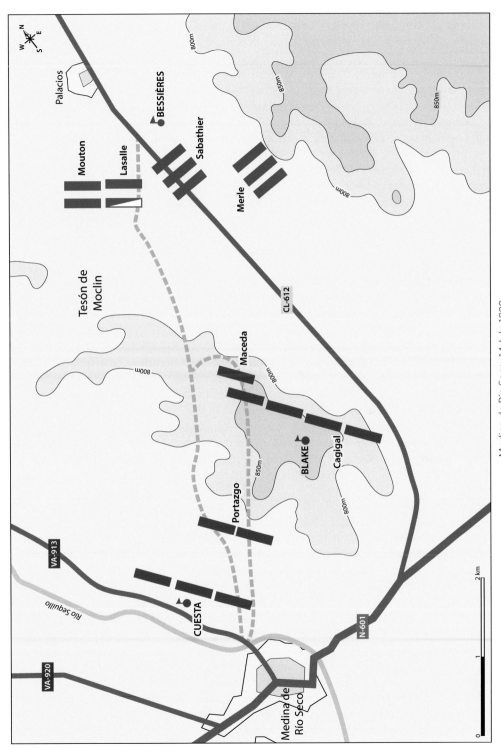

Medina de Río Seco, 14 July 1808.

echelon in what in ordinary circumstances would have been quite a strong defensive position with the Army of Castile, by far the weakest component of their order of battle, tucked away well out of danger far in the rear. However, the circumstances were far from ordinary, for the French were in not, as the Spanish commanders blithely assumed, coming at them from the direction of Valladolid: far from it, indeed. Thus, as commander of all the French troops in the region, Bessières had stolen a march on the Spaniards. Gathering together such troops as he could – a mere 13,500 men, many of whom, however, were high-quality veterans – he had marched north to Palencia, from where in the evening of 13 July he swung south-west to take the Spaniards in flank. This proved a stroke of genius, Blake and Cuesta being taken completely by surprise. Afforded a few hours' notice by a message that arrived in the small hours, the former ordered Portazgo's division to fall back on Cuesta so as to present Bessières with a refused flank, but neither of the two commanders seem to have realised Blake's intention for, instead of forming a defensive line blocking the northern approaches to the Spanish position, they rather held their troops back in the low ground in the rear, thereby leaving the Paramo de Valdecuevas completely exposed. To put it mildly, it was not a happy situation.

That this was the case was revealed almost as soon as the French arrived on the field early in the morning of 14 July. At first, true, it seemed that the Spaniards might be attacked from the direction they initially expected, for rather than immediately taking the forces arrayed on the Paramo de Valdecuevas in flank, leading elements of Bessières' army – the infantry divisions of *général de division* Pierre Merle and *général de division* Georges Mouton – filed across the front of the Paramo and then faced right from their line of march to attack it head-on. What followed showed that, but for the French commander's decision to march on Medina de Río Seco from Palencia, Cuesta and Blake might have secured a defensive victory for, positioned on what had become the extreme left of the French array, Merle was initially held in check by the masses of troops defending the lip of the Paramo.

However, this small success was almost immediately rendered meaningless, for on the right Mouton was able to seize the ridge that had originally been held by the 4th Division of the Army of Galicia. To all intents and purposes, then, the Spaniards had already lost the battle, but defeat was now converted into utter disaster. In brief, bringing up the rear of the French line of march had been a mixed division of cavalry and infantry commanded by the dashing hussar-general, *général de division* Antoine Lasalle, and, in accordance with Bessières' orders, this force had swung to its right and, hidden from Blake and Cuesta by yet another undulation in the ground, was now bearing down on the Spanish array from the north. Pouring over the crest concerned, its mounted element – *général de brigade* Auguste de Colbert's brigade of *chasseurs à cheval* – now thundered forward across up the gentle slopes leading to the heights held by the 1st Division of the Army of Galicia and the Vanguard. Needless to say, the result was complete humiliation for the Spaniards. Caught in flank and rear with no time to form square, the troops concerned dissolved in flight, while many of them were put to the sword or taken prisoner by Colbert's victorious horsemen, the only unit to escape with its ranks in good order being the Voluntarios de Navarra light-infantry regiment, and then only because its commanding officer had the presence of mind to get his men into square.

With the destruction of the Spanish right at the hands of Merle and Lasalle, around half of the troops Cuesta and Blake had been put out of action. However, something might yet have been saved from the wreck as the way was still clear for the Army of Castile and the 4th

Still pretty much in its original condition, in 1808 this track formed the main road from Palencia to Medina de Río Seco. On the left can be seen the lower slopes of the ridge originally held by the 4th Division of the Army of Galicia while the knoll in the middle distance was in all probability employed by Bessières as his command post in the early stages of the battle. (Author's collection)

The Tesón de Moclín and the Paramo de Valdecuevas viewed from the vicinity of the low ground which constituted the second position of the 4th Division of the Army of Galicia: the yawning gulf which allowed Colbert's cavalry to take Jado Cagigal and Maceda in flank and rear is all too obvious. (Author's collection)

The open ground stretching north from the old road from Palencia to Medina de Río Seco across which Colbert launched the cavalry charge which destroyed the troops of Maceda and Jado Cagigal. (Author's collection)

The area beneath the Tesón de Moclín which witnessed the destruction of the 4th Division of the Army of Galicia by Colbert's cavalry. (Author's collection)

Division of the Army of Galicia to retire from the field in good order. However, precluded by the configuration of the ground from observing what was happening on the summit of the Paramo de Valdecuevas, the Marqués de Portazgo evidently decided that it was still his duty to do what he could and therefore ordered his division to advance on Mouton's troops on the ridge to the north of the Paramo. Gallant gesture though this was, it was utterly futile. Formed in columns of attack, Portazgo's men advanced in good order and pressed home their assault with vigour in spite of being assailed by heavy fire from Mouton's divisional artillery battery, but, just as they were coming to grips with their opponents, disaster struck yet again. Thus, now rallied from their pursuit of the broken Spanish right, Colbert's cavalry launched a second charge into their right flank that routed them in their turn with heavy losses.

With all three formations of the Army of Galicia broken beyond repair, all that was now left to the Spaniards was the hopelessly unprepared Army of Castile. This, too, could now have escaped, but, propelled by nothing more than a concern for his personal honour, Cuesta threw his men into the attack in their turn. Facing them was the infantry component of Lasalle's division (the infantry brigade of *général de brigade* Just Sabatier) and a detachment of infantry of the Imperial Guard that had formed part of the escort that had been dispatched to Madrid with Murat when the Spanish capital was occupied in March. All of the men concerned being first-class troops, there could be but one outcome in the clash that followed, and, notwithstanding a brave show on the part of its unfortunate recruits, the Army of Castile, too, was soon in full flight, the triumphant French forces in the meantime descending on the unfortunate town and subjecting it to a most brutal sack which saw widespread rape and murder and ended in the destruction of at least 40 houses by fire.

Thus ended the Battle of Medina de Río Seco. Spanish casualties had amounted to 2,500 men and 13 guns, while the French had lost just 400 men and, in the process, cleared the way for Joseph Bonaparte, who had a few days earlier crossed the frontier into his new kingdom, to proceed to Madrid, which he finally entered on 20 July. As for Blake and Cuesta, the former fell back on Galicia, while the later made for Salamanca only to be stripped of his command two months later as a result of a dispute with the nascent provisional government known as the Junta Central. That said, the battle was anything but the decisive victory that Napoleon initially envisaged it to be. On the contrary, not only was the army broken at Medina de Río Seco but one Spanish army among several, but exactly one week later *Teniente General* Francisco-Javier Castaños was to be found taking the surrender of the 17,000 French troops who were to be taken prisoner at Bailén.

Medina de Río Seco Today

The battlefield of Medina de Río Seco is both one of the most unspoiled of all the historical sites pertaining to the Peninsular War and at the same time the most beautiful, and therefore deserves to be far better visited than is actually the case. Being quite extensive, it is easier to visit for those possessed of motor transport, but, as the author can testify, the most rewarding way of doing so is to go on foot: the going is very good throughout and few of the gradients any problem to anyone who is reasonably able-bodied; that said, to attempt the full circuit would certainly involve a full day's walking and necessitate the carriage of a full complement of food and, especially, water, it going without saying, too, that it is not an undertaking that should be considered in the full heat of summer.

The obvious point from which to start a tour of the battle itself is the town of Medina de Río Seco, and all the more so if the visitor is reliant on public transport, in which respect there are good bus services from Valladolid and Madrid, but it is recognised that those travelling by car might prefer to so arrange matters that they tackle the battlefield more in accordance with the above narrative; if so, the logical route would be to begin at the neighbouring village of Palacios de Campos and then drive south on the CL-612, this being the route followed by Merle and Mouton as they filed along the front of the Army of Galicia. If it is required to get an impression of the positions held by Jado Cagigal and Maceda, this can be followed as far as its junction with the main road from Valladolid (the N601), but otherwise take the unmade road that branches off to the right about half a mile south of the village: keep left at the fork that will be encountered after a few hundred yards, and this leads directly to the saddle that separates the Paramo de Valdecuevas and its northern extension, including, most prominently, the Tesón de Moclín. Having explored the area round about, it is then possible to drive straight on to Medina de Río Seco.

Let us rather presume, however, that the visitor is reliant on his or her own two legs. As such, the best place to begin is the town itself, an atmospheric place which conserves many buildings of the period including the churches of Santa María, Santiago de los Caballeros and Santa Cruz – this last the site, or so it is said, of the gang-rape of many nuns – and two of original mediaeval gateways. Particularly notable, meanwhile, are the arcades which line the main street (the Calle Angel Peralta) while some of the older dwellings display evidence of the mud and straw 'daub' that filled the gaps between the beams which acted as the framework for their construction. Finally, there is a monument to the battle dating its original form from 1908 in the Parque Duque de Osuna on the southern edge of the old town, though, like many similar examples erected in the same era, it is keener to highlight the suffering of the civilian population rather than the efforts of the regular army.

To reach the battlefield, leave the town at the Plaza del Arco Ajujar and cross the little river on which the town is built, turn right and then take the first turning to the left. Follow this straight on in the direction of the high ground straight ahead, this being the Paramo de Valdecuevas. At the farm at the end of the road (this marks the approximate site of Blake's command post), fork right across the plateau – the ground, of course, occupied by Jado Cagigal and Maceda – until the steep slope which marks the latter's eastern and south-eastern faces. At this point, turn left and follow the narrow path along the edge of the fields until it drops down to a saddle crossed at right angles by an unmade road, noting, in the process, the isolated knoll in the valley below, this presumably being employed both by Merle's divisional battery as a convenient site from which to bombard the troops holding the Paramo and by Bessières as a command post. Meanwhile, the road, of course, is the one mentioned above as a convenient route for those wishing to follow in the footsteps of the French from Palacios de Campos. Across the road is the prominent knoll known as the Tesón de Moclín. Easily ascended, and used as his command-post by Bessières in the latter stages of the battle, this offers commanding views of not just the battlefield but also wide areas in every direction. Meanwhile, stretching away to the north is the ground occupied by Mouton, the low ridge visible perhaps 1,000 yards away in the direction of the town being the position allotted to the division of the Marqués del Portazgo and the shallow depression below the spot that witnessed the destruction of said formation. Returning to the track, turn west and follow it back to Medina de Río Seco. Just before the town is reached, the visitor will pass the municipal cemetery, this marking the approximate position of the right wing of the Army of Castile as the latter was deployed at the start of the battle.

The Paramo de Valdecuevas viewed from the direction of the highroad from Valladolid; had the French launched their attack in the manner expected, they might have faced a much harder fight. (Author's collection)

The main street of Medina de Río Seco. (Author's collection)

The church of Santa María, one of various places of worship which witnessed scenes of gang-rape in the aftermath of the Battle of Medina de Río Seco. (Author's collection)

3

Bailén
16–19 July 1808

Situated in the upper valley of the River Guadalquivir in northern Andalucía, Bailén was the scene of a major French defeat at the start of the Peninsular War. Sent to occupy Cádiz in May 1808, a French army commanded by *général de division* Pierre Dupont de l'Etang advanced as far as Córdoba, which it took by storm after defeating a small force of Spaniards at Alcolea. While at Córdoba, however, Dupont heard, first, of the approach of a much larger force of Spanish regulars under the commander of all the Spanish forces in Andalucía, *Teniente-General* Francisco-Javier Castaños, and second, of a series of attacks on his communications in La Mancha by hastily organised bands of irregulars. Much alarmed, he therefore fell back to the small town of Andújar. Unwilling to mount a frontal attack on Dupont, the Spanish commander then resolved on a risky attempt at encirclement, sending the divisions of *Mariscal de Campo* Teodoro Reding and *Mariscal de Campo* Antoine de Malet, Marqués de Coupigny, eastwards along the southern bank of the River Guadalquivir in order to get behind the French, while a smaller column made its way through the foothills of the Sierra Morena – the east-west chain of mountains separating Andalucía from Castilla la Nueva – in the hope of preventing them fleeing due north. There followed a comedy of errors: the Spanish encircling force defeated a small French division – that of *général de division* Jacques Gobert – at Mengíbar and cut the road to Madrid, only to retreat back across the river in the face of a second division sent to clear the road by Dupont. Had they been followed up, all might have been well, but the commander of the troops concerned – *général de division* Dominique Vedel – wrongly assumed that the troops had moved north-east to occupy the pass that carried the main road to Madrid across the Sierra Morena and set off in hot pursuit, leaving Reding and Coupigny free to re-occupy Bailén. Uncertain as to what was happening in his rear, meanwhile on the evening of 18 July Dupont decided to evacuate Andújar and join Vedel.

The stage was now set for a battle whose significance was subsequently to be blown up out of all proportion. Marching through the night, Dupont reached a range of low hills that ran to the west of Bailén near dawn the next day only suddenly to be fired upon by Spanish pickets. With the way blocked, the French commander could only deploy for battle. Possessed as he was of some 10,000 men, he should easily have been able to break through: the Spaniards had themselves been taken by surprise and were deployed in an improvised line that was everywhere overlooked by the French positions. But in the event, encumbered

Part of the battlefield of Mengíbar: the field in the foreground is to this day known as the *sitio de la matanza* or 'the site of the slaughter'. (Author's collection)

The ridge occupied by Dupont's army viewed from the Spanish right-centre. (Author's collection)

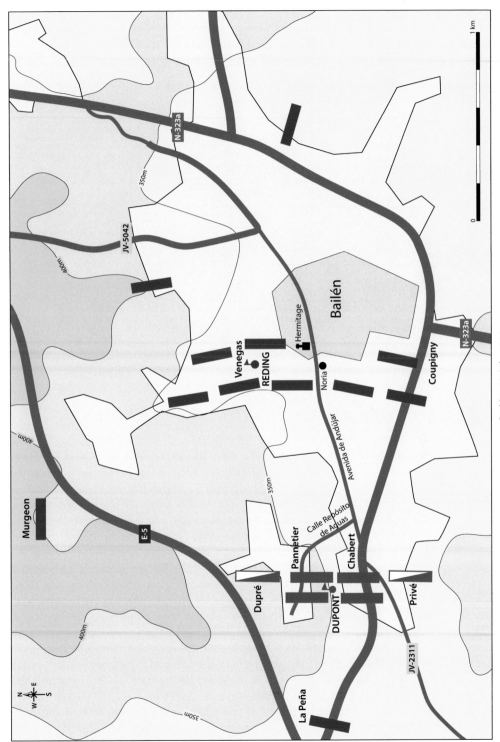

Bailén, 19 July 1808.

The northern half of the battlefield of Bailén: the French left flank extended to the vicinity of the white building in the distance while the area in the foreground witnessed repeated French cavalry charges. (Author's collection)

as he was by an enormous baggage train laden, or so it was said, with much plunder, Dupont panicked. Brought up piecemeal, his troops, who were in any case mostly second-line units of limited quality, were easily repulsed, a vital factor in their defeat being the fact that the 8- and 12-pounder guns that constituted the bulk of the Spanish pieces far out-classed the 4-pounders which was all Dupont had with which to answer them. By late afternoon, then, the French were in disarray. Dupont himself was wounded, some 2,000 other men were down including cavalry-brigade commander, *général de brigade* Claude Duprés, and the survivors were exhausted, demoralised and tortured by heat and thirst (not only was it a blazing summer day in one of the very hottest parts of Spain, but the invaders' only source of water was a spring far to the rear). To the west, meanwhile, Castaños' other two divisions had advanced from Andujar and were now closing in for the kill, matters being made still worse by the fact that two Swiss regiments in Spanish pay which had been forcibly incorporated into Dupont's command suddenly raised their muskets in the air butts-uppermost and rejoined their erstwhile masters. As for the Spaniards, assured of plentiful supplies of water by the fact that a deep well was situated right in the midst of their front line and much stiffened by the imperturbable behaviour of Reding, who was senior to Coupigny and had therefore assumed command of the battle, they were in fine fettle.

With matters in this state, the only thing that could have saved Dupont was the return of Vedel. That general, however, had marched his men as far as the town of La Carolina well to

The well in the centre of Reding's line that sustained the Spanish army throughout the battle.
(Author's collection)

The olive groves in the rear of Dupont's position in which Dupont's exhausted men took shelter in the closing stages of the battle. (Author's collection)

Situated well to the rear of Dupont's army, the River Rumblar (or Herrumblar) was the only source of water available to the French troops (Author's collection

the north, while he made his way back in the most dilatory of fashions and that despite the fact that the cannonade from Bailén could clearly be heard in the distance. In consequence, when Vedel at last came up, having taken 12 hours to cover the 20 miles that separated him from Dupont, dismayed by the failure of one last attack in which his only élite battalion, the 500-strong Marins de La Garde, had been thrown back in its turn, his superior had already requested an armistice. In the negotiations that followed, it was finally agreed that Vedel's column should lay down its arms along with that of Dupont, but that, in exchange, the 17,000 men involved in the capitulation should all be repatriated to France (terms, alas, which were not honoured: apart from Dupont and a few other officers, the prisoners were eventually sent to the island of Cabrera where many of them died of starvation).

All this, of course, was a major humiliation for Napoleon, opponents of his rule being everywhere much encouraged and Joseph Bonaparte, who had arrived in Madrid just one week before, persuaded to flee to the shelter of the River Ebro and raise the siege of Zaragoza. Not surprisingly, then, Dupont and the other senior officers who were repatriated to France were promptly thrown into prison in disgrace, while the Emperor immediately set about planning the massive counter-offensive that was eventually to see him recapture the Spanish capital. However, for the Allies it was a double-edged sword: not only was the full force of the imperial wrath called down on Spain, but, understanding of what had actually happened in the campaign being almost totally lacking, much over-confidence was engendered in the Spanish camp, whilst the exaggerated expectations encouraged in London later created great problems for the Anglo-Spanish alliance. Meanwhile, many misapprehensions of the time have been carried forward into our own days, it still being possible to come across works in English and Spanish alike which appear to believe that the victory was the work of armed civilians, when the fact is that almost all the Spaniards who actually fought in the battle were drawn from the regular army, raw recruits though some of them may have been. There is a local legend which insists that the inhabitants of Bailén turned out to

The post-house situated a few miles to the west of Bailén on the road to Andújar where Dupont formally surrendered to Castaños on 21 July 1808. (Author's collection)

ply the defenders with food and drink, a claim commemorated in the town's coat of arms, featuring, as this does, an urn shot through by a musket ball as it was supposedly being proffered to Reding by an elderly woman named María Bellido, but this story is likely to be at least in part the work of invention. What is the case, however, is that, in one of the first cases of its kind, the Junta of Seville ordered that all those combatants who had taken part in the campaign should receive a special medal, regardless of their rank.

Bailén Today

Bailén, alas, is not an attractive town, and there is almost nothing left of the built environment of 1808 other than the parish church and a small hermitage in the Calle Bénito Galdós, of which the former contains the tomb of Castaños and the latter (supposedly) the remains of mortally wounded French general, Claude Dupré (Castaños, by contrast, lived to the ripe old age of 94, not departing this world until September 1852). Other points of interest, meanwhile, include the town's museum to the battle (also in the Calle Bénito Galdós) and the somewhat over-blown monument that graces (or otherwise!) the nearby esplanade known as the Paseo de las Palmeras. Of the battlefield itself, alas, there is also little to see. By following the Calle Bénito Galdós away from the town centre in a westerly direction along the former's continuation – the Avenida de Andujar – for approximately 500 yards, the visitor will eventually come to a roundabout. Immediately on the left will be seen a traditional well known as the Noria de la Huerta de Don Lázaro: this was the water-source that kept the Spanish forces sustained throughout the battle, and also marks the approximate site of Reding's front line. When the author first visited the town in 2001 the area to the right – the scene of much of the fiercest fighting – consisted of open fields, but this has now been heavily developed in favour of new housing. However, one area that may still remain may be found to the left of the Calle Andrés Torrejón, this being constituted by a street running at right angles to the Avenida de Andújar which is undeveloped on its western side and therefore offers unrestricted views of the French positions. Having taken advantage of these, return to the Avenida de Andújar, turn right and carry on to the Calle Depuradora de Aguas. At this point turn right and follow the road up the hill past the Mirador restaurant: the remaining portion of the battlefield is on the right. Finally, at the water purification plant at the end of the Calle Depuradora de Aguas, turn left into the olive groves. This is, for the author, by far the most evocative part of the walk: it is easy, indeed, to imagine Dupont's exhausted men slumped in the shade of the trees. Finally head south to the old main road which may be followed back to the Avenida de Andújar and thence the town centre.

Further Reading

O. Hayes, *The Battle of Bailén* (Surbiton: Bretwalda Books, 2014)

4

Somosierra

30 November 1808

For Napoleon the news of the defeat at Bailén and the panic-stricken retreat by which it was followed came as a massive body blow. With his prestige in shreds, he responded in forthright fashion, rushing thousands of troops of the *grande armée*, many of them hardened veterans, to the Spanish frontier from their quarters in Germany, and instilling fresh life into the improvised forces that had waged the first campaigns of the war: Spain, then, would be punished for her insolence. Along with the reinforcements came many of the best commanders at France's disposal including no fewer than six *maréchaux* – Jean de Dieu Soult, Michel Ney, Jean Lannes, Claude Perrin (aka Victor), Edouard Mortier and François Lefebvre – but the emperor was not disposed to leave anything to chance: on the contrary, if there was revenge to be obtained, the credit was going to fall to him and him alone. On 6 November, then, he arrived hotfoot from Paris at the headquarters of the reborn Army of Spain and took personal command of the large mass of troops whose task, he had decided, was to burst through the centre of the Spanish forces arrayed against him in a great crescent stretching from the Basque provinces to the eastern frontiers of Navarre and march on Madrid via the highroad that connected it with the French frontier at the tiny village of Hendaye, while at the same time throwing out substantial bodies of troops to each flank to deal with the Spanish armies on the left and right of the breakthrough.

Composed in many instances of raw troops, commanded by generals who were, at best, men of mediocre talent, short of supplies, beset by winter weather for which they far from properly equipped and heavily outnumbered, the Spaniards had no chance in the face of such an onslaught and in consequence sustained heavy defeats at Gamonal and Espinosa de los Monteros, leaving Napoleon free to head for the Spanish capital at the head of a force composed of the Imperial Guard and the corps of *maréchaux* Victor and Lefebvre together with various formations of cavalry, the whole ensemble amounting to some 40,000 men. To defend Madrid, the Spaniards could only muster some 16,000 men, of which the most important component was a stray division of the army destroyed at Gamonal commanded by Bénito San Juan. That said, they did enjoy a strong defensive position in the form of the pass of Somosierra, a deep cleft in the mountains north of Madrid from which the Spanish capital could be reached in two to three days of hard marching. It was here, then, that, San Juan resolved to make his stand, but, having done so, he badly bungled his dispositions, placing fully a third of his troops in the town of Sepúlveda despite the fact that this

The Puerta de Somosierra looking north from the position of the last Spanish battery. (Author's collection)

The site of the last of the three batteries the Spaniards built to block the Puerta de Somosierra.
(Author's collection)

stood a considerable distance to the west of the northern entrance of the defile and could play no possible part in its defence. Why San Juan took this decision has never been properly explained, but it is probable that he was anxious to block a side road that ran from the Madrid highway along the northern flank of the mountains to the more westerly Pass of Guadarrama, several days' march away though this was. His arrangements for holding Somosierra itself, true, were sensible enough, his 16 guns being divided between four

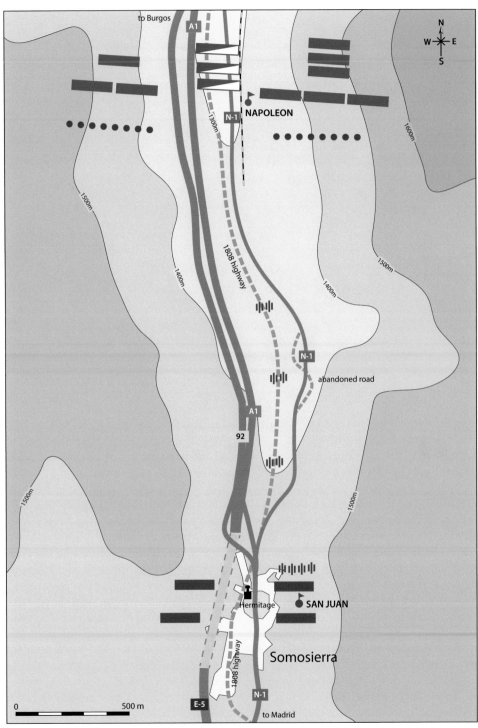

Somosierra, 30 November 1808.

The hermitage that marks the summit of the Puerta de Somosierra; note the bullet-hole on the arch above the door. (Author's collection)

successive firing positions along the highroad chosen in such a way that each one was covered by the one behind, and the heights on either side, and, indeed, the pass itself, furnished with detachments of infantry, but from the start the Spanish position was desperately vulnerable, and there was therefore little chance that it could withstand a serious assault.

Arriving before the pass on the foggy morning of 30 November, Napoleon was anything but dismayed by what he saw and quickly dispatched substantial forces of infantry to clear away the Spanish troops holding the high ground overlooking the pass from east and west, and the troops concerned – the nine battalion-strong division of *général de division* François Ruffin – were soon making excellent progress: rough and steep though the ground was, it offered no real obstacle to troops moving in open order, while the defenders were completely out-matched by their opponents. To Napoleon, however, this was seemingly not apparent (either that, or he simply lost patience and decided to force the pace of operations). Turning to one of his *aides de camp*, a *colonel* de Piré, he ordered him to direct his personal escort, a squadron of Polish light horse attached to the Imperial Guard commanded by *major* Jan Kozietulski, to charge the full length of the defile and clear the way for the army. Aghast at this prospect – it was a basic maxim of military lore that cavalry should never seek to take artillery batteries head on – Piré and several other officers, including, not least, Napoleon's chief-of-staff, *maréchal* Berthier, protested that the task was impossible, only for the Emperor to fly into a rage and insist that his orders were obeyed forthwith: nothing, he said, should be beyond the capacity of his Poles.

What followed, to borrow a phrase associated with the equally foolish Charge of the Light Brigade, was magnificent, but anything but war. Galloping headlong into the defile in column of fours (so narrow was the road that any other formation was impossible), the squadron, which numbered no more than eight officers and 206 men, immediately came under heavy fire, amongst the first to fall being Kozietulski, whose horse was shot from under him. The Poles having quickly cleared a hastily excavated cut in the road, the first three Spanish batteries were taken without difficulty, but the unit was in considerable disorder and its horses badly blown, and there therefore followed a pause of some few minutes, a fact that has enabled some accounts to claim that the squadron having in effect been fought to a standstill, the Spaniards in the final battery were cleared by a second squadron of the regiment that Napoleon had dispatched to support Kozietulski's men. However, while more horsemen were indeed sent into the defile, the survivors of the original squadron managed to recover their momentum. In a very few minutes, then, the Poles emerged from the defile, and, albeit not without a fierce fight with the Spanish gunners which cost one of their surviving officers, Andrzej Niegolewski, no fewer than nine bayonet wounds, put the troops holding the summit of the pass to flight, the additional cavalry sent up in their support being left with nothing else to do than pursue the mob of fugitives which was all that was left to San Juan southwards in the direction of the nearby town of Buitrago de Lozoya. With six of its eight officers dead or wounded, along with anything from 50 to 100 of the rank and file (accounts differ in this rerspect), Kozietulski's squadron had effectively been destroyed as a fighting force, and all for an objective that could have been taken at much less cost with the aid of infantry alone. That said, having suffered over 2,000 casualties and lost all their guns, the defending forces were in a state of complete disintegration (so bad did the situation become, indeed, that, accused of treason, San Juan was some days later murdered by a group of his own soldiers), while the road to Madrid was wide open, the Emperor going on to take the capital on 4 December. As for the Poles, as crazy as the orders they had been given had been, they could bathe in the glory of having carried out a task that had been deemed well-nigh impossible, being rewarded by elevation from the ranks of the Young Guard to those of the Old, not to mention a number of crosses of the Legion of Honour, the first such decorations the unit had ever received. Among the men so decorated was Niegolewki, Napoleon supposedly being so impressed with his courage that he took the example of the much-coveted award that he wore on his breast and pinned it to the Polish officer's uniform jacket with his own hands.[1]

---

1   To a large extent this account of the action at Somosierra has been compiled from the numerous Polish accounts put together by Lalowski and North. Meanwhile, one source that does not figure is the memoirs of Philippe de Ségur. In this work Ségur includes a dramatic account of the charge which features him riding all the way to the summit of the pass at the head of Kozietulski's men, only to fall badly wounded at the climax of the action. This claim, alas, is completely mendacious, the reality being that Ségur was rather cut down outside the mouth of the defile by a shell fragment while bringing the Poles the order to advance. In the past, the men concerned have often been referred to as lancers, but they were not converted to such a role until the following year, and in consequence were armed with sabres, carbines and pistols alone.

A suitably wintry view of the summit of the Puerta de Somosierra looking north; the line of the old road is just visible running down the slope in the middle distance (Paddy Griffith).

Somosierra Today

Situated at the northernmost extremity of the Madrid region on the main motorway from Madrid to Burgos, the Basque country and the French frontier, the pass of Somosierra is easily located, though the highway now passes beneath the summit by dint of a lengthy tunnel. To reach the scene of the action, leave the motorway at Junction 5 and follow signs for Robregordo and Somosierra. Unfortunately, the road across the pass that was in use before the tunnel was built has done much damage to the defile up which the Poles charged, but the line of the original road is still discernable and can be followed without too much difficulty. Still extant, albeit much restored, is the hermitage that stood at the summit in 1808, while a short walk to the east from said hermitage will take the visitor to a level area that offers a good view of the ascent and was almost certainly the site of the final Spanish battery.

Further Reading

M. Lalowski and J. North, *Somosierra, 1808: the Legendary Charge of Napoleon's Polish Guard Cavalry* (privately published, 2020).

J. de Neef, *An Audacious Charge: a Classic Study of the Battle of Somosierra, 1808* (privately published, 2020).

5

Zaragoza
June 1808 – February 1809

A major city on the southern bank of the River Ebro in Aragón possessed of no defences other than a mediaeval wall and a crumbling mediaeval castle known as the Castillo de la Aljafería, Zaragoza was a leading centre of the Spanish insurrection of 1808, power there having been seized by a young officer of the Guardias de Corps named José Rebolledo de Palafox y Melcí (by convention, normally referred to just as 'Palafox'). A scion of a prominent noble family with strong links to the city, Palafox has always been regarded as one of the greatest heroes of the Spanish struggle against Napoleon, but in reality he was a complex character whose leadership, we shall see, was to prove sorely lacking.

Zaragoza was an early target of the French, who mounted their first attempt at its capture on 15 June having first routed disorderly assemblies of patriotic volunteers sent out from the city by Palafox at Mallén and Alagón, in which last the Spanish commander was lightly wounded. It should be noted that other than a few invalids, an anti-bandit patrol known as the Fusileros de Aragón and a small number of refugees from the garrison of Barcelona who had made their way to Zaragoza after the Catalan capital was taken over by the French, Palafox had no regular troops at his disposal whatsoever. Yet, furious at the deposition of Ferdinand VII, persuaded by the stories circulating respecting the Dos de Mayo that the French were bent on the massacre of every single Spaniard and galvanised by moves such as the proclamation of the much-revered image of the Madonna known as the 'Virgin of the Pillar' as the city's *capitán-general*, the populace was determined to defend itself. A simple escalade, this first attack was therefore driven off with heavy losses, but on 28 June regular siege operations began against the city under *général de division* Jean-Antoine Verdier. With the defenders distracted by a catastrophic explosion in their main powder magazine, the invaders drove the Spaniards off the heights that dominated the city from the south. With this preliminary move out of the way, on 2 July 3,000 troops attacked the walls, only to find that the defenders, who had by now been reinforced by a regiment of line infantry from Catalonia, again put up a desperate resistance. Indeed, the invaders were once again repelled with heavy losses, their defeat being accompanied by the emergence of one of the greatest popular icons of the Spanish struggle against Napoleon in the person of Agustina of Aragón – more precisely, Agustina Zaragoza Domenech – a Catalan girl who singlehandedly saved a key position from the enemy by seizing a linstock from a dying gunner (reputedly her husband) and firing a cannon into the very faces of the advancing French. Much discouraged, Verdier now resigned himself to engaging in conventional siege operations. Despite a series of sorties, by 31 July all was ready for the bombardment of the city. With 60 guns in place, whole sections of the latter's flimsy defences were swept away, and in the afternoon of 4 August the French attacked again. This time there was no mistake: protected until the last minute by their trenches, the assault columns scrambled through the various breaches and poured into the streets. Yet, inspired by the demagoguery of José Palafox, the defenders remained as defiant as ever. In the face of furious opposition, the attackers were forced to fight their way yard by yard towards the heart of the city. Had they been able to keep going, they might well have triumphed, but the attack ran out of steam, and the end of the day found the French confined to a narrow finger of territory stretching from the walls as far as the central promenade and market-place known as El Coso. What might have happened next is difficult to say: Verdier's forces were in no fit state to press on, but the Spaniards were too disorganised to do more than keep up a steady fusillade and make spasmodic rushes at one French position or another. In short, fresh troops might yet have won the day for Verdier, but on 12 August he received news of the French defeat at Bailén and decided to abandon the siege forthwith. By 13 August, then, the invaders were gone.

A view all but unchanged since 1808: the imposing silhouette of the Pilar basilica as viewed from the original bridge across the River Ebro. (Author's collection)

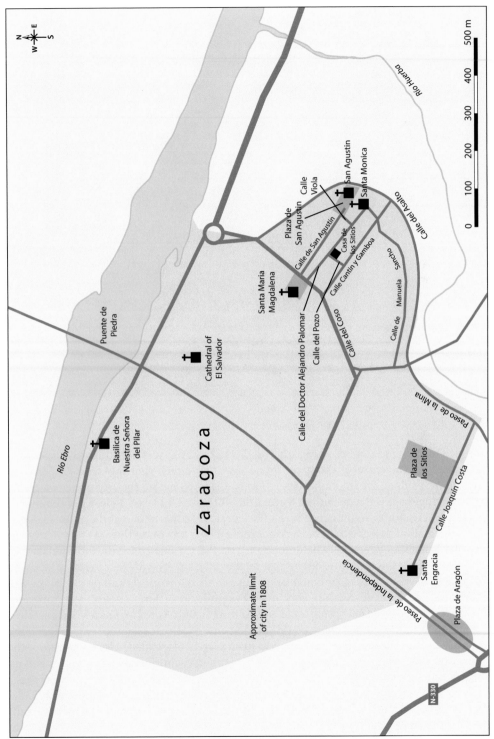

Zaragoza.

The River Huerva: though little more than a muddy ditch, this watercourse still constituted a useful obstacle in respect of troops attacking the south-eastern sector of the defences. (Author's collection)

So much for the first siege of Zaragoza. Napoleon, however, was not a man to forget such setbacks and, in the wake of the great French counter-attack that took the Emperor all the way to Madrid, on 20 December 40,000 men appeared before the city under *maréchal* Mortier. Facing them was a defending force of 32,000 troops, the vast majority of them regiments of conscripts and volunteers who had been raised in the course of the autumn, while the city's mediaeval defences had been strengthened by a line of earthworks and entrenchments that linked together the Aljafería castle and the various convents and monasteries that lay just outside the walls. Inside the city, meanwhile, streets had been barricaded, doors and windows blocked, walls loopholed, and houses linked by tunnels and passageways. But neither these preparations nor the continued braggadocio of José Palafox, a commander whose undoubted genius for propaganda and self-publicity was unfortunately not matched by even the slightest military talent, could save the city. By the close of the year, then, all the approaches to the city south of the Ebro had been closely blockaded, Monte Torrero – the high ground that overlooked the defences – overrun and considerable progress made on the attackers' trenches and gun emplacements. Nor was much done to stop their progress: though plenty of troops were available, the only sorties that took place consisted of suicidal rushes by mere handfuls of men. Very soon, in fact, Palafox was exposed in all his mediocrity. All the troops in Aragón having been concentrated in Zaragoza, it was found that

The author demonstrating the art of camouflage at the foot of the walls that line the Paseo del Asalto; high though the ramparts were, they lacked any towers from which attackers could be subjected to flanking fire, whilst at the same time being desperately vulnerable to artillery. (Author's collection)

there were none left for a relief force, whilst such was the overcrowding in the city that populace and troops alike soon fell prey to a devastating epidemic of typhus. To the misery of disease was soon added that of bombardment, for on 10 January the French opened up on the city with their siege batteries. After 17 days of incessant cannonades, moreover, with the besieging forces now headed by the redoubtable *maréchal* Lannes, the walls were stormed amidst scenes of heavy fighting. As before, the defenders fought on, but the city was doomed. Despite scenes of desperate heroism – in a foretaste of battles far in the future, the French had to fight their way into the city house-by-house, blowing holes in partition walls and methodically slaughtering the defenders of each room – the invaders could not be checked, whilst the ravages of typhus and starvation had very soon brought the city to its knees. As for the civilian populace, with the bombardment continuing unmercifully, all it could do was cower in such sanctuaries as the basilica of Nuestra Señora del Pilar and the neighbouring cathedral of El Salvador, illusory though the shelter was which they provided, as witness the terrible scenes witnessed in the former when a bomb fired from a mortar crashed through the roof and destroyed the chapel of Santa Ana. The last straw, however, was a sudden attack on the hitherto unassailed suburb on the northern bank of the river, a lifeline through which a considerable quantity of supplies had continued to reach the defenders, that soon had the few troops which had been left to hold it fleeing in panic across the bridge that led to the city-proper. At this fresh disaster, now desperately ill of typhus, even Palafox realised that all was lost, and he therefore ordered his surviving followers to lay down their arms.

On 20 February 1809, then, the guns at last fell silent, and the few thousand defenders still on their feet marched into captivity in France, though some few managed to escape on the way, including, not least Agustina of Aragón, who eventually made her way to Seville where she was feted as a species of mascot by the Junta Central. As for Palafox himself, borne away to close confinement in the Chateau de Vincennes, he survived his illness, but did not return to Spain till 1814. On both sides, meanwhile, the losses had been terrible – the Spanish death-toll alone came to some 54,000 – while the city had been reduced to ruins.

Zaragoza Today

Were he to return to his home city, it is probable that José Palafox would have some difficulty finding his way around, for Zaragoza has become a thoroughly modern metropolis. Inevitably, then, much of the built environment as it existed in the early years of the nineteenth century has long since been torn down, while such were the ravages of the siege that even buildings that might have been expected to survive like churches and convents were in many cases demolished rather than restored to their former glory. That said, there remains much to see including the Castillo de la Aljafería (now a cultural centre), the much-battered Puerta de Carmen (the only gate in the city walls not torn down in the course of the nineteenth century), the bridge across the Ebro that gave access to the northern suburb of San Lazaró, the much-contested church of Santa Engracía and, in the imposing Pilar basilica, the Virgin of the Pillar, this last being housed in a tiny niche bordered by a step worn away by the knees of countless generations of pilgrims. These can all be found easily enough, so the focus here will be on guiding the visitor through the narrow streets of the district

A house pockmarked by musket balls in the Calle de la Viola; meanwhile, note the narrowness of the street to the left. Exploring such thoroughfares makes it easy to envisage the difficulties the French encountered in making progress towards the centre of the city. (Author's collection)

The convent of Santa Monica: until it was stormed on 30 January by a group of engineers who had blown a hole in the rear wall of the chapel, defenders stationed here could enfilade any French troops who entered the city via the breach at the southern end of what is today the Calle Cantín y Gambos. Meanwhile, of the 21 nuns resident in the convent at the start of the second siege, only 14 survived to the surrender. (Author's collection)

The plaza and monastery of San Agustín, an area which saw scenes of bitter fighting in the course of the second siege. (Author's collection)

of La Magdalena, this being the area of the old city that contains the most atmospheric memories of the sieges and witnessed some of the fiercest house-to-house fighting. To access this district, begin at the church of Santa Engracia on the Paseo de la Independencía and, passing to its left, walk slightly south of east along the Calle San Clemente. After a short distance the visitor will reach the Plaza de los Sitios and, with it, the city's chief monument to the sieges. From the Plaza de los Sitios, take the Calle Moret and at the end of this last turn left onto the aptly-named Paseo de la Mina, just across the road from which will be observed the River Huerva, a tributary of the Ebro that saw fierce fighting in the first assault on the city. Follow the Paseo de la Mina and its continuation, the even more aptly named, Paseo del Asalto, along the line of the old city wall of which there remain a number of impressive fragments. On reaching the Calle Cantín y Gambos – the site of one of the chief breaches in the defences in the sieges of 1808 and 1809 alike – turn left and then immediately right into the Calle Manuela Sancho: the church straight ahead is the Convento de Santa Mónica, the defence of which is portrayed in famous paintings by Nicolás Mejía Marquéz and Jules Girardet. Having passed said convent, turn right into the Plaza de San Agustín, this last being dominated by the monastery of the same name, although all that is left from the time of the sieges is the facade of the church and one wall of the monks' living quarters. As with its neighbour, Santa Mónica, the tale of its defence is commemorated in fine art in the form of a highly symbolic painting by César Alvarez Dumont dating from 1887 showing a nobleman, an ecclesiastic and various members of the populace banding together in defence of the church's pulpit. From the monastery walk the length of the square noting, en route, the bullet marks scarring the walls of the brightly coloured buildings on the left, and, at the further end, turn left to return to the Calle Doctor Alejandro Palomar. At the junction, turn right and head westward deeper into the heart of the old city. Very shortly thereafter the visitor will come to a large building on a street corner. Known as the Casa de los Sitios, this continues to bear the marks of heavy fighting, and, in particular, the fire of defenders posted in the buildings on the Coso and, immediately beyond it, the church of Santa María Magdalena, another ecclesiastical building that was rebuilt after the war. A block beyond this will be found the Coso and, with it, the furthest point of the French advance into the city in both the sieges, from whence it is but a short walk to the river and the Pilar basilica.

Finally, for those interested in the history of art, it is worth pointing out that the sieges of Zaragoza generated more paintings than any other episode of Spain's war against Napoleon. In this respect, mention has already been made of the canvasses produced by Mejía. Alvarez and Girardet centred on the defence of the convent of Santa Monica and the monastery of San Agustín, but there are also such works as Louis Lejeune's depiction of the French attack on the church of Santa Engracia and Maurice Orange's study of the surviving defenders marching out of the in the wake of the city's surrender, not to mention numerous attempts to capture the moment when Agustina of Aragón saved the day and thereby won her place as the quintessential national heroine, not to mention the best-known Spanish participant in the Peninsular War. Without exception, however, all of this output is marred by a fixed determination to retail a series of images that spoke to a particular view of the Spanish War of Independence: thus, setting aside the fact that Agustina is invariably portrayed as a beautiful young woman, something of which there is no evidence one way or the other, we see the common people rallying en masse to the defence of the *antiguo regimen* under the leadership of the Church and the nobility, while common to all is the display of the

The 'Casa de los Sitios': a seventeenth-century palace that would have been the home of a wealthy noble family, it was left unrestored as a memorial to the heroism of the defenders. (Author's collection)

Roundshot impacts in the eastern face of the Pilar basilica; along with the nearby cathedral and many other churches, the basilica became home to hundreds of desperate civilians. (Author's collection)

Marks of musket balls in the Plaza de San Agustín. (Author's collection)

most conspicuous heroism. In reality, of course, the situation was far more complex, and more benefit will therefore be derived from Francisco Goya's equestrian portrait of José Palafox. Thus, a man who in his heart believed that the insurrection against Napoleon was a catastrophe and by 1808 had become possessed of the darkest and most pessimistic of views in respect of the people of Spain, Goya came from Aragón and in the wake of the first siege travelled to Zaragoza from his home in Madrid. On meeting the Spanish commander, however, the famous artist does not appear to have been won over by his braggadocchio, and, much as he had a few years earlier with his well-known group-study of the Spanish royal family, crafted a work that suggested a reality that was very different from the image: what we see, then, is not a clean-cut martial hero, but rather a complex mixture of ostentation and ambition, indeed almost a caricature.

Further Reading

R. Rudorff, *War to the Death: the Sieges of Saragossa, 1808-1809* (London: Hamish Hamilton, 1974)

C. Esdaile, *The Peninsular War: a New History* (London: Penguin, 2002)

6

Sahagún de Campos
21 December 1808

Though almost always referred to in British sources as Sahagún, the action described in this chapter should properly be referred to as Sahagún de Campos, this being the full name of the Leonese village outside which it was fought on 21 December 1808. The first engagement to take place between British and French troops in Spain in the Peninsular War and a rare display of tactical virtuosity on the part of British cavalry – an arm of service that was all too prone to get out of control on the battlefield and, as Wellington put it, 'gallop at everything' – Sahagún was occasioned by the decision of the new commander of the British forces in Spain and Portugal, Lieutenant General Sir John Moore, to take a more active role in the campaign of November–December 1808 than had hitherto been the case.

Before telling the story of Sahagún, however, we must first delve into its antecedents. For a very short action – it lasted only a few minutes – the combat has a background that is inordinately long and complicated. In brief, following the evacuation of the army of *général de division* Jean-Andoche Junot from Portugal in the wake of the Convention of Sintra, the British government resolved that Moore should take his troops to Spain with a view to them ultimately taking their place alongside the Spanish armies on the River Ebro. This, however, was not to be undertaken without due prudence: on the contrary, rather than plunging deep into the interior of the *meseta*, the British commander was rather ordered to transfer his forces by a mixture of land and sea to the northwestern province of Galicia where they could join up with an additional division which was being sent out from England under Lieutenant General Sir David Baird in the shelter of the rugged mountains which character-ised the region and at the same time acquaint themselves with the situation in the country in more detail, reliable information in respect of this last being in short supply.

This plan of campaign was perfectly sensible, but Moore was on extremely bad terms with the Secretary of State for War and the Colonies, Lord Castlereagh, and was a man avid for glory after many years of frustration in which he had repeatedly been denied the fruits of victory and, most recently, exposed to complete humiliation in the course of an abortive expedition to aid Britain's Swedish allies against the Russians. Fearing that following the government's orders to the letter would cost a great deal of time, he in consequence decided to march directly across the frontier rather than concentrating all his forces in Galicia. This was not, in fact, so bad an idea: spread across central Portugal as they were, his troops could for the most part be concentrated for battle much more quickly than would be the case were they to be sent via Galicia, while the point Moore had chosen as the place where they should be mustered – the famed cathedral and university city of Salamanca – was far enough from the Ebro to be free of any danger even if the French should make a sudden offensive movement. Yet in the event the plan miscarried very badly: marching by direct routes across central Portugal, much of the British army arrived at Salamanca early in November, but this was not the case of a large contingent under Lieutenant General Sir John Hope which included all the cavalry and most of the artillery that, for reasons that are too complex to go into here, ended up marching almost all the way to Madrid before finally doubling back and heading for Salamanca. Whether or not the problem could have been averted is a matter that remains hotly debated, but, even had Hope's column got to Salamanca more quickly, it would have made little difference in that Baird's division was for some weeks blocked from landing by the Junta of Galicia for fear that the costs of supplying it would be exorbitant, the result being that the troops concerned were also badly delayed.

All this made for a very uncomfortable position, albeit one which Moore had in large part brought down upon his own head. Without the troops of Hope and Baird, the British commander had no hope of taking the field successfully, while, Napoleon having by now taken the offensive in the north, the military situation had started to deteriorate in the most dramatic of fashions. To make matters worse, meanwhile, it was all too obvious that the roseate dreams that had been entertained in Britain of the Spanish people rising en masse to confront Napoleon with fire and steel had been wildly overstated, if not invented altogether. Thus, the reality was very different, there being no sign either of any popular enthusiasm or of any attempt on the part of the civil authorities to raise fresh recruits. As the days passed, more and more reports started to come in of terrible Spanish defeats, defeats that could not but leave the road to Salamanca wide open, and all this with Moore's forces scattered from the frontiers of Galicia to the vicinity of Madrid. Faced by this situation (which he blamed on everyone but himself), the British general was plunged into ever greater gloom and on 28 November, ignoring the increasingly desperate appeals of the British ambassador, John Hookham Frere, he sent orders to Baird to turn back and retire on Galicia, whilst at the same time readying the men under his direct command at Salamanca to retreat across the frontier into Portugal as soon as Hope's command, by now only a short distance away, had come in from the east.

Almost immediately however, the situation changed, for Moore heard, first, that part of the Spanish forces were being rallied in the province of León under the *Teniente-General* Pedro Caro y Sureda, Marqués de la Romana, a general who had won much acclaim in Britain for bringing out the Spanish division that had been sent to Denmark in 1807 at the behest of Napoleon in support of the insurrection in Spain and Portugal and leading it to safety with the help of the Royal Navy, and, second, that the population of Madrid was evincing a determination to defend the city from the oncoming masses of invaders. To retreat in such circumstances clearly being absolutely out of the question, Moore therefore resolved to move against Napoleon's communications with the French frontier, these last being protected only by the single corps of *maréchal* Jean-de-Dieu Soult. Picking up Baird's men en route, then, he was soon marching north at the head of an army of 30,000 men.

There followed the battle of Sahagún. In brief, on 20 December elements of the cavalry screen which Moore had thrown out in front of his advancing troops discovered that there was a brigade of French light cavalry commanded by one *général de brigade* César Debelle

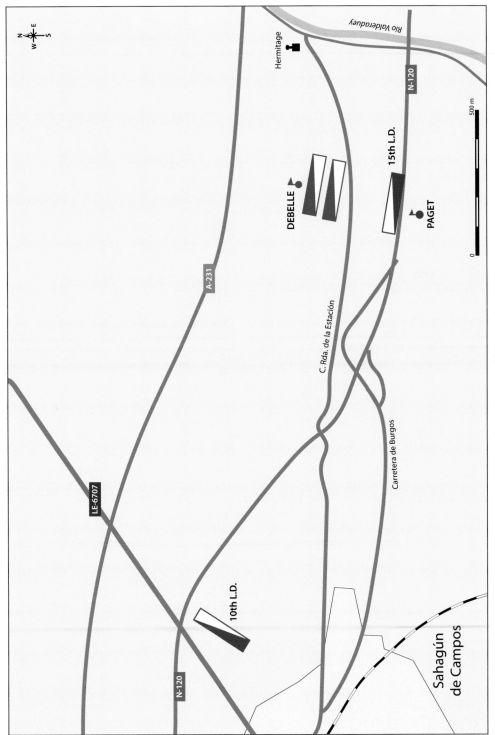

Sahagún de Campos, 21 December 1808.

stationed at the village of Sahagún. Quickly discovering what was afoot, the commander of Moore's cavalry, Lieutenant General Henry, Lord Paget, decided on an immediate attack at the head of the only units he had to hand, namely the 10th and 15th Regiments of Light Dragoons – at least, such was their official designation: in fact, like several of their fellows, both units had been allowed to redesignate themselves as hussars, it being by this term that they are often referred. The 10th was dispatched in a wide encircling movement to the west together with a four-gun detachment of horse artillery, while, led by Paget himself, the 15th rode straight for the settlement. Battle was joined in the cold and misty dawn of 21 December. Having been told by the survivors of a picquet that had been overrun by Paget in the course of his approach that he was about to come under attack, Debelle had got his 750 men mounted up, but he had not had done much more than start moving them out of the village by the time that the 15th Light Dragoons appeared in the fields to the south. In consequence, although the 15th could muster no more than 400 troopers, he and his men had little chance and that despite the facts, first, that they enjoyed the protection of a ditch and, second, that their assailants were so chilled by their ride through the night that many of them could scarcely hold their sabres. Still attempting to deploy into line as the British cavalry charged to shouts of 'Emsdorff and victory!' (the regimental battle-cry, Emsdorff being a small action that took place in July 1760 in which the regiment had played a prominent part), they were swept away in an instant, the light dragoons being much assisted by the fact that Debelle's men made no attempt to counter-charge, rather seeking to repel their assailants with a volley of fire from their carbines. Indeed, resistance seems to have been all but non-existent, large numbers of the unfortunate riders being cut down as they fled. Enraged, perhaps, by the cold and their exhausting ride through the night, the victors appear to have been inclined to show little mercy – one eyewitness describes bodies lying in heaps and British horsemen killing men trying to surrender – but eventually exhaustion prevailed sufficiently for the many survivors who were trapped on the banks of a small river that crossed the path of the French retreat a mile or so to the east to be permitted to throw down their arms.

To put it mildly, this was a signal triumph, some 350 Frenchmen having been killed, wounded or taken prisoner at the cost of just four men dead and 21 wounded. French casualties would have been significantly higher had the 10th Light Dragoons not been so delayed in their march that they only arrived as the fighting was coming to an end. Yet, if it was a signal triumph, it was also an empty one, for a mere three days later news arrived at Moore's headquarters that Napoleon had at last discovered the whereabouts of the British army – something that had hitherto eluded the emperor – and was marching in pursuit with every man that he could muster. Knowing that he could not make a stand against the threat that now menaced him, Moore responded in the only way he possibly could, namely turning his troops around and heading for the safety of Galicia post-haste, thereby initiating the famous 'Retreat to Corunna'. This last, alas, was an episode that the British commander handled very badly, pushing his men onwards at a speed that was quite unnecessary and in the process suffering serious losses. Thus, Napoleon only pursued him as far as Astorga, thereafter dispersing his forces and leaving the campaign to the corps of *maréchal* Soult alone, while the terrain through which the British army fell back was replete with positions that could easily have been held for a day or more. All that being the case, it is probably just as well that Moore was mortally wounded in the battle outside La Coruña that concluded the campaign on 16

The battlefield of Sahagún looking east from the embankment of the N120: the road on the right is the old highway, while the 15th Light Dragoons charged from right to left across the fields shown in the foreground. (Author's collection)

The battlefield of Sahagún looking west along the line of the old highway. Debelle's brigade formed up in the fields on the right, while on the left can be perceived the remains of the ditch which protected its front line. (Author's collection)

The hermitage of the Virgen del Puente. (Author's collection)

The bridge across the River Valderaduey that blocked the retreat of Debelle's brigade. (Author's collection)

Old houses in the centre of Sahagún. (Author's collection)

January 1809. As for Paget, successful though his generalship had been, not just at Sahagún but also at a subsequent rearguard action that took place at Benevente, personal differences with Wellington – notably the fact that following his return to England the noble lord ran off with the wife of the latter's youngest brother, Henry Wellesley – meant that he never saw service in Spain and Portugal again. Only in 1815 did necessity allow the rift to be repaired, Paget, now Lord Uxbridge, returning to the field to take command of Wellington's cavalry in the campaign of the Hundred Days and, indeed, arguably at least, save the day at Waterloo, where, famously enough, he lost a leg in the closing moments of the battle.

Sahagún de Campos Today

Isolated in the vast expanses of the rolling wheat region known as the Tierra de Campos – literally 'the land of the fields' – Sahagún is far removed from the usual haunts of those bent on touring the sites of the Peninsular War and will very likely only ever be visited by devotees of Sir John Moore. This is a pity, for, not least because as an important stopping place on the pilgrim's road to Santiago de Compostela, the town is an attractive place that can boast a number of interesting buildings dating from well before the Napoleonic period, while the battlefield is all but unchanged. To reach this last, starting in the centre of the old town, take the Avenida de la Constitución eastwards in the direction of the railway station and at the Calle del Arco, turn left. Immediately after crossing the bridge over the railway, turn right on the Ronda de la Estación and follow this eastwards out of town. Once over the by-pass (the Carretera de Burgos), this follows line of the old road to Carrión de los Condes, Palencia and, ultimately, Burgos, or, in other words, the route by which Debelle sought to escape Paget's clutches. Having passed beneath the N120 (the Carretera de Burgos' successor), a broad area of open fields opens up on the left, this marking the area where the French attempted to confront the 15th Light Dragoons. Put to flight, they for most part galloped eastwards parallel to the Ronda de la Estación and this should be followed eastwards until a turning is reached beside the river mentioned above. Turning left here, the visitor will after a very short distance reach the mediaeval hermitage of the Virgen del Puente with, immediately beyond it, a small bridge that in 1808 was the sole means of crossing the river, it being at this choke point that most of the prisoners were rounded up.

Further Reading

D.W. Davies, *Sir John Moore's Peninsular Campaign, 1808-9* (Dordrecht: Springer 1974)

P. Haythornthwaite, *Corunna, 1809: Sir John Moore's Fighting Retreat* (Oxford: Osprey Books, 2001)

C. Summerville, *March of Death: Sir John Moore's Retreat to Corunna, 1808-1809* (Barnsley: Frontline Books, 2003)

Portsmouth Napoleonic Society, 'The action at Sahagún, 21st December 1808', <https://www.pns1814.co.uk/Sahagun.htm>, accessed 25 March 2023.

7

Medellín

28 March 1809

A heavy Spanish defeat, the battle of Medellín was one of *maréchal* Victor's greatest victories. Reinforced by a division of dragoons, in early 1809 Victor's corps of the French Army of Spain had been sent to march on Lisbon in accordance with the instructions Napoleon had issued for the pacification of Spain and Portugal in the wake of his decision to return to France following his failure to catch up with the army of Sir John Moore. On nearing Badajoz, however, Victor found himself facing the new commander of the Spanish Army of Extremadura, *Teniente-General* Gregorio García de la Cuesta, a position the latter owed to nothing more than the fact that he happened to be in Badajoz at the time of the fall of Madrid and was therefore seized upon by the junta of that city as a replacement for the unfortunate San Juan. As we have seen, a tough and determined soldier with an excellent record from the so-called War of the Convention of 1793–1795, Cuesta was by nature very aggressive, whilst he also knew that he was feared and distrusted by the Junta Central (the provisional government of Patriot Spain, which had been forced by Napoleon's great counter-offensive to flee from its initial base at Aranjuez to Seville) on account of a bitter dispute that had arisen in respect of the choice of the delegates sent to the Junta to represent his initial base in Old Castile. As if this was not enough, in the fevered atmosphere that reigned in Patriot Spain, a general who did not evince sufficient fighting spirit or was simply defeated by superior forces, was at serious risk of being put to death: setting aside the fate of San Juan, at the outset of the rebellion Cuesta himself had come close to being lynched when he tried to counsel (on grounds that were eminently practical) against the idea of a revolt. Yet another issue, meanwhile, was that the area was in the grip of intense agrarian unrest, the neighbouring town of Don Bénito having just experienced a serious peasant rising. Having initially fallen back in the face of Victor's 13,000 infantry and 4,500 cavalry as they marched southwards from the River Tagus, Cuesta therefore resolved on an offensive.

On 28 March 1809, then, Victor found himself under attack at the town of Medellín, the site of an important bridge across the River Guadiana. Although the French commander's troops were much better than those of Cuesta, whose men were mostly raw recruits, his position was not a comfortable one: caught by surprise, he had the Guadiana at his back, whilst he was also somewhat outnumbered, the Spanish army consisting of 20,000 infantry and 3,000 cavalry, offset though this numerical advantage was by the fact that the French had 42 cannon and howitzers to the Spaniards' 30. Meanwhile, Cuesta had also adopted a sensible battle plan in that he had deployed his forces in a crescent-shaped formation with its flanks resting on the Guadiana on the one hand and a minor tributary of that river called the Ortiga on the other, the idea being that it would launch a concentric attack on the French in which every step that it advanced would thicken its line. To say that there were no faults in this scheme would be foolish: the terrain was very open and the initial Spanish line extremely thin, whilst much would depend on the troops maintaining their alignment with one another as they moved forward. However, if the French were to be attacked at all, it is hard to see what else could have been done, while Cuesta did at least take the precaution of forming his infantry battalions into lines of double depth, with the men arrayed in six ranks rather than the normal three, in the hope that this would give them greater stability.

Following an initial cannonade of about one hour, the Spanish advance began around 2:00 p.m. Initially, indeed, all went well for the Spaniards. Showing much courage, they pressed home their attack in the face of the much superior French artillery fire and drove back Victor's first line, this being composed of the cavalry divisions of *généraux de division* Antoine Lasalle and Victor de Fay de Latour-Maubourg supported by a number of infantry battalions drawn from the troops of the Confederation of the Rhine attached to Victor's army; astonishingly enough, meanwhile, two regiments of French dragoons were driven off by musket fire when they attempted to charge a section of the Spanish array. Nor did it help that many of the infantry had to be kept in square on account of the fact that Cuesta had intermingled his horse and foot, thereby enabling them to lend one another close support. Whether the Spaniards could ever have carried the day is unclear, for Victor had a perfect view of the battlefield from his headquarters on the terrace in front of the castle that overlooked the town and had therefore been quick to rush fresh troops to the front from the substantial numbers of men he had kept in reserve. At this point, however, disaster struck. The exact circumstances remain unclear, but some Spanish cavalry suddenly broke and left a gaping hole in the line. Seeing their opportunity, the French pounced: within moments

The bridge over the River Guadiana at Medellín. (Author's collection)

Medellín, 28 March 1809.

The castle overlooking the town of Medellín whose terrace served *maréchal* Victor as a command post. (Author's collection)

The plain on which the Battle of Medellín was fought viewed from the castle. Now dotted with small-holdings, in 1809 it was rough pasture all but devoid of trees. In the far distance on the left can be seen the town of Don Bénito, the scene of intense agrarian disturbances that may have spurred on Cuesta in his attempt to gain a victory. (Author's collection)

their horsemen were pouring through the gap and rolling up the Spanish infantry on either side. Caught in flank and rear, the Spaniards broke and ran, suffering appalling casualties in the process: by the end of the day they had lost fully 10,000 men as well as 20 of their 30 pieces of artillery. French losses, by contrast, numbered no more than 1,000. As for Cuesta himself, he was ridden down by some fugitive cavalry whilst trying to rally his men (with effects that famously were still to be visible when the British encountered him in the campaign of Talavera four months later). Yet the French profited little from their victory: unable to get Badajoz to surrender, Victor suspended his advance and was eventually forced to withdraw to the Tagus valley for want of supplies, while the receipt of large numbers of fresh troops meant that Cuesta was soon able to take the field once more. In this, however, there was little comfort for the unfortunate inhabitants of Medellín, the town being pillaged so severely by the French that over half its houses were reduced to ruins and most of its population forced to flee.

Medellín Today

Still a very small town, Medellín is most famous as the birthplace of the *conquistador*, Francisco Pizarro, a large statue of whom dominates the main street, whilst it is also known for its impressive Roman theatre. By contrast, the battle was for many years almost forgotten and it was not until the bicentenary that its victims were commemorated by the striking monument that may be found near the bridge across the River Guadiana. As for the battlefield, open country though much of it still remains, it has to be said that it is not the best place to visit. Being flat as a pancake, it is difficult even to photograph, while matters are not helped by the fact that the rough grazing and scrub of 1809 have been swept away in favour of intensive horticulture. Rather than attempting to walk the field, then, the visitor is rather advised to ascend to the castle, from which vantage point the same view can be enjoyed as that which allowed Victor to marshal his forces so effectively. That said, some reasonable views may be obtained from the verges of the Ex206 (the highway to Don Bénito), running, as this does, right across the middle of the battlefield. As said road crosses the Río Ortiga at one point, it also offers a means of judging how much of an obstacle it posed to troops trying to cross it; in so far as this is concerned, it is the opinion of the author that Cuesta's hope that it would prove a major obstacle was far from visionary: not only are the banks quite steep, but the gully through which the stream flows is a good six feet deep, while the fact that the battle was fought in late March means that it could well have been in spate. That individual horsemen might have been able to negotiate it is not in doubt, but any mounted troops trying to advance across it *en masse* would necessarily have been thrown into great disorder.

8

Oporto
28 March and 12 May 1809

The initial capital of the Portuguese insurrection, Oporto witnessed two episodes of violence in the Peninsular War, namely the storming of the city by the forces of *maréchal* Jean de Dieu Soult on 29 March 1809 and its subsequent recapture by the yet-to-be-ennobled Lieutenant General Sir Arthur Wellesley less than two months later. To begin with the former, its origins lay in the orders given by Napoleon to Soult in the wake of the Battle of La Coruña, namely that he should leave Galicia to the troops of *maréchal* Michel Ney, take his corps south and march on Lisbon. Absurdly over optimistic though this scheme was, the French commander did his best to comply. Despite being forced to leave the bulk of his artillery and transport behind for want of sufficient draught animals, on 18 March he crossed the frontier south of Orense, thereby outflanking the defenders of the fortress that blocked the main road from Galicia into Portugal at Valença. Pressing on in the face of desperate resistance from the local militias known as the *Ordenança*, Soult captured the minor fortress of Chaves and then swung westwards towards the sea. Having first crushed the opposing army of *Tenente-General* Bernardino Freire de Andrade at Braga, by the last week of the month he was closing in on Oporto. Situated on the northern bank of the River Douro, this last had been fortified by the erection of an extensive system of redoubts and other earthworks on a ridge of high ground that overlooked the city. However, garnished though the defences were with large numbers of guns, they were too extensive for the forces available to the local civil and military authorities, while most of the troops concerned were in any case little more than raw levies lacking in training and discipline alike. When Soult attacked on 29 March, then, he was able to break through the Portuguese line without the slightest difficulty, his 18,000 troops then proceeding to pursue the fleeing defenders into the streets below. Completely out of control and enraged by weeks of privation, the soldiery proceeded to sack the city unmercifully in the face of which behaviour more and more people fled downhill towards the river in the hope that they would be able to reach the safety of the opposite bank.

Sadly enough, at this point military disaster was topped by tragedy. While some of the luckier refugees managed to find boats to take them across the majority were left with no option but to crowd onto the only available crossing, namely a ramshackle bridge of boats, the general panic being rendered all the greater by the arrival on the quay of a number of French cavalry. With far too many people trying to get across the bridge at once, the

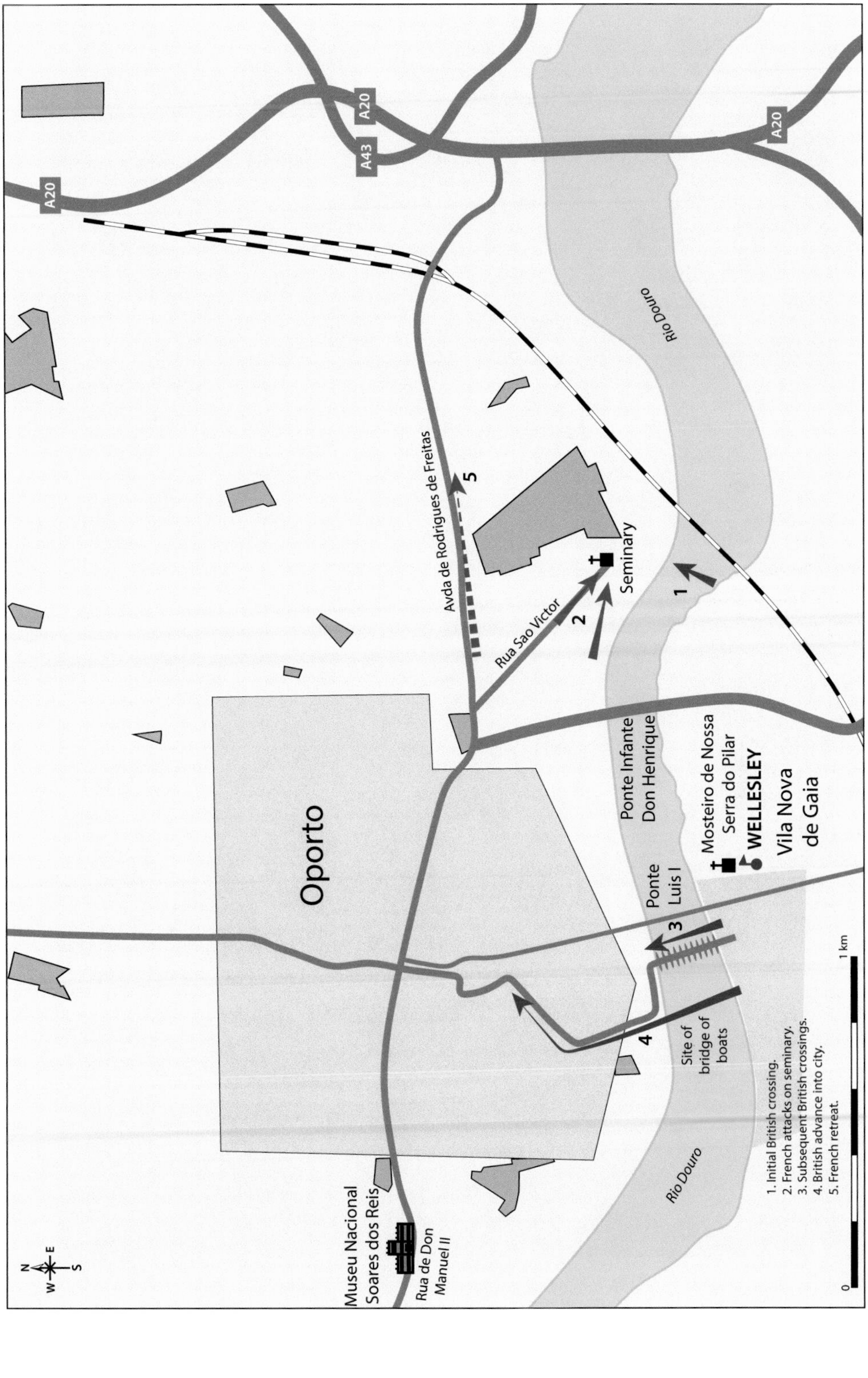
A20
A43
A20
A20
Rio Douro
Avda de Rodrigues de Freitas
5
Rua Sao Victor
2
Seminary
1
Ponte Infante Don Henrique
Mosteiro de Nossa Serra do Pilar
WELLESLEY
Vila Nova de Gaia
Oporto
Ponte Luis I
3
4
Site of bridge of boats
Rio Douro
1. Initial British crossing.
2. French attacks on seminary.
3. Subsequent British crossings.
4. British advance into city.
5. French retreat.
0
1 km
Museu Nacional Soares dos Reis
Rua de Don Manuel II
N
W
E
S

Oporto, 28 March and 12 May 1809.

The site of the massacre beside the River Douro showing the street from which terrified fugitives poured onto the quayside with the French cavalry in hot pursuit. (Author's collection)

The approximate site of the pontoon bridge; meanwhile, the boats in the foreground are very similar to those used to ferry Wellesley's troops across the Douro. (Author's collection)

inevitable happened in that one of the pontoons was driven beneath the fast-flowing waters by the excessive weight whereupon the entire edifice was torn apart and large numbers of the refugees hurled into the river, several hundred of the unfortunates concerned either succumbing to drowning or being shot down by the vengeful soldiery as they struggled to reach the shore. How many were lost in this tragic episode in particular is unknown, but the Portuguese death toll for the day as a whole has been calculated as some 8,000 men, women and children, the French also capturing 200 guns and enormous quantities of supplies.

Impressive as the feat of capturing Oporto was, it marked the limit of Soult's success. Thus, isolated in the depth of Portugal without the slightest idea as to what was happening elsewhere in the Peninsula amidst many signs that the Portuguese were recovering from their initial reverses (on 25 March, *Tenente-General* Francisco Silveira had succeeded in recapturing Chaves and taking prisoner the whole of its 1,300-strong garrison), the French commander decided that he could advance no further and therefore went onto the defensive until such time as he had heard from the forces of *maréchal* Victor, supposed, as these were, to be marching on Lisbon from the east, not that they had even crossed the frontier at this point. Indeed, the very day that Soult stormed Oporto, Victor was routing Cuesta's Army of Extremadura at Medellín. In consequence, the initiative passed to Sir Arthur Wellesley, who had on 2 April been appointed to the command of all the British forces in Portugal. Having landed at the Portuguese capital some 20 days later, the new arrival was soon marching north at the head of 18,000 men to attack Soult whose communications with the Spanish frontier were simultaneously threatened by a division of Portuguese troops headed by the new commander of the Portuguese army, William Carr Beresford.

What followed was a masterpiece. Although the screen of troops he had thrown out south of the Douro was quickly driven in, Soult considered himself to be quite safe as the bridge had not been restored, while every boat that could be found had been seized and taken over to the northern bank. Had he known of Beresford's column, the *maréchal* might have been more worried, but at this point he was wholly ignorant of the fact that it had taken the field. That the city could not be held indefinitely was clear enough, but, send off some of his troops though the *maréchal* did, he saw no need for undue haste and continued to defy Wellesley with the remainder of his forces, these last numbering some 11,000 men, the vast majority of them infantry or gunners.

When Wellesley arrived in the transpontine suburb of Vila Nova on 11 May, it therefore at first looked as though he would be stymied, but the next morning a small number of wine-barges were discovered a little way off, and it was not long before a daring plan had been drawn up. In brief, surveying the scene from the imposing convent directly overlooking the site of the pontoon bridge, the British commander realised that a large bend in the river just to the east of the city meant that there was a good chance that an attempt to get troops across to the northern bank in that area would not be observed by the French. While it was clearly a considerable risk, it was decided that, although no more than 100 men could be carried over at a time, the boats should be used to put a battalion across with instructions, if possible, to seize the prominent cluster of buildings – as it transpired, the diocesan seminary – that could be seen standing on a bluff just outside the eastern-most extremity of the city. Had there been French troops in the seminary, the plan would almost certainly have come to grief at an early stage, but, happily enough, it was completely empty, while the French did not discover what was going on until a garrison of several hundred men had been installed

The monastery of Nossa Serra do Pilar. (Author's collection)

The seminary as viewed from Nossa Serra do Pilar. (Author's collection)

The seminary as viewed by its French assailants; in 1809 it is likely that the garden to the left (now a cemetery) was surrounded by a high stone wall. (Author's collection)

within the walls. Needless to say, a brigade of infantry was sent to launch a counterattack, but the men concerned were beaten off without difficulty, and that despite the fact that the officer appointed to command the garrison, Lieutenant General the Honourable Edward Paget, had to be carried back across the river with a shattered arm. A battery of French guns that was brought to support the attack was quickly forced to withdraw by the fire of Wellesley's artillery, most of which had been concentrated on the slopes above Vila Nova. Determined to retake the seminary, Soult then brought up a second brigade to deal with the interlopers, but the garrison had since been substantially reinforced, and once again the attackers were forced to withdraw to the safety of the city, while their commander, *général de division* Maximilien Foy, was badly wounded. In calling up the men concerned, however, Soult had left the city's quaysides unprotected, and, much angered by the calamities that they had suffered at the hands of the invaders, the populace rushed to the river, seized all the boats they could find and rowed them across to Vila Nova post-haste. Very soon, then, more British infantry were pouring across the river and pushing uphill towards the city's cathedral. As if this was not enough, meanwhile, a brigade of infantry and a single under-strength regiment of cavalry – the 14th Light Dragoons – got across the Douro some miles further inland and closed in on the only road by which the French could hope to effect their escape, namely the rough track that led into the rugged hills to the east. In theory, the main road to the north was also an option, but the fact that there was still a Portuguese garrison in Valença meant that getting across the frontier in that direction would have been very difficult, if not impossible.

A street typical of the narrow thoroughfares leading up from the quayside to the centre of the city. It was up such passages that the men of Wellesley's army who were brought across the river by the inhabitants advanced to get to grips with the French. (Author's collection)

The Museu Nacional Soares dos Reis: formerly known as the Palacio dos Carranças, it was used by *maréchal* Soult as his headquarters. (Author's collection)

With matters in this state, Soult could only give the order to evacuate Oporto forthwith and his troops were soon fleeing eastwards in great disorder, the only reason that so many of them got away being that Wellesley had too few horsemen across the river to mount an effective pursuit. In fairness to the 14th Light Dragoons, the regiment did launch a gallant charge in an attempt to do what it could, but the only result was that it was beaten off with the loss of one third of its strength. Yet the French defeat had still been serious enough, Soult having suffered some 600 men killed or wounded together with another 1,800 taken prisoner whilst at the same time managing to inflict only 125 casualties on his assailants. Nor was this the end of the his travails: forced to make use of routes that were ever more impracticable, by the time he had reached the safety of the Spanish frontier, another 4,500 men had in one way or another fallen by the wayside, the invaders also having been stripped of all their guns and baggage. In the Anglo-Portuguese camp, by contrast, all was jubilation, the only cause for regret being that several of Wellesley's subordinate commanders, including, not least, Beresford, had shown little in the way of energy and initiative.

Oporto Today

Portugal's second city, Oporto is a modern metropolis that has expanded far beyond the area that it occupied in 1808, and it is therefore impossible to trace the redoubts and other fortifications that were stormed by the French on 29 March 1809; that said, the quay which led to the bridge of boats is still intact, while it is also graced by a monument to the tragedy that it witnessed. Also easily accessible are the chief sites of Wellesley's liberation of the city, namely the monastery of Nossa Serra do Pilar, which served as the British commander's headquarters and the seminary which saw such bitter fighting, this last being situated on the Largo do Padre Baltasar Guedes at the eastern of the Rua do Sao Victor. In viewing the former, the visitor should ignore the numerous cannon-ball strikes that pockmark its façade, these rather having been inflicted in the civil war of 1828–1834. For a spectacular walk between the two, it is worth taking the Ponte María: this crosses the river just east of the monastery and offers spectacular views of the area where the first British troops crossed to the northern bank. Finally, also worth visiting is the Museu Nacional Soares dos Reis in the Rua de Dom Manuel II: an eighteenth-century palace, it was here that Soult had his headquarters.

Further Reading

O. Hayes, *Oporto, 1809* (Banstead: Bretwalda Books, 2013)

D. Buttery, *Wellington against Soult: the Second Invasion of Portugal, 1809* (Barnsley: Pen and Sword, 2016).

9

Alcántara

14 May 1809

Alcántara was one of the smaller actions of the Peninsular War and has its origins in the formation of the unit known as the Loyal Lusitanian Legion in the wake of the Portuguese insurrection against the French. The brain-child of a number of exiles who had fled the French invasion in the autumn of 1807 and escaped to England, it was intended that this should be an independent force of all arms – infantry, cavalry and artillery – led in part by British officers that could harass the occupation forces and win time for the leaders of the uprising to raise a new army to replace that of the Braganças, this last having been disbanded by the French other than a few picked elements that had been marched off to join the *grande armée* as the Légion Portugaise. Eager to be seen to being doing whatever it could to support its Portuguese allies, the Portland administration quickly swung behind the scheme and made available a full set of arms and equipment, whilst also providing money for the production of the dark green uniforms in which it was decided that officers and men alike should be dressed. As for a commander, the post was given to Lieutenant Colonel Sir Robert Wilson, an extremely flamboyant character who had made a name for himself in the War of the First Coalition and had since been employed as a liaison officer in both Prussia and Russia. Wilson was authorised to recruit a small staff of British officers, at the head of which he proceeded to sail to Oporto, the city in which the Portuguese insurrection had begun and still remained the *de facto* capital of Patriot Portugal despite the liberation of Lisbon following the Battle of Vimeiro. At this point, however, serious problems began. At full strength (some 3,000 men), the Legion was supposed to consist of three battalions of infantry, a regiment of cavalry and a battery of artillery – and it had been blithely assumed that the patriotic enthusiasm that was held to prevail in Portugal would produce all the men required without delay, but, in the event, nothing could have been further from the truth. Exactly as had been the case with Spain, the idea of a populace ardent to take up arms for God, king and country was found to be woefully misplaced, the uprising having rested on factors that were far more complex than hatred of Napoleon. So far as military service was concerned, indeed, few men could be found who were willing to enlist in anything other than part-time militias tied to the defence of their own towns and villages, the result being that even the Portuguese authorities were struggling to find the men they needed to rebuild the regular army. Rank outsider as he was, then, Wilson proved completely incapable of realising his intentions, and the fact is that he would have been left with no men at all had he not been given several hundred Galicians who had been rounded up as vagrants after fleeing across the frontier in a bid to escape the conscription which had been imposed by the provincial junta that had taken control of their home province.

It was not just a question of manpower. An inveterate glory-hunter, Wilson had seemingly been possessed by a vision of himself as an independent commander who would be left free to fight what amounted to a private war, and he was therefore outraged to discover that the insurgent administration that had coalesced around the figure of the Bishop of Oporto was determined to incorporate the Loyal Lusitanian Legion into its own forces. Taking such elements of the proposed formation as he had managed to organise – a small infantry battalion, a single squadron of cavalry and a tiny artillery battery consisting of just two 4-pounder guns – with him, then, Wilson fled to the fortress of Almeida, which at time was home to a small British garrison whose commander he hoped to persuade to join him in a series of raids against the enemy forces holding Salamanca and its environs. Yet here, too, Wilson met disappointment, Lieutenant General Sir John Cradock, the rather lack-lustre commander that Sir John Moore had left to hold Portugal following his march into Spain, quickly deciding to pull the two infantry regiments concerned back to Lisbon.

To put it mildly, Wilson was now in a very difficult position, but he had no intention of just sitting quietly behind the walls of Almeida and instead resolved to bamboozle the commander of the French forces in Salamanca, *général de division* Pierre Lapisse, into thinking that he was faced by a much large force than was actually the case. Sending small parties of his men forward into the plains of southern León, he therefore directed them to make as much of a nuisance of themselves as they could, the result being a number of minor actions in which small detachments of French troops found themselves under attack by troops whom they for some time presumed to be British regulars. For good measure, meanwhile, Wilson also sent part of his solitary infantry battalion to hold the Puerta de Baños, thereby cutting communications between Lapissse and his parent commander, *maréchal* Victor, the remainder of the latter's forces – in essence, II Corps – currently being deployed far to the south in observation of the fortress of Badajoz.

According to Wilson's admirers, all this amounted to a great strategic success in that it dissuaded Lapisse from marching on Ciudad Rodrigo and Almeida. The only problem was that the French commander had no intention of undertaking any such operation, the single infantry division that was all that he had at his disposal being wildly insufficient to try anything so foolhardy, not that his orders allowed him to try anything of the sort in any case. Nor did he have much difficulty out-smarting Wilson in that, ordered to join Victor preparatory to the march on Lisbon via Badajoz and Elvas that the orders issued by Napoleon prior to his departure for France after his pursuit of Sir John Moore directed the *maréchal* to undertake, Lapisse made as if to attack Ciudad Rodrigo, thereby persuading Wilson to recall the men he had sent to hold the Puerta de Baños and in the process open the way for the troops concerned to march south.

To reach Victor, however, they had to get across the River Tagus, and in this respect the only means by which they could do so was the Roman bridge that spanned the river beneath the northern walls of the minor border fortress of Alcántara. Inadequately protected in terms of fortifications and garrisoned only by a town militia, this last was an easy target, and on 12 April 1809 Lapisse's troops stormed the feeble barricade that had been erected to protect the approaches to the bridge, poured across the river under the cover of a heavy

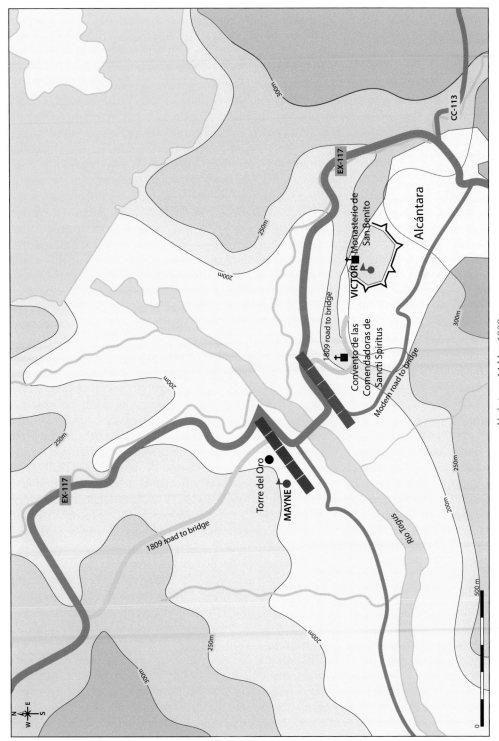

Alcántara, 14 May 1809.

cannonade and broke into the town which they then proceeded to sack in the most unmerciful of fashions, (amongst the booty, be it said, was a recipe-book stolen from the beautiful convent of San Bénito which gave French cuisine an item which can still be encountered in Parisian restaurants today, namely Perdrix à la Mode d'Alcántara).

Sacking Alcántara was one thing and holding it quite another, the next morning therefore seeing Lapisse's troops take the road they needed to follow to join Victor at Mérida. Hard on their heels, meanwhile, was the Loyal Lusitanian Legion, this last marching across the bridge and entering the town almost before the last of its attackers had left its southern gate. Having been called to the headquarters of the newly-arrived Lieutenant General Sir Arthur Wellesley to advise him on the situation in northern Portugal, Wilson was not himself present, but his deputy, Lieutenant Colonel William Mayne had received some reinforcements in the shape of the Idanha Nova militia regiment and a single company of cavalry, this little force having marched over the frontier from the nearby Portuguese fortress – again, a very minor place – of Castelo Branco. With the new arrivals, meanwhile, came orders from the British commander to hold the crossing against any attempt to retake it and use it to strike into Portugal, Mayne very sensibly deciding that the best way to achieve this was to leave the town to its own devices and withdraw to the steep bluffs overlooking the bridge from the north, the slopes of which were garnished by an eighteenth-century watch-tower known as the Torre del Oro. Most of the troops at his disposal were infantry, of course, and the 1,500 men concerned were hastily put to the construction of such field defences as could be thrown together, but there were also six guns, the two cannon which Wilson had brought from Oporto having at some point been supplemented by four Portuguese 4-pounders. As for the handful of cavalry which Mayne had at his disposal, they were dispatched to watch the road from the south, the bridge in the meantime being prepared for demolition.

As can be imagined, the news that there were Portuguese troops in Alcántara came as a considerable shock to Victor who jumped to the completely erroneous conclusion that they were the advance guard of an enemy force that was advancing to attack him from the north, one of the many problems that he was labouring under being that that he had absolutely no idea what was happening inside Portugal, all that Wellesley had actually done in respect of the Tagus valley being to send some 11,000 British and Portuguese troops to garrison Castelo Branco. Almost immediately, then, Lapisse's unfortunate division found itself marching back along the same road it had just traversed in the opposite direction accompanied by, not only a division of dragoons and some additional artillery, but also *maréchal* Victor himself, the whole force outnumbering Mayne by some six to one.

Battle was joined early on 14 May when the French encountered the thinly-stretched Portuguese cavalry screen, the riders concerned promptly taking to flight and clattering back through the town and over the bridge at high speed. Pushing through the streets under fire from Mayne's cannon, the attackers soon gained the buildings overlooking the river and opened up with their own artillery, while in the meantime getting ready for the unavoidable task of storming the bridge (running, as it did, through a narrow gorge, the river was quite unfordable). Covered by the fire not just of Victor's guns, at least some of which were 8-pounders that completely outclassed the weapons available to Mayne, but also hundreds of French infantrymen, the assault column duly charged down the ramp that led to the bridge and negotiated the sharp turn at the bottom that was the only way of reaching it, but was shot to pieces as it tried to reach the far side and eventually scrambled back to the safety

The southern face of the defences of Alcántara: poorly designed and in a bad state of repair, the latter had little chance of repelling even opponents equipped with nothing but field artillery. (Author's collection)

The Puente de Alcántara as viewed from the foot of the bluff on which the town is built; note how the bridge is completely overlooked the heights on the northern bank. (Author's collection)

of the town. Thereafter the action settled into nothing more than a prolonged exchange of fire. In such an exchange, of course, sheer numbers dictated that the French would overcome their opponents, while their advantage was boosted still further by the fact that many of their men had been able to find good cover in buildings such as the large convent that directly overlooked the bridge (while it was true enough that 10 men in each company of the Legion's infantry were equipped with Baker rifles rather than muskets, the number concerned was not enough to make a difference). Sure enough, with casualties mounting steadily, at around midday the morale of the Idanha Nova regiment suddenly collapsed whereupon the whole unit turned and fled. Seeing this, Mayne attempted to blow the bridge, but the explosion left it sufficiently passable for troops moving two abreast to get across. With this, the game was up, and Mayne therefore ordered the green-coated legionaries to retreat post-haste covered by the fire of a single gun that managed to delay the advance of the French across the river for a full hour before finally being spiked and abandoned. Also left behind were some 300 dead and wounded, although the French, who were too mauled to pursue Mayne's men with any degree of seriousness, had lost far more, one source going so far as to put their casualties at 1,400.

Thus ended the combat of Alcántara. Re-occupied by Portuguese forces later the same month, the town remained in the hands of Napoleon's opponents for the rest of the war. As the only crossing of the Tagus for many miles though, the precaution was taken of completing the demolition of the span of the bridge that had been damaged by Mayne and bridging the resultant gap with a remarkable 'flying bridge' which could literally be rolled up

The ramp leading from the town of Alcántara to the bridge across the Tagus. Note the almost total absence of cover on the side of the road overlooking the river: formed in close column, the French could not but have suffered heavy casualties as they charged down the slope. (Author's collection)

The town of Alcántara viewed from the bridge; safely ensconced in the buildings, the French were able to pick off their Portuguese opponents more-or-less at will. (Author's collection)

and hauled in should the crossing ever be threatened from the north. Meanwhile, the town was much traversed by the Anglo-Portuguese army as its forces moved up and down the frontier in accordance with the events of the campaign. As for the Loyal Lusitanian Legion, after a furious battle which saw Wilson try desperately to defend its independence from the Portuguese authorities, and, in particular, the British commander of the Portuguese army, Beresford, it was eventually incorporated into the Portuguese army as additional battalions of *caçadores*. Wilson himself thereupon returning to England in high dudgeon. There is, however, an amusing sequel to the story. Passing through Castelo Branco in the course of his journey to Wellington's headquarters prior to the action, Wilson appears to have encountered a young Scottish commissary named John Downie with a highly chequered past – having begun his career as a slave trader on the newly-conquered Caribbean island of Trinidad, he had gone on to serve as the private secretary of the South-American revolutionary, Francisco de Miranda – and so impressed him with his tales of derring-do that Downie decided to emulate him and form a private army of his own in the form of the so-called Loyal Extremaduran Legion. Even more ephemeral than its Portuguese counterpart, this force never achieved real substance, but Downie's thoroughly unscrupulous efforts to turn his dream into reality make for an entertaining story, involving him, as they did, in successfully bamboozling, not just Richard and Henry Wellesley (at the time concerned,

A typical street in Alcántara; with the exception of the power cables, almost nothing has changed since 1809. (Author's collection)

The convent of San Bénito; positioned directly above the bridge, it offered the French excellent positions from which to lavish fire on the Portuguese troops manning the slopes on the far side of the river.
(Author's collection)

British Foreign Secretary and British ambassador to Spain), but also Wellington himself, while Downie ended up as a Spanish general and, not just that, but governor of the Alcazar of Seville.

Alcántara Today

A remote town even by Spanish standards, Alcántara is a pretty place but has little to offer the casual tourist other than the bridge and the stunningly beautiful convent of San Bénito, from whose terrace it may be assumed that *maréchal* Victor directed the fighting. Possessed of excellent views of the river though it is, San Bénito is not to be confused with the convent mentioned above as overlooking the bridge, this last being rather the Convento de las Comendadoras de Sancti Espiritus: abandoned following the final dissolution of Spain's religious orders in the 1830's, this is now little more than a ruin, but its commanding position can still be appreciated. For the Peninsular-War 'buff', by contrast, there is much to see: not only is the main scene of the action completely untouched and extremely easy both to find and to interpret, but many stretches of the town's defences have survived, it being all too clear why it could not have been held against a determined attack from any direction other than across the river.

Further Reading

R. Chartrand, *Oldest Allies: Alcántara, 1809* (Oxford: Osprey, 2012)

M. Glover, *A Very Slippery Fellow: the Life of Sir Robert Wilson, 1777-1849* (Oxford: Oxford University Press, 1978)

10

Talavera

27–28 July 1809

Despite being a clear victory that inflicted terrible damage on the French forces engaged in the action, Talavera was in many ways a disappointing battle, the campaign which led to it having been embarked on with the highest hopes. The story begins with the aftermath of the expulsion of the army of *maréchal* Jean de Dieu Soult from Portugal in May 1809. In brief, having completed his immediate orders, which simply called for the defence of the proverbial 'oldest ally', Lieutenant General Sir Arthur Wellesley resolved on an offensive in central Spain in company with an Army of Extremadura rebuilt after its near annihilation at Medellín to a strength of some 35,000 men, but still commanded by the fiercely combative *Teniente-General* Gregorio García de la Cuesta. However, it took time to make the initial arrangements, and it was not until mid-July that all was ready. In outline, the Allied plan, which had grown considerably in scope and ambition, called for the 23,000-strong Spanish Army of La Mancha, headed by *Teniente-General* Francisco-Javier Venegas, to march on Madrid from its base at La Carolina in the Sierra Morena and thereby pin down *général de division* Horace Sébastiani's corps defending the southern approaches to the capital, as well as the small central reserve headed by King Joseph, while Wellesley and Cuesta struck eastwards up the Tagus valley and attacked the corps of *maréchal* Victor, which we last saw fighting the Loyal Lusitanian Legion at Alcántara but had since fallen back to a position closer to Madrid. Given that Victor had but 19,000 men, it could be assumed that he would be crushed whereupon Joseph and Sébastiani would be forced to retreat. Joseph and Sébastiani might, of course, ignore Venegas and join Victor, or Victor ignore Wellesley and Cuesta and join Joseph and Sébastiani, but, even if they came to be (something that did not seem especially likely given that it would in either case lead to the fall of Madrid), neither possibility was especially worrying, for both the Allied forces had an easy line of retreat available to them and therefore ought to be to slip away unscathed before the French came up with them. All that was required for victory to be obtained, then, was for all three Allied commanders to press the French hard while at the same time taking care to watch out for a surprise French counter-strike.

In almost no respect, however, did this plan succeed. Coming up against Victor east of the undistinguished riverside town of Talavera de la Reina in a strong position behind the River Alberche on 22 July, Wellesley and Cuesta agreed to attack him the next day, only for the Spaniards to fail to move at the appointed time. Finding that Victor had in consequence been able to pull out safe and sound, Wellesley was furious. Why the Spanish general refused to move is not quite clear, but he may well have come to entertain genuine doubts about attacking across a river that was notoriously prone to flash-flooding whenever summer storms broke out in the mountains in which it rose. If so, however, he failed to communicate his decision to his British counterpart, and it is therefore just possible that he suspected that he was being led into a trap: not only did he have many enemies in the Junta Central who would have been only too glad to see him removed from his command, but he was also highly mistrustful of Wellesley whom he regarded either as an agent of the Junta or, alternatively, a rival who was out to usurp his command. Whatever the reason for what had passed, the result was disastrous, for the British commander refused point-blank to advance any further than the Alberche, a decision which also rested on a number of other considerations that were already weighing heavily on his mind. In so far as these were concerned, there were first of all two issues that pertained to the Spaniards in that the Army of Extremadura was all too obviously for the most part composed of raw recruits who were ill-armed, ill-equipped, lacking in training and officered in many instances by men with no experience of war, while, fairly elderly even as it was, Cuesta was still suffering from the effects of the injuries he had sustained at Medellín and was therefore arguably in no state to lead an army in the field. On top of all this, meanwhile, there was the problem of food and transport: Wellesley had only agreed to advance into Spain in return for the Spaniards agreeing to meet the needs of his army in full, but, through no fault of their own perhaps – notoriously lacking in resources at the best of times, the Tagus valley had in the past few months been stripped of everything it could offer by the French – this was something that they had completely failed to do, the result being that his men were staring famine in the face.

If Wellesley had been furious before, it was now the turn of Cuesta. Unable to shift his ally from his decision, the Spanish commander decided to press on eastwards anyway, only on 25 July suddenly to run into not just Victor but also King Joseph and Sébastiani. What, then had gone wrong? The answer lay with Venegas, who had not only advanced in the most dilatory fashion, but also turned aside to engage in useless demonstrations against Toledo (a town that is near impregnable against troops coming from the south). What motivated this conduct is unclear, but one possibility is that Venegas had decided to sabotage Cuesta's operations out of sheer spite and another that, for one reason or another, he had been given secret instructions to hang back. Whatever the explanation, the result was that 46,000 men were therefore soon heading for Wellesley and Cuesta. It was not just with the men actually facing them that the two generals would be forced to contend, however. Albeit briefly, we must now turn to events further north. In so far as these were concerned, following his expulsion from Portugal, *maréchal* Soult had done what he could to refit his battered corps and then turned north to assist Ney in suppressing the Spanish forces he had been battling in Galicia ever since the province had been occupied following the evacuation of the army of Sir John Moore. Almost immediately, however, Soult had decided that the real battle lay in the Tagus valley and he had therefore turned his men around and headed back into León, an outraged Ney responding by evacuating Galicia and marching south in hot pursuit. Given that the western parts of Old Castile were already held by the corps of *maréchal* Edouard Mortier, the net result was that another 50,000 French troops were poised to march south across the mountains that fringed the northern edge of the Tagus valley and take Wellesley and Cuesta from the rear.

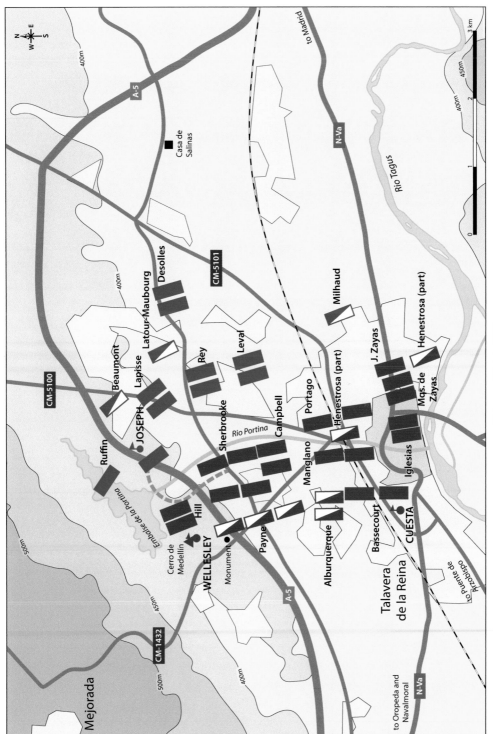

Talavera, 28 July 1809.

The eastern face of the Casa de Salinas; Wellesley attempted to observe the French advance from the low tower beside the tree. (Author's collection)

A detail of the courtyard of the Casa de Salinas. (Author's collection)

To put it mildly, then, the prospects for the Allied cause did not look good. Indeed, it was only a matter of luck that things were not still worse, Cuesta's hopelessly outnumbered forces only being saved from destruction by some sustained French bungling. By dint of a hasty retreat, however, the morning of 27 July found them streaming back across the Alberche and heading for a defensive position selected for them by Wellesley a little further west, it being the view of the latter that the line of the river was indefensible. Covering the Spanish retreat, meanwhile, was the British division of Major General John Mackenzie. This formation, however, was neither as alert or as well-posted as it might have been, while the countryside around its headquarters – a substantial Renaissance palace called the Casa de Salinas – was obscured by groves of olives, pines and holm-oak. Eager to see what was going on, Wellesley had ridden out to this building and mounted the low tower that surmounted its eastern face when suddenly a swarm of French infantry burst out of the scrub and attacked Mackenzie's troops. In the subsequent scrimmage the British commander came very close to being captured or even killed – clattering down the stairs into the courtyard below, he just got out of the rear gate before the French came rushing in from the other side – whilst over 400 men became casualties, but he succeeded in rallying the division and bringing it safely back to the main Allied line.

To the accompaniment of a constant cannonade, both armies now began to deploy for battle. Moving up from the east through country covered by the same sort of scrub that had so hampered Mackenzie at the Casa de Salinas, the French occupied a position running from a low hill called the Cerro de Cascajal southwards across the plain that extended to the Tagus. Stationed at the edge of the scrubland and olive groves through which the French had come, their right and centre had an excellent field of fire and could move on the Allies over open ground, but their left was less well-defined, the olives, pines and holm-oaks covering the entire position and extending forward in a great belt that encompassed the town of Talavera and merged with the position occupied by the Allies.

If the terrain did not especially assist the French, it did not wholly favour the Allies either. For most of its length their position was marked by a small stream called the Portiña, but, except where it ran through a narrow ravine between the Cerro de Cascajal and a somewhat steeper and higher eminence running more-or-less east-west known as the Cerro de Medellín that buttressed the Allied left, this was no obstacle whatsoever. Just before it plunged into the olive groves and scrubby woodland that cloaked the southern end of the battlefield, it was overlooked by a low knoll called the Pajar de Vergara, but otherwise the

A panorama of the battlefield taken in 1995 from the northern outskirts of Talavera; the Cerro de Medellín is in the centre and the much lower Cerro de Cascajal to the right; in the past 30 years much of the land in the foreground has been built over. (Author's collection)

position was protected only by the Cerro de Medellín. Some further help was derived from the groves and enclosures that filled the space between said knoll and the Tagus, but, if these hampered cavalry charges and artillery bombardments, they at the same time exposed the defenders to the danger of being taken by surprise, masked their own cannon and made it very difficult to manoeuvre. Meanwhile, most of the centre was extremely vulnerable to cannon fire, for, except on the rather narrow Cerro de Medellín, which was all but cleft in two by a deep re-entrant that cut into its southern slopes, there was no reverse slope of the sort that Wellesley so much favoured.

The Cerro de Medellín viewed from the Cerro de Cascajal; note the brick water-tower: this marks both the site of the repulse of Ruffin's night attack and the crest that sheltered Hill's division during the French bombardment. (Author's collection)

The eastern slopes of the Pajar de Vergara; although the knoll was bare in 1809, the vegetation gives a good idea of the groves that shielded the Spanish army just to the south. (Author's collection)

Held by the British from the Cerro de Medellín to the Pajar de Vergara and the Spaniards from the Pajar de Vergara to the Tagus, the Allied position, then, was really rather mediocre. As if this was not enough, the Spaniards were clearly in many cases extremely brittle – in a famous incident that took place in the late afternoon or early evening, four battalions took to their heels at the sound of their own muskets after letting fly a massive volley at some French cavalry that had appeared far in the distance. Finally, the Allies were badly outgunned, Joseph, Victor and Sébastiani having brought 80 cannon to the battlefield and Wellesley and Cuesta only 55. The French were somewhat outnumbered, true – Wellesley and Cuesta could muster some 53,000 men to their 46,000 – but the rather slight advantage that this amounted to was completely nullified by the fact that, as the attackers, they could mass the bulk of their forces against the British or the Spaniards alone whilst containing the rest of the Allied array with a mere handful of cavalry (another branch of the service in which Wellesley and Cuesta were distinctly over-matched, at least in terms of quality).

Whilst either the British or the Spaniards could have been the target of the blow that followed, for a variety of reasons it fell upon the former. In this, at least, the Allies were fortunate. Far better trained than the Spaniards and much heartened by their success in Portugal, the British could rely upon the tactical genius of Wellesley, whilst the weeks that had passed since the Oporto campaign had seen the formation of the army into permanent divisions. However, *maréchal* Victor – the only one of the three French commanders on the field at this point – had never faced the British in battle. Determined to seize the lion's share

Part of the summit of the Cerro de Medellín showing the cleft which provided Hill's infantry with cover during the French bombardment; this area was also the epicentre of the fighting which followed the night attack of 27 July. (Author's collection)

The summit of the Cerro de Cascajal looking south towards Talavera; French artillery positioned here inflected terrible damage on Wellesley's exposed troops. Meanwhile, the Pajar de Vergara may be glimpsed in the far distance on the right-hand side of the photograph. (Author's collection)

of the glory, he did not even wait for the rest of the French army to come up. Hardly had night fallen, then, when the division of *général de division* François Ruffin moved forward against the Cerro de Medellín. Apparently positioned in the wrong place, the defenders were taken by surprise and the scrub-covered slopes of the hill soon became the scene of a confused night action. Riding up to find out what was going on, the genial and well-liked divisional commander, Major General Rowland Hill, was almost captured, and it was only after fierce fighting that the French were driven off.

Troublesome though it may have been, the attack on the Cerro de Medellín had therefore been a failure. However, alerted to the danger though the defenders now were, Victor had not finished. Thus, at five o'clock in the morning the massed batteries of French artillery opened fire on Wellesley's troops. Under cover of this terrible cannonade, Ruffin's troops again rolled forward across the Portiña. Arrayed in three columns of battalion, they were soon moving up the steep slope on the further bank, assailed by no more than the fire of Hill's skirmishers, there being very few Allied guns that could be brought to bear upon them. Waiting for them behind the crest of the slope they were ascending, however, were 4,000 British infantry. No sooner had they breasted the rise, then, than the attackers were assailed by a crashing volley that virtually wiped out their leading ranks. To their credit, Ruffin's men did not break straight away, but attempted to deploy and even managed a volley or two of their own, but, after a brief exchange of fire, Hill's six battalions charged their shaken opponents, and, in a matter of moments, the entire French division was fleeing in disarray.

Needless to say, the repulse of Ruffin's troops caused consternation among the French commanders, but their response was marked by deep disagreement as to what should be done. Knowing that Soult was poised to cut their opponents' communications, Joseph, Sébastiani and the king's chief adviser, *maréchal* Joseph Jourdan, had been opposed to an assault from the beginning, but their hands had been forced by Victor, an impetuous commander who had only become a *maréchal* two years' before and was possessed of

The lower slopes of the Cerro de Medellín in the vicinity of the Portiña. (Author's collection)

something of an inferiority complex (an ex-ranker of no great intellect, he was the butt of many jokes). Desperate to redeem his reputation, the latter therefore continued to advocate the destruction of the enemy, and, after much argument, it was this position that carried the day, for Joseph was frightened at the idea of what Napoleon might do if the British, in particular, were allowed to escape, and was just at this very moment informed that Soult would take rather longer to reach the Tagus valley than had originally been hoped. In consequence, preparations began for another assault. Chief amongst these was a heavy bombardment which caused terrible casualties in the troops manning the flat ground between the Cerro de Medellín and the Pajar de Vergara, a great many men being torn apart, decapitated, or stripped of arms or legs and that despite the fact that many of them had been ordered to lie down to avoid the worst of the enemy fire. Very soon, then, large numbers of wounded were being carried to the field hospitals that had been established in the rear, one of them in no shelter more complicated than the pool of shade cast by a large cork tree. The scene was not all one of complete mayhem, however. The day being scorching hot, the Portiña became a natural magnet for both sides, and so scores of soldiers were soon creeping to its banks festooned with the water-bottles of themselves and their comrades. All along its course, then, men who had just been trying to kill one another and would soon be trying to do the same again found themselves scooping liquid from the same stagnant pools and even sharing food wine and tobacco and trying to talk to one another.

A scene that has probably not changed in more than 200 years: the ravine at the foot of the Cerro de Medellín; little more than a muddy trickle, the Portiña was the only source of water on the battlefield. (Author's collection)

Unfortunately, the fraternisation could not last forever. By 2:00 p.m., indeed, all was ready for the new attack. While two of Victor's three infantry divisions – those of Ruffin and *général de division* Eugène Villatte – threatened the Cerro de Medellín by moving along the long valley that flanked its northern slopes, the two that Sébastiani had brought to the field – those of *généraux de division* Jean Leval and Gabriel Rey – together with Victor's third division – that of *général de division* Pierre Lapisse – surged forward towards the Allied centre. The result was the bloody crisis of what was already a very bloody day.

The remains of a small farm in rear of Wellesley's centre that was pressed into service as a field hospital; note the dried grass in the foreground: by the end of the day, much of the battlefield was in flames.
(Author's collection)

North of the Cerro de Medellín, Wellesley was not much tested, for, anticipating the French move, he had sent most of his cavalry into the valley, where they were reinforced by a large contingent of Spanish troops sent over at his request by Cuesta (who, it must be it said, behaved as an absolutely model ally throughout the battle). Advancing a little way, the French perceived that one of the two British cavalry brigades that had been sent to watch Wellesley's northern flank was riding towards them, and they therefore halted and deployed all their units in square. Undaunted the cavalry – a mixture of British and German light dragoons that together made up the brigade of Brigadier General George Anson – charged on, only to meet disaster. According to every British account, the horsemen suddenly encountered a hidden watercourse and were thrown into terrible confusion. This has been argued by certain Spanish historians of a nationalistic disposition to be a piece of fabrication, but, be this as it may, there is no question that the charge failed. Thus, reaching the French squares, the British cavalry had no chance of breaking any of them and for the most part wheeled aside, leaving a suicidal remnant to plunge on down the valley and be overcome by some French horse that had been waiting in reserve. Fortunately for the Allies, however, such was the array of troops that was still guarding the far end of the valley that Ruffin and Villatte decided that discretion was the better part of valour and made no attempt to resume their advance.

Far more important was the situation in the centre where the attack had been preceded by a further heavy bombardment. Arrayed side-by-side with Leval on the left, Rey in the centre and Lapisse on the right, the French moved forward in lines of battalion columns (the first – composed of Dutch and German troops – in a single line and the second and third in two, one behind the other). Preceded by their skirmishers, the columns moved forward, but, as they did so, they were subjected to heavy artillery fire, the Pajar de Vergara having

The Cerro de Medellín viewed from the north-west on a rather gloomy February morning: it was from approximately the position from which the photograph was taken that Anson's brigade set off on its doomed charge. (Author's collection)

been reinforced by a number of Spanish guns. All along the front, meanwhile, the end result was the same. On the British right, the division of Brigadier General Henry Campbell, supported by a few Spanish battalions that were also caught up in the attack, met their assailants with a rapid succession of volleys, brought them to a halt and then forced them to retreat with a spirited bayonet charge which captured a battery of light artillery that was being brought up for the purpose of close support. Coming up against the crack division of Lieutenant General John Sherbrooke – it was entirely composed of units of the Guards and the King's German Legion – however, the divisions of Lapisse and Rey were subjected to rather different tactics. Allowed to approach to within 50 yards, they were assailed by a single volley only and immediately charged by the redcoats. Cut down by the hundred, the French turned and ran, but at this point things again went wrong. Keyed up by long hours of lying motionless under artillery fire, Sherbrooke's troops rushed after their opponents, only to run straight into their supports. Disordered and outnumbered, they were immediately

Created by damming the Portiña, this reservoir marks the area in which Anson's brigade came to grief in its attack on the divisions of Ruffin and Villatte. (Author's collection)

routed with heavy casualties. Much encouraged, the French followed them up, but the only reserves that the British had left in the centre moved up and formed a fresh line, while, from his vantage point on the Cerro de Medellín, Wellesley rushed a single battalion down the slope to join them. Allowing Sherbrooke's men to fall back through their ranks, these troops then confronted the troops who had followed them across the Portiña and engaged them with a heavy fire that quickly brought them to a halt. There followed a prolonged firefight, but, assailed by British cavalry as well as infantry, the French could eventually take no more and fell back.

Even now the battle was not over, however, for, as the remnants of the divisions of Lapisse and Rey retired, that of Leval was moving forward again. However, raked by artillery fire from the Pajar de Vergara, the advancing troops were again brought to a halt by the musketry of the defenders, whilst the attack was finished off altogether by Cuesta's troops who sallied out in some number and assailed the French left flank, the high point of this exploit being a spirited cavalry charge that not only inflicted many casualties but overran what remained of Leval's divisional artillery. For the French this was the end. Very few of the infantry – the only troops who could make any impression on the Allied position – were still fresh; over 7,000 men had been killed or wounded; 17 guns had been captured; and the entire army was badly demoralised. Desperate for victory to the last, Victor demanded that the battle be continued, but Joseph, Sébastiani and Jourdan over-ruled him, pointing out that the Allies were still intact and that there was even a danger that they might counter-attack. In consequence, though sporadic firing continued for some hours, by the middle of the night the entire French army was in retreat amidst widespread shouts, or so it was said, of 'A Bayonne! A Bayonne!'

The area at the foot of the Cerro de Cascajal where Sherbrooke's division ran into trouble after repulsing Lapisse and Rey. (Author's collection)

Behind them they left some much-scarred opponents, not to mention scenes of absolute horror. Over 5,000 British troops – one quarter of the force engaged – had been killed or wounded, as had several hundred Spaniards, while large numbers of men who had been left lying on the field were burned to death in grass-fires started by smouldering wadding. Truly it had been a pyrrhic victory, while it was also one whose fruits were quickly erased. Wellesley and Cuesta were forced to abandon the campaign and retreat across the River Tagus when news broke that Soult's three corps had crossed the mountains and were massing at the town of Plasencia deep in their rear, while the French not only retook all the guns that they had lost, but also scooped up all the British wounded as prisoners. Finally, as if this was not enough, rather than retiring on the Sierra Morena post-haste, on 11 August Venegas allowed himself to be caught at the town of Almonacid de Toledo, the result being a resounding Spanish defeat. With the atmosphere further marred by furious quarrels between the British and the Spaniards with regard to who was responsible for the debacle, it was a dispiriting end to what had turned out to be the most disappointing of campaigns.

Talavera Today

The battlefield of Talavera has not been dealt with very kindly by the passage of time. The olive groves and holm-oaks of 1809 have long since been ripped up in favour of intensive horticulture; the town has grown massively; a motorway runs through the Allied centre; the bare and rocky Cerro de Medellín is for the most part covered in pine woods; the Cerro de Cascajal is crowned by a substantial mansion; the Pajar de Vergara is hidden beneath a farmstead; and the site of the British cavalry charge is now a substantial reservoir. Nor is much of the field even accessible to visitors except by permission of the owners, a particular loss in this respect being the Cerro de Medellín. Visiting the battlefield is therefore a matter of driving from one place of interest to the next, a task that is rendered far from easy by the many minor roads that criss-cross the site in every direction. Essentially, the 'stands' available to the visitor are three-fold, namely the Casa de Salinas, the area between the Cerro de Cascajal and the Cerro de Medellín and the ground at the western end of the valley from which the British cavalry advanced to attack Ruffin and Villatte.

Logically enough, the best place to begin the tour is the Casa de Salinas (now called the Casa de las Torres and not to be confused, as certain authors have done, with either the Finca la Torre or the Casa Rural Ermita de Salinas). Standing proud in the midst of empty fields, this is best found as follows. Assuming that the visitor is arriving from Madrid on the E90 (Autovía del Sur-Oeste), at Junction 115 take the CM-5100 and drive south in the direction of Talavera. Having crossed over the railway line, turn left at the first junction and head east past the station on the CM-5001 (signposted San Román de los Montes); soon turning north-east, this heads out of town via a succession of modern housing estates. Immediately after the last of said estates, turn right onto an unnumbered road running beside a canal and take the fourth turning to the right: marked by its two distinctive pinnacles, the Casa de las Torres will then be seen directly to the fore. Unfortunately, the house is private property and is not open to visitors, but it is possible to walk around the outside of the complex and view the tower (actually little more than a bastion) from which Wellesley watched the French.

A street in the old part of Talavera: after the battle, eye-witnesses described such thoroughfares as being so choked with wounded that it was impossible to get through without treading on them.
(Author's collection)

The view of the Casa de Salinas (actually the Casa de las Torres) that greets the visitor travelling from Talavera on the CM-5001; the tower from which Wellesley watched the French advance is on the far side of the complex. (Author's collection)

To view the rest of the battlefield, the visitor should return to the town via the same route as before and then turn back onto the CM-5100. At the junction just beyond the railway station, turn left onto the CM-4132 (signposted Segurilla) and take the first right (signposted Embalse de la Portiña) and follow this northwards: crowned by a distinctive circular building and, further to the left, an obelisk erected in 1909 to mark the spot from which Wellesley directed his troops, the Cerro de Medellín is ahead and to the left, while the road, now no more than a track, follows the line of the Portiña and eventually turns up onto the lower slopes of the Cerro de Cascajal. Open to visitors to explore for themselves, the area round about is worth exploring in some detail and all the more so as, on the French side of the Portiña at least, the terrain is not much changed from the condition it would have been in 1809; meanwhile, the banks of the reservoir offer a pleasant spot for a little rest and recreation. Finally, for those of an energetic description, it is possible to walk clock-wise along the water's edge to the vicinity of the area in which Anson's brigade met its fate: some distance beyond the far end of the reservoir and approximately opposite the line of the Portiña a shallow ravine marked on maps as the Arroyo de Atalaya will be observed running down from the hills to the north, this very probably being the obstacle mentioned in all the eye-witness accounts as having caused such havoc.

Given that it is not possible to access the summit of the Cerro de Medellín, the last part of the battlefield that is worth visiting is the area of Anson's cavalry charge. To reach this destination, return to the CM-4132 and turn right. After crossing the western traces of said hill, the road drops down into a broad valley: it was from here that Anson launched his attack, while the slopes to the north were garrisoned by the Spanish division of Bassecourt, this having been sent over from the right by Cuesta in response to the appeals of a Wellesley greatly worried by the threat posed by the advance of Ruffin and Villatte to his left wing. The bottom of the valley being constituted by open pastures and scrubland, it is possible to follow the route of the cavalry for some considerable distance.

The essay in disrespect and poor taste erected to commemorate the battle in 2009: rather than a memorial to the dead, it is seemingly rather designed as a hymn to the ceramic industry for which the area is noted. (Author's collection)

So much for the battlefield. Setting aside the obelisk on the summit of the Cerro de Medellín, there are also two monuments to the battle, of which the first, erected in 1990 as the result of a public outcry after human remains were uncovered during the construction of the motorway, stands in a small park just beside the junction which links the latter with the CM-4132: designed to represent three piled muskets (one for each of the three armies involved in the battle) and around 100 feet high, it also offers an attractive ceramic map of the action. For the second monument, return to Talavera and head for the Jardines del Prado in the south-eastern part of the town (a relic of the scrub and olive groves that cloaked the position of Cuesta's army). Inaugurated in 2009 as part of the commemoration of the bicentenary of the battle, this can only be described as a disgrace which is worth visiting only for the intense amusement which is likely to be derived from viewing it. Nearby, however, is the much more dignified sight constituted by the basilica of Nuestra Señora del Prado: marking the eastern limit of the town in 1809, this was one of the various churches pressed into service the hundreds of wounded from the battlefield.

Further Reading

A.W. Field, *Talavera: Wellington's First Victory in Spain* (Barnsley: Pen and Sword, 2006)

R. Chartrand, *Talavera, 1809: Wellington's Lightning Strike into Spain* (Oxford: Osprey, 2013)

11

Ocaña

19 November 1809

The biggest battle of the Peninsular War fought between French and Spanish troops alone, Ocaña was a major disaster for Allied cause that had profound consequences for the history of Spain. Beset by internal enemies, in the autumn of 1809 the Junta Suprema Central was desperate for a victory. Against British advice, it therefore resolved on a concentric advance on Madrid. Of the three forces involved, the largest was the 60,000-strong Army of the Centre which was posted in the mountains that divided New Castile from Andalucía under the command of *Teniente-General* Juan-Carlos Areizaga, a complete nonentity who had won the favour of the Junta by leading a mission to his native province of Navarre in the hope of stimulating an insurrection. The one hope that this force had of success was to hurl itself on the French so as to take them by surprise: with winter coming on, the latter had gone into cantonments and were not expecting an attack. However, after a rapid initial march that took him to within a few miles of the capital, Areizaga failed to press home his advantage and after some indecisive manoeuvring fell back to the small town of Ocaña where he then elected to turn at bay, and that despite the fact that it offered little in the way of a defensive position. Commanded by *maréchal* Jean de Dieu Soult, the French attacked on 19 November with 33,000 men. Hungry and low in morale after many days of marching and counter-marching to little purpose, short of cavalry, deployed in an open plain stretching eastwards from the town with their right flank completely 'in the air', lacking the training necessary to allow them to manoeuvre in the presence of an enemy, and possessed of a commander who was lacking any experience of independent command and paralysed by fear and indecision – far from attempting to encourage his men, Areizaga spent the battle watching the fighting from the safety of one of the town's church towers – the Spaniards had no chance. Whilst the French infantry pinned down their front line, a division of dragoons crushed the cavalry that protected their right wing and then rolled the entire army up from the flank. Some formations fought well enough and eventually got off the field in some sort of order, but, by the end of the day, Areizaga had lost a third of his army along with 60 guns and all of his baggage, whilst many other troops deserted in the days that followed. At under 2,000 men, meanwhile, Soult's casualties had been minimal. Nor, meanwhile, was Ocaña the only disaster to result from the Junta Central's ill-judged offensive. In distant Old Castile, the Duque del Parque's 26,000-strong Army of the Left had struck out from its base at Ciudad Rodrigo in the direction of Salamanca, which last it managed to occupy in the wake of a rare Spanish victory at Tamames. Having pushed on a little way towards Madrid, however, Del Parque heard news of Ocaña and in consequence turned for home, only to be taken by surprise by a force of French cavalry at Alba de Tormes on 29 November and put to flight with heavy losses.

The battlefield of Ocaña as viewed looking north from the position of the Spanish right wing; it is probable that there would have been more trees in 1809, but otherwise the ground is little changed. (Author's collection)

The open fields occupied by the Spanish right wing at Ocaña; unable to form square with sufficient alacrity, the Spaniards were routed with terrible losses. (Author's collection)

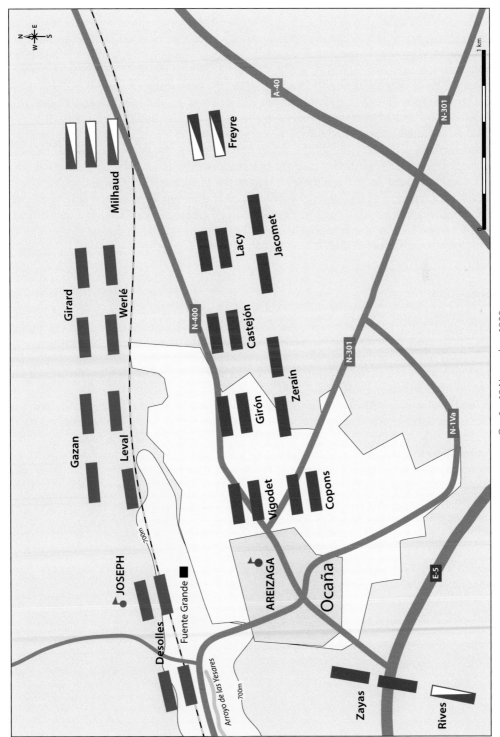

Ocaña, 19 November 1809.

For the Allied cause, all this represented an unparalleled catastrophe. With few troops left to protect it, Andalucía was open to invasion and, with it, Patriot Spain's chief repository of the sinews of war (with the exception of Cádiz, the whole region was duly overrun in January 1810). Gone too, meanwhile, was all possibility of the Spanish regular army launching major campaigns in its own right, the fact being that for the rest of the struggle it could do little more than seek to defend such fortresses as remained in Patriot hands, conduct guerrilla operations and second the operations of Wellington's forces. As for the history of Spain, setting aside the resentment and hostility engendered by the relegation of the Spanish army to an essentially secondary role in the defeat of the French invasion (an issue that helps to explain said force's extraordinary propensity to engage in military coups in the period after 1814), Ocaña brought in its train the downfall of the Junta Suprema Central, which was in January 1810 replaced by a council of regency, and at the same time helped ensure that the new parliament which had in any case been scheduled for election in 1810 fell into the hands of Spain's small faction of committed liberals, the result being the revolution that produced the famous Constitution of 1812.

Ocaña Today

Chiefly known for the major prison that was built on its southern outskirts in the 1880's, Ocaña is in most respects a rather undistinguished little place, its only historical monument of any note being the enormous sixteenth-century water-works that were constructed to take advantage of a natural spring in the ravine that runs westwards from the vicinity of the town itself and in 1809 protected the Spanish left flank from attack. According to tradition, on the morning of the battle, Areizaga's cavalrymen drove their horses down to drink from the great tanks which dominate the interior to this day. As for the Spanish position, this ran eastwards along the present-day N600, at the time of the battle a country road that ultimately led to Cuenca. The terrain is so flat that there are few vantage points for those wishing to view the field other than a bridge about a mile from the town which takes said road across the old railway from Madrid to Valencia, why Areizaga chose the spot to fight an enemy that was much superior to him in terms of cavalry being a question that remains all but impossible to answer.

12

The River Côa

24 July 1810

The Battle of the River Côa marked the end of almost a full 12-month period in which barely a single British or Portuguese soldier had fired a shot in anger in the Peninsular War. The product of the situation that pertained after the unfortunate Talavera campaign, this was a very sore point in so far as the Patriot authorities were concerned and had caused great tension with respect to the alliance with Britain. Had Wellington had his way, meanwhile, the interval would have dragged on even longer, but, as we shall see, it was ended much against his will by the actions of one of his most turbulent subordinates. As for the action that followed, it produced a bloody draw, but not without some very worrying moments for the Allied cause which at one point threatened a serious defeat that could have precipitated Britain's withdrawal from the Peninsula. That this did not occur was the fruit, above all, of the fighting qualities of Wellington's infantry, a resource that does much to explain the long string of victories that followed and ultimately led to the expulsion of the French.

For the origins of the Battle of the Côa, we must look at developments in the French camp in the wake of the conquest of Andalucía in January 1810. That this was achieved with such speed – the whole campaign was over in barely a fortnight – was in part because the French were able to march on the Sierra Morena with the vast majority of the troops who had hitherto been holding central Spain; in brief, the corps of *maréchaux* Victor, Horace Sebastiani and Edouard Mortier. If this was so, meanwhile, it was because of the catastrophic defeat which Austria had suffered in the campaign of Wagram, the peace treaty to which this led confirming Napoleon's control of the European mainland from the coasts of the Atlantic to the frontiers of Russia. With further conflict against the eastern powers a very distant prospect, if, indeed, it was a prospect at all, Napoleon could concentrate all his attention on Spain and Portugal. Enormous numbers of new conscripts having been called up in the course of 1809, there were plenty of troops available for this purpose, and the closing months of the year had therefore seen thousands of fresh recruits, together with some veterans drawn from the army that had defeated Austria, file across the frontier. Of these the men who were newly mobilised went to units that were already in Spain with a view to making up their losses from battle and disease, while several of the formations that were sent from Germany were posted to other parts of the country, so it would be wrong to think that all the men concerned were intended for use against Lord Wellington as the Anglo-Portuguese commander was now styled, having been raised to the peerage in the wake of

Talavera. That said, the accession of fresh strength was such that it became possible to think of a fresh march on Lisbon, this being something that the humiliations of 1808 and 1809 had made a real fixation for Napoleon, so much so, indeed, that the emperor initially gave out that he was going to come to Spain to take command of the new campaign himself. In the event, however, this did not occur, not least because of his decision to divorce Josephine and embark on a search for a new bride. In the end, then, the task was handed to André Masséna, possibly the most competent of all Napoleon's marshals, who was given command of a new Army of Portugal composed of two of the corps that were already in the Peninsula, namely II Corps of *général de division* Jean Reynier and VI Corps of *maréchal* Michel Ney, together with a formation commanded by *général de division* Jean-Andoche Junot that had hitherto been serving with the *grande armée* as the 'Corps of Reserve of the Army of Germany' but was henceforward styled VIII Corps, all this amounting to a force of some 68,000 men.

It having been decided that Masséna should base his advance on Salamanca, two preliminary operations had to be first to be undertaken. Thus, although there was no Spanish field army in the region, there remained Spanish garrisons in the border fortresses of Astorga and Ciudad Rodrigo, it being axiomatic that these should be dealt with before any attempt to cross the frontier. As a result, the spring and early summer were completely taken up with reducing these two fortresses, it not being until Ciudad Rodrigo was taken on 9 July that Masséna could start bringing his troops up to the frontier, a process in which the lead was taken by Ney's VI Corps, this being a force consisting of some 24,000 men consisting of three infantry divisions, a single cavalry division and six batteries of artillery with a total of 48 howitzers and field guns.

Facing this imposing array was a single division of Wellington's army, namely the so-called 'Light Division' of *Brigadier General* Robert Craufurd, this having been tasked with the job of manning a line of outposts in the 20 miles of territory separating Ciudad Rodrigo from the Portuguese frontier, and, with it, the vital fortress of Almeida, while the rest of the army waited for the French attack much further back. Also in attendance was a cavalry brigade and a single battery of horse artillery, but in the event the units concerned played almost no part in the battle. Consisting of two small infantry brigades, each of which mustered a mere two-and-one-half battalions instead of the usual three or four, the Light Division numbered just 4,000 men and was therefore desperately outnumbered. That said, the units which made it up – the 1/43rd, 1/52nd and 1/95th Regiments of Foot and the 1º and 3º Batalhões de Caçadores – were some of the best troops in the whole Anglo-Portuguese army, all of them being highly-trained light infantry capable of fighting in open as well as closed order, and, in the case of the green-uniformed 95th and some of the caçadores, equipped not with the old 'Brown Bess' musket but rather the Baker rifle, a much superior weapon that could be fired with great accuracy up to a range of 300 yards, the only problem being that, for various reasons, it took much longer to load. For all its many qualities, however, the Light Division was in serious danger, that this was so being entirely the fault of Robert Craufurd. Thus, in accordance with the orders that he had received from Wellington, 'Black Bob', as he was known, should now have retired across the Côa, a river that, if of no great width, was extremely fast-flowing and ran at the bottom of a deep ravine just inside, and parallel to, the frontier. Despite the fact that the only crossing was a single stone bridge of a very narrow nature, however, Craufurd refused to budge and instead kept his men echeloned along a gentle ridge that ran along the brink of the ravine. That this was

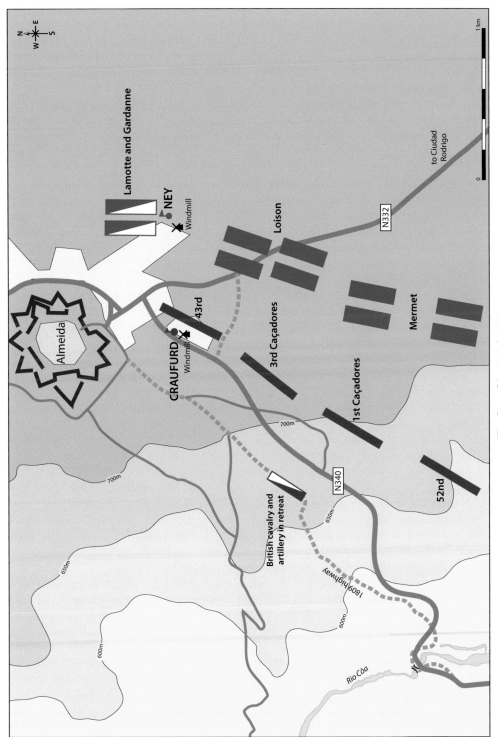

The River Côa, 24 July 1810.

folly in the extreme was clear enough, but why the general should have been so stubborn is harder to explain. As he was never required to make a case in defence of his conduct, we cannot know for certain, but he had great confidence in his troops, who had already worsted the French in a handful of minor skirmishes, and was also a very dissatisfied figure who had been slow to achieve promotion and was also obsessed with restoring the honour he felt he had lost when he was caught up in the capitulation of Whitelocke's expeditionary force in Buenos Aires in July 1807. All this being the case, it seems safe to assume that he believed that he could obtain the glory of giving the enemy a bloody nose without incurring much in the way of risk, an assumption that is all the more likely given that, even when the enemy hove into view, he seems to have wildly under-estimated the number of troops which were marching to attack his positions, believing that he was being attacked by no more than a single infantry division with some attached cavalry rather than an entire corps. There was at least some excuse for this – when the day dawned it proved to be very dull and drizzly, the result being that, Ney having drawn up his infantry divisions one behind the other in a single massive column, Craufurd may genuinely have been unable to see what was facing him – but the fact remains of little credit in respect of his picketing arrangements; all too clearly, something was badly amiss.

The simple fact, then, is that Craufurd was gravely at fault. In defence of his attitude, it should be pointed out that, by remaining east of the Côa, he had kept open the road to the fortress (which was situated on the further side of the river), thereby allowing convoys of supplies to be got within the walls until the very last minute, but the ability of Almeida to hold out for a few more days was scarcely worth the potential loss of the Light Division. In short, no amount of special pleading is enough: Craufurd was both in a bad position and acting in blatant defiance of his orders, and it is probable that it was only Wellington's lack of subordinates of real quality that saved him from a court-martial in the days following the battle.

All that said, it is to this last that we must now turn. Raining heavily as it was, the hussars Craufurd had sent out on picket duty did not spot the oncoming masses of enemy troops until the latter were literally on them, but enough men got away to raise the alarm, the Light Division then leaping to arms with its usual speed and efficiency. Even then, it is possible that the beleaguered Anglo-Portuguese could have made good their escape without a fight, but, beguiled still further by the fact that the position they occupied was a maze of small enclosures that offered excellent possibilities to men trained in skirmish tactics, their commander now heaped folly upon folly by deciding to stand and fight. Very soon, however, it became clear that this was a serious mistake. In theory, the left wing of the defenders rested on the fortress of Almeida, and the hope was that its guns would deter the French from pressing their attack in that sector, but Ney was ever an aggressive commander, and he therefore ordered one of his cavalry regiments to gallop into the gap between the glacis and the first of the Light Division's troops and then wheel down the road towards the bridge, thereby threatening to envelop the whole of Craufurd's position. Very quickly, then, the defenders began to fall into disorder and the British commander was left with no option but to order a retreat to the bridge. First to go were the cavalry and artillery, the latter having had the opportunity to fire no more than a handful of shots, the infantry following in their wake as best they could, though not without putting up a desperate rearguard action. For all concerned, the quickest way to the bridge was the road that zig-zagged down into the gorge

Part of the position which Craufurd chose to defend at Almeida: the hills in the far distance are on the other side of the Côa. (Author's collection)

Almeida as viewed from Craufurd's left flank; the French cavalry advanced into the low ground in the middle distance. (Author's collection)

from Almeida, and, with so many men trying to make their way along it and more joining all the time, it was only a matter of time before things went badly wrong. In brief, just before reaching the bridge, the road made a sharp turn to the right, and just at this very point one of the artillery battery's caissons overturned, thereby completely blocking the way. Cleared away though the offending vehicle eventually was, the net result was that the infantry ended up clumped together around the crossing in straits that appeared ever more difficult.

Craufurd was now facing disaster, but at the last minute he was saved by the presence of mind of the commander of his first brigade, Lieutenant Colonel William Beckwith. Thus, gathering together all the British infantry he could find, Beckwith led them up to the top of a steep knoll immediately overlooking the bridge and formed them into a solid defensive line that held the French at bay long enough for, first, the cavalry and the artillery and, then, the two Portuguese battalions to cross to the far bank of the river and take up positions from which they could provide covering fire while the rear-guard broke away in their turn. However, as it transpired, the drama of the moment was far from over, for, just as the last of the light infantry and rifleman reached the foot of the knoll, several companies of the 52nd who had been stationed at the southernmost end of the British line and had been delayed in their withdrawal were spotted running down the hillside in a desperate attempt to reach the bridge before they were cut off. To make matters worse, meanwhile, at that very moment the leading French infantry burst over the crest of the knoll and opened fire on the mass of troops below, Without hesitating for an instant, Beckwith and one or two other officers got together some of the men around them and led them back up the slope, managing, not only

The steep slopes and rough scrubland that lay in rear of Craufurd's position as viewed from the knoll overlooking the bridge; the Light Division was initially drawn up along the most distant skyline, while the road that was its only line of retreat can be seen in the middle distance. (Author's collection)

The sharp turn where the road was blocked by an overturned caisson; at the time of the battle, the cut-off to the right did not exist. (Author's collection)

The monument to the battle erected to mark the bicentenary in 2011 and, beyond it, Beckwith's knoll. (Author's collection)

The bridge across the River Côa and, beyond it, the steep slopes from which the men of the Light Division shot so many of the French attackers. (Author's collection)

to drive the enemy off the knoll, but also to hold it long enough for the stray companies of the 52nd to scramble to safety.

Duty done, the men who had taken part in this impromptu counter-attack now filed across the bridge in their turn. However, if anyone expected that the battle would now come to an end, they were sorely mistaken. Not content with securing his objective, which had consisted of nothing more than driving the Light Division away from Almeida, Ney appears to have decided that his opponents were in such disarray that one more effort would turn a reverse into an outright defeat. Mustering his troops anew, then, he proceeded to send an infantry battalion to rush the bridge in the hope that it would open the way for him to cross the river in force. In this, however, he was to be sorely disappointed. Far from being out of the fight, the Light Division had recovered its equilibrium, while it now occupied a position that was so strong that there was no way the French could take it by storm, the bridge being directly overlooked by rocky slopes that were now crammed with riflemen and light infantry who were only too eager to take their revenge for the alarms and excursions of the last two hours or more. The result, then, was that the attack was stopped in its tracks, the men concerned being cut down in droves, and all the more so as Craufurd had got his artillery battery into action, this being arrayed across the road in such a way as to enfilade the crossing. However, this reverse checked Ney not a whit, and, determined to succeed, he therefore repeated the process not once but twice, on each occasion again incurring heavy losses. Finally convinced that there was no chance of victory, at length the *maréchal* called off his troops, the battle

The Côa gorge viewed from the position from which Craufurd's artillery enfiladed the bridge; although this last is obscured by the line of the modern road, its position is marked by the modern monument in the left background. (Author's collection)

The road leading down to the bridge on the western side of the river; having escaped the French attack, Craufurd's horse-artillery took up position at the top of the slope. (Author's collection)

petering out in a prolonged exchange of fire between the forces lining each bank of the river. In all, Craufurd's losses came to 333 men killed, wounded and taken prisoner and Ney's to 527.

The Côa Today

If one excepts the modern bridge that now spans the river a few yards from its predecessor, the battlefield of the Côa is all but completely unspoiled and can be walked in its entirety without difficulty. Assuming that the visitor has first taken the opportunity to visit the town of Almeida and take in the view of the gorge that its southern ramparts afford, the first stage is to drive out of town on the N332 (signposted Vilar Formoso) and head uphill past the municipal sports-centre. Just beyond this complex a narrow lane will be encountered on the right-hand side of the road, this giving access to the position held by Craufurd's left wing, and, more specifically, the 43rd Foot, and, beyond it, an excellent sample of the cluttered terrain over which the Light Division conducted its retreat; meanwhile, note the nearby windmill, this being one of several such structures that dotted the field in 1810. Returning to the N332, the visitor should then drive back towards Almeida and turn left at the junction with the N340 (signposted Guarda) and follow the road down to the modern bridge across the river, on the further side of which and a little uphill will be found an area that offers some convenient parking, it then being possible to walk back down to the old bridge following the line of the original road. Having passed under the modern bridge, the old one will be found directly in front, though it should be noted that the edifice one sees today is not actually that of 1810 but rather a reconstruction dating from the 1820's, albeit one that appears to have been almost identical to the original. Immediately at the end of the bridge will be found the modern monument to the battle and, above it, the knoll fought over by Beckwith, while a short stroll along the old road, which for a little distance follows the riverbank, will take the visitor to the sharp turning which caused the Light Division so much trouble in the course of the retreat. Finally, it is well worth attempting the steep climb that leads to the summit of the knoll, this offering dramatic views both of the road back to Almeida and the steep slopes defended by Craufurd in the closing stages of the battle.

The battlefield of the Côa is, of course, very close to several other Peninsular-War sites, including, most notably, Fuentes de Oñoro, but special mention ought to be made of the Real Fuerte de la Concepción. Situated a short drive from Almeida just inside the Spanish frontier at the village of Aldea del Obispo, this was first established in 1664 but in its current form dates from 1735. Garrisoned as an outpost by the Anglo-Portuguese army, it was evacuated and partially blown up on 21 July 1810 and thereafter saw no action. Allowed to fall into ruin in the course of the nineteenth century, it has since been fully restored and is now a luxury hotel called the Hotel Eurostars Fuerte de la Concepción.

13

Buçaco

27 September 1810

The Battle of Buçaco was a major tactical defeat for the French forces in the Iberian peninsula and in some respects the worst setback that the cause of Napoleon Bonaparte had yet received there. Bailén, of course, had much more of an impact, but the forces available to Dupont had been much smaller than those available to the French commander at Buçaco, *maréchal* André Masséna, while the latter was a figure of infinitely greater talent and prestige. That said, Buçaco did nothing to change the course of events, with the fact that Masséna was able to resume his march on Lisbon after just two days doing much to assuage the pain of what occurred, so much so, indeed, that in some French accounts the battle has even been hailed as a victory.

In terms of the narrative of the Peninsular War, Buçaco follows on directly from the Battle of the Coa. Before going any further, however, it is first necessary to say something about the strategy which Wellington had settled on with respect to the defence of Portugal. In brief, this was four-fold. Thus, first, the Portuguese army was to be rebuilt and, at the same time, reformed to a standard sufficient to allow it to take its place in the line of battle alongside Wellington's British troops; second, the militia and the second-line home-defence force known as the *ordenança* were to readied for guerrilla operations against the French lines of communication; third, those areas of the country directly threatened with French invasion were to be evacuated and subjected to a ruthless scorched-earth policy; and, fourth, Lisbon itself was to be protected by a thick belt of field fortifications centred on the town of Torres Vedras. From all this, it is often concluded that right from the beginning Wellington intended to retreat all the way to Lisbon come what may. This, however, was not the case. On the contrary, mindful of the appalling cost to the Portuguese population should it indeed prove necessary to devastate the countryside and force the populace to flee, the British commander had every hope that supply difficulties and the need to take Almeida would combine to halt Masséna at the frontier, failing which he hoped to turn back the invaders by fighting a battle in one of the many defensive positions offered by the rugged terrain through which the French would necessarily have to march if they wanted to reach Lisbon. That this was the case puts Buçaco in a completely different light from the one in which it is pictured in many of the standard accounts. Thus, while most of the arguments concerned have at least some measure of truth, none of them fit the bill in its entirety. Critics claim that Wellington decided to turn and fight with a view to doing no more than blooding the remodelled Portuguese army, gaining more time for his campaign of devastation, calming the distinctly riot-prone population of Lisbon, stilling the growing criticism of his defensive plan in the Portuguese council of regency, reassuring the Perceval administration in London, or even engineering a justification for the enormous cost of building the Lines of Torres Vedras. However, the fact is that what the British commander was really after was a smashing victory that would end the campaign at a stroke.

Be all this as it may, let us pick up the story from the moment that the guns fell silent on the evening of 24 July. With the Anglo-Portuguese army showing no signs whatever of intervening on the fortress' behalf, Almeida was quickly blockaded, though such were the difficulties encountered in bringing up sufficient supplies that formal siege operations were not opened until the middle of August. Nor was this the end of Masséna's problems, for the ground was so stony that it took another 10 days to prepare the batteries needed by the siege artillery. In the ordinary course of events, so powerful a fortress as Almeida should have taken some time to overcome, a result that could have rendered a march on Lisbon completely out of the question, but the course of events on this occasion proved anything but ordinary. Thus, a mere 13 hours after Masséna's heavy guns opened fire on the walls, a chance shell ignited the defenders' powder magazine, the consequence being a massive explosion that reduced every building in the place to ruins, atomised the mediaeval castle in which the powder had been housed and killed 500 of the garrison. The walls still

One of the outer gates of the fortress of Almeida: a formidable fortress held by a strong garrison; in ordinary circumstances it should have defied Masséna's army for many weeks. (Author's collection)

Buçaco, 27 September 1810.

Part of the remains of the castle that housed Almeida's powder magazine; after the war the site was levelled, leaving only the foundations and the ditch. (Author's collection)

stood, true, but the surviving troops were in a state of shock, many guns had been smashed beyond repair and all the foodstuffs in the place destroyed. The governor, a British officer named William Cox, tried hard to prolong the defence for a further couple of days, but, led by one or two officers who had a grudge against the British general who had been given the command of the Portuguese army, Lieutenant General William Beresford, the troops mutinied, Cox therefore had no option but to surrender.

With Almeida out of the way, Masséna was now free to march on Lisbon. That said, getting his three corps moving was no easy business. Thus, not only had still more food had somehow to be gathered, but the baggage wagons needed to carry it could only be brought forward by stripping all the infantry divisions of one of their two attached batteries of field artillery. No sooner had the advance begun, meanwhile, than men began to fall by the wayside for reasons of illness or want of food, Wellington's devastation of the countryside having proved effective enough to cause the French serious problems. In this situation, Masséna's only hope was to take the Anglo-Portuguese army unawares and bring it to battle in circumstances that favoured the invaders, but their opponents offered them no such opportunity and were therefore left free to turn at bay on ground of their own choosing, namely the towering Serra do Buçaco, a nine-mile long ridge north-east of Coimbra that lay firmly athwart the French line of march and presented a formidable obstacle, the slopes being everywhere very steep and the countryside below a tangled mass of scrub seamed with gullies and ravines.

The village of Moura as viewed from the position of the Light Division: the tangled terrain stretching into the distance is typical of the ground that Masséna had to contend with in his advance from Almeida. (Author's collection)

The village of Sula as viewed from vicinity of Moura; in 1810 there were far fewer trees while the buildings shown in the left-hand side of the photograph did not exist. With regard to the position of Wellington's troops, the Light Division was originally deployed just to the rear of the heights in the left background. (Author's collection)

To hold the line constituted by the *serra*, Wellington had only 52,000 men and 60 guns, but his problems were greatly lessened by the fact that the somewhat larger French army – in all, Masséna had some 58,000 men under his command – could only assault his positions in two places, namely the spur by which the road the invading army had been following reached the summit just above the little village of Sula, together with another to its left that was separated from it by a deep cleft in the hillside, and a minor track some distance to the south that led up to the centre of the ridge from the hermitage of Santo António do Cântaro (note that there neither was then nor is now any village of this name). Not surprisingly, then, both points were well defended, with the former being left in the hands of the redoubtable Light Division and several independent Portuguese infantry brigades, and the latter in those of the 3rd Division of Sir Thomas Picton, a commander known to be quite extraordinarily belligerent, while Wellington himself established his headquarters in an imposing convent of the Order of Barefoot Carmelites known as Santa Cruz do Buçaco that stood on the western slopes of the ridge near the village of Luso. Running either along or just below the summit, meanwhile, was a further track that could be used to move troops from one sector of the line to another in the event of a sudden emergency, while the pronounced reversed slope ensured that the defenders would be hidden from the oncoming French until the last moment as well as well protected from enemy artillery fire. Finally, as if all this was not enough, so steep were the slopes that any attackers would have to negotiate that it could be guaranteed that any troops who reached the summit would do so 'blown' and in a state of some disorder.

To put it mildly, then, the Buçaco position represented a formidable obstacle, and one which Wellington was absolutely confident he could defend. Nevertheless, when Masséna reached the area immediately to the east of the *serra* on 25 September, spurred on by contempt for the Portuguese and also lacking any experience of fighting the British, let alone Wellington, he abjured any attempt at manoeuvre in favour of a head-on attack that would see *général de division* Jean Reynier's II Corps ascend the ridge from the hermitage while *maréchal* Michel Ney's VI Corps headed up the Sula spur, *général de division* Jean-Andoche Junot's VIII Corps in the meantime being held back in reserve. In all, then, the assault would be delivered by just 40,000 men, but, to the last, Masséna was absolutely convinced that his men had only to reach the summit for the entire Anglo-Portuguese army to break and run and that despite the fact that he had only the vaguest idea of Wellington's dispositions and, indeed, strength.

It took the best part of two days to get the French forces into position, and so the battle did not begin until the misty morning of 27 September. To begin with the assault of Reynier's corps, and all the more so as it stepped off some time before that of Ney, its two infantry divisions, those of *général de division* Etienne Heudelet de Bierre and *général de division* Pierre Merle, advanced determinedly up the slopes ahead of them, harassed by the light and rifle companies of the 3rd Division, but having reached the summit, they immediately ran into serious trouble. Thus, advancing up the track in a column just one company wide – a formation dictated by the need to ensure that the troops concerned did not drift apart as they negotiated the generally very irregular hillside in the morning mist – the first battalions of Heudelet's men had no sooner reached the crest of the ridge than they were flayed by the fire of two batteries of guns and at the same time confronted by a brigade of Portuguese infantry belonging to Lieutenant General Thomas Picton's 3rd Division that had

The Serra do Buçaco viewed from the vicinity of the hermitage of Santo Antonio do Cântaro; in 1810, it would have been largely free of trees. (Zack White)

been stiffened by the temporary attachment of a battalion of redcoats. Had the troops facing them resorted to the tactic that became such a hallmark of Wellington's army – namely, a single volley followed by a bayonet charge – it is probable that they would have been swept away at once, but instead the defenders resorted to fire alone, and the leading battalions were therefore afforded the time they needed to deploy into line, thereafter engaging their assailants in a prolonged fire-fight. To their right, meanwhile, the troops of Merle's division had advanced up the slopes of the *serra* in a very similar formation via a minor re-entrant in the slope, only to be much slowed down by the broken nature of the ground, and at the same time both drifting to their left, thereby losing still more time, and becoming deprived of all semblance of order. Had they managed to keep their formation, maintain a better pace and head straight up the hill, they might have achieved a great deal, for it so happened that they were heading for a wide gap in the line of the defenders. However, if there was one man among Wellington's generals who was capable of dealing with such a crisis, it was Picton. Realising what was afoot, the latter had managed to rush in troops from both sides and the unfortunate French were therefore simultaneously hit by a hail of musketry from one flank and a bayonet charge from the other, this last being the work of the famous 88th Foot or Connaught Rangers, a unit which rejoiced in the nickname of 'The Devil's Own'. Utterly dismayed, the single regiment that had actually managed to reach the summit turned and

The final ascent of the track ascended by Heudelet's division; already tired and underfed, the troops would have been exhausted by the time they reached the summit. (Zack White)

The area in which Merle's division emerged onto the summit looking towards the track ascended by Heudelet's division; this last ran just beyond the modern road seen descending to the left. (Zack White)

fled only immediately to crash into the men coming up behind with the result that, within a matter of moments, the entire division was rushing pell-mell back the way they had come, leaving behind them large numbers of killed, wounded and prisoners.

Disastrous as this outcome was for the French, the fighting in Picton's sector was not quite over. Thus, seemingly due to a misunderstanding in respect of his orders, the commander of the second brigade of Heudelet's division, *général de brigade* Maximilien Foy, had not followed its fellow into the fray, but had rather halted his men further down the slope. Apprised of his error by an angry Reynier, Foy immediately rushed to the support of the beleaguered units of his fellow brigadier, *général de brigade* Antoine Arnaud, that were still holding out at the summit and managed to either drive back or put to flight the Portuguese troops who were the only forces standing in his way, but, just at the opportune moment, the remaining defenders were rescued by the arrival of the first units of the 5th Division of Major General James Leith, the latter commander having realised that, there being no sign of any attack upon his own men, his duty was to move to the support of Picton. Struck in flank by a full British brigade, Foy's troops collapsed in their turn, while they were soon after joined in flight by the four battalions of Arnaud's brigade that had made the first attack (the other four, it seems, had been held back in reserve).

So much for the fighting above Santo António do Cántaro. What, though, had been going on with respect to Ney's corps? In response to the orders it had received from

Old huts on the outskirts of Sula: the tangled terrain greatly favoured the skirmishers from the famous 95th Rifles and other units who so harassed Loison's troops. (Author's collection)

Masséna, this had not advanced until the men of Heudelet and Merle had been seen to reach the summit of the sector of the *serra* facing them. Like that of Reynier, the attack was made on a frontage of two divisions, with that of *général de division* Jean Marchand on the left and that of *général de division* Louis Loison on the right, each of the formations concerned being tasked with advancing up one of the two spurs that ran down from the summit of the ridge. In this sector, the lead was taken by Loison who set off up the right-hand spur towards Sula with his two brigades side-by-side in columns of battalion preceded in each case by a skirmish screen consisting of their four *voltigeur* companies. Fiercely contested though their progress was by an equally thick skirmish screen that had been sent down from the heights above by the commander of the Light Division, Brigadier General Robert Craufurd, the division eventually cleared Sula and, despite being pounded by the fire of several batteries deployed at the head of the ravine that separated the two spurs, pushed on up the slopes beyond, only to be struck by a disaster that was just as absolute as anything which had happened in respect of Reynier's corps. In brief, lying hidden in a sunken road just above Sula were the two light infantry battalions of the Light Division, namely the 1/43rd and the 1/52nd Regiments of Foot, both of them crack units which were well up to strength despite their recent blooding at the River Coa, and, at a signal from Craufurd, who had mounted a small rocky outcrop that stood on the very sky-line, they now jumped to their feet, delivered a single volley on the disordered masses in front of them, and finally charged with the bayonet, their opponents falling in large numbers and, like Merle's men before them, fleeing the oncoming enemy with the utmost speed. All that was left, then, was the division of Marchand, but this could no more achieve success than that of Loison. Thus, pushing up the spur assigned to it with its two brigades one behind the other in the face of determined resistance from a variety of light troops, it initially attempted to move around the head of the ravine separating the two spurs so as to support Loison, but was checked by the fire of three batteries of artillery that Wellington had placed at that very spot, and therefore reverted to its original course and pressed straight on up the slope. Here, too, however, the French were stymied. Deployed across their path were the four line battalions of Pack's independent brigade, but, Portuguese though they were, they did not break and run in the manner that Marchand presumably expected and instead held their ground, their assailants then losing all momentum thanks to a foolish decision to deploy into line. Fortunately for the troops concerned, Pack's forces do not seem to have been trained in the volley-plus-bayonet charge tactic mentioned above, and the result was a fierce firerfight that cost both sides heavy casualties. To all intents and purposes, however, the battle was all but over, and so, recognising defeat, Ney ordered Marchand to disengage, the latter then withdrawing in good order.

Unfortunately for the inhabitants of central Portugal, who went on to suffer a humanitarian disaster that was possibly even greater than that unleashed by the terrible earthquake that struck Lisbon in 1755, Buçaco was not the strategic success for which Wellington seems to have hoped. A commander of great talent and determination, Masséna refused to retreat and instead sent out cavalry patrols to seek a way of outflanking the Anglo-Portuguese position. This being encountered soon enough in the form of a narrow pass some miles to the north whose defence had been entrusted to a force of Portuguese militia which had failed to arrive in time. The French then were soon on the move once more, Wellington therefore

Sula as viewed from the position of the Light Division; having taken the village, Loison's men were still faced by a steep ascent. (Author's collection)

The rocky out-crop from which Craufurd ordered the 43rd and the 52nd to advance; according to legend, waving his hat as he did so, he shouted, 'Now 52nd: avenge the death of Sir John Moore'. (Author's collection)

The spur which witnessed Marchand's attack: so steep is the ascent that it is astonishing that the men concerned fought as well as they did. (Author's collection)

being left with no option but to retire to the safety of the Lines of Torres Vedras. Yet the fact that the Anglo Portuguese army had to evacuate its positions is no reason to account the battle a French victory. On the contrary, at almost 4,500 men, Masséna's casualties were heading for four times the 1,252 suffered by their opponents, while, at the end of the day, the Anglo-Portuguese army remained in much the same state of order and morale as it had at the start. To look at matters from another point of view, meanwhile, if 45 French battalions had gone into action, the equivalent number for their opponents was just 24. In fairness, the French had been hampered by the inability of their artillery, such as it was, to influence the course of the battle, not to mention the strength of the defensive position where they faced, but, as witness the failure of make use of Junot's corps and, at a lower level, the muddle which had characterised the attack of Heudelet's division, there had also been severe failures of generalship. If victory was to be achieved, then, much more was needed, but whether even so skilled a general as Masséna could deliver this was a moot point.

The windmill above Sula. (Author's collection)

The entrance to the military museum at
Buçaco. (Author's collection)

The spot where the track from Santo Antonio do Cántaro crosses the road from Luso before ascending the *serra*. (Zack White)

Buçaco Today

Much of the Serra do Buçaco having long since been forested, the battlefield of which it is the centre-piece is something of a disappointment. That said, particularly in the area of Loison's attack, it is still possible to follow many of the events of the battle. However, the best place to begin a visit is the Museu Militar do Buçaco, this being situated in the eastern outskirts of Luso (in 1810 a tiny village, but now a sizeable town thanks, not least, to its emergence in the late nineteenth century as an important spa). To find it, drive through the town on the N234 (signposted Mortagua), and, near the summit of the pass, double back on the N234-4 (signposted Estrada Forestal): the museum will be found a short distance along on the right. Just across the road from the museum, meanwhile, a turning to the left – the Rua Duque de Wellington – leads up the rear slope of the *serra* to the chief monument to the battle, a white obelisk topped with a star that marks the spot from which Wellington watched the advance of Marchand's division in the final stages of the battle. Somewhat further along the N234-4, meanwhile, is the Buçaco Palace Hotel, this originally being a summer residence of the last king of Portugal that was constructed on the basis of the remains of the convent in which the British commander established his headquarters: although the complex as a whole is much altered, the church and the cloister remain untouched and are open to visitors.

From the hotel, return to the N234, turn right and after a short distance park on the left side of the road at the turning marked 'Moinho de Sula', said windmill standing at the end of a short track a few yards further on; nearby will be found the clump of rocks from which Craufurd directed the attack of his two redcoat battalions. From the parking place, meanwhile, walk northwards along the Rua do Moinho and, just past the cluster of buildings, take the track to the right that leads downhill to Sula, the centre of a bitter struggle between the skirmishers of Craufurd and Loison. On reaching the T-junction at the end, turn left into the main street (the Rua Principal) and follow it to the end: in 1810, this was the road that was being followed by Masséna's army, the modern highway rather dating from the early years of the twentieth century. Oman and the many writers who have followed his account therefore being quite wrong to associate the attack along the main road with Marchand's division rather than that of Loison.

From Sula, whose many modern additions along the crest of the slope almost completely cover the ground on which the 43rd and 52nd broke Loison's division, return to the parking place by the windmill, and turn left onto the N234, this offering a number of spots from which photographs may be taken of the position of the Light Division high above. At the entrance to the village of Moura a turning to the right signposted Moinho do Moura leads to a windmill from which Masséna is believed to have watched the attack of Ney's corps. Finally, to reach the scene of Reynier's fight, return to the N234-4, but, instead of following it toward the museum and hotel, turn very sharply to the left and follow the road along the crest of the ridge, keeping right at the first fork in the road and left at the second (it was, of course, this road that Wellington relied on to rush troops from one sector of his line to another in the event of an emergency). Eventually, a crossroads is reached, this marking the spot at which the track from Santo Antonio do Cântaro reached the summit, and, with it, the area where Heudelet's attack came to grief (to find the site of Merle's defeat walk north along the tree line: after a short distance, this turns sharply to the right and, a little way further on, just as sharply to the left, the spot where Merle reached the summit being marked by the shallow gully that soon afterwards falls away to the right). At the crossroads, meanwhile, the track ascended by Heudelet can be picked out beside the road to the left, almost immediately crossing over this and dropping down into the trees: completely impassable even to off-road vehicles, the going it offers is extremely difficult even for walkers, so much so, indeed, that it is even downright dangerous. To reach Santo Antonio do Cântaro, then, rather than taking the modern road that took the place of the original track (a snare and a delusion as it soon strikes sharply south-eastwards and takes the unwary visitor on a very long detour), turn back in the direction of Luso and head north until a junction is reached with a road that angles back very sharply to the right and immediately heads downhill. By taking said road, it is possible to drop diagonally down the eastern side of the *serra* to the low ground at its foot. Once the descent flattens out, continue in the same direction until a junction with a road that turns back very sharply to the left, this last being the Rua do Poço. After some distance, this leads to a small cluster of buildings of which one is the hermitage (if using Google maps, search under Capela de Santo António do Cântaro). As for the track followed by Heudelet's division, for some little distance this runs westwards from the chapel immediately beside the Rua do Poço but then turns sharply to the right and curves round to reach the road by which the visitor descended the *serra* about a kilometre from the junction with the Rua do Poço. This done, it crosses the latter and rises straight up the hillside. However, though traces of it remain all the way to the summit, attempting to follow in the footsteps of Heudelet is not recommended, such an enterprise being one that is most definitely only for the truly dedicated, very fit, and utterly heroic.

Further Reading

R. Chartrand, *Bussaco, 1810: Wellington Defeats Napoleon's Marshals* (Oxford: Osprey 2001).
D. Buttery, *Wellington against Masséna, 1810-1811* (Barnsley: Pen and Sword, 2007).

14

Fuentes de Oñoro

3–5 May 1811

The Duke of Wellington was a great general, possibly, indeed, the greatest general in the whole history of the British Army, but even the most proficient commanders are capable of the occasional fumble, the battle of Fuentes de Oñoro being a case in point. Fought on 3–5 May 1811 on the very frontier of Spain and Portugal, this saw the Anglo-Portuguese forces pushed harder than had ever been the case before or since, even Wellington going so far as to concede that it was the moment in his career when he had come closest to defeat. What makes this last all the more extraordinary, meanwhile, is the fact that his opponents had just come through an experience as traumatic as anything the Napoleonic Wars had to offer. In the event, the British general was able to recover from the error that could have cost him the battle, and even to snatch a victory of sorts, but, to purloin the phrase so often used of Waterloo, it was a close run thing, and, by extension, one that makes for a particularly interesting story, the fact that the site is especially well preserved also making it a prime choice for the battlefield tourist.

To understand the battle of Fuentes de Oñoro, it is necessary to begin with a brief account of events in the wake of the earlier contest at Buçaco. As we have seen, having invaded Portugal at the head of 68,000 men, *maréchal* André Masséna had attacked Wellington in the exceptionally strong position the latter had taken up on the ridge of that name, only to be thrown back with heavy losses. Nothing daunted, however, Masséna had found a way to outflank his opponents and the result was that Wellington was soon falling back on the fortified belt known as the Lines of Torres Vedras which he had had thrown up to protect Lisbon and at the same time create an impregnable redoubt that would be proof against the very largest invading army. The Lines having been described on numerous occasions, we need not say much about them here, but, in brief, they consisted of two lines of redoubts stretching along a line of hills that ran all the way from the enormously wide estuary of the River Tagus to the Atlantic ocean, these defences having been further augmented by scarping the slopes of the heights on which they stood and blocking the ravines in between with abattis and inundations. As his forces retired, meanwhile, the Portuguese continued to lay waste the countryside into which the French were advancing so as to deny them the food on whose requisition they had necessarily been counting. Having been unable to catch Wellington before he entered his defences, Masséna quickly realised that there was no way he could force his way in, and, short of food as he was, it therefore might have been expected that he would immediately retire to Spain, this being something that was very much what his British opponent had been anticipating. The French commander, however, was a redoubtable individual, who was, as witness his long defence of Genoa in 1800 in the face of rampant starvation, no stranger to adversity. Far from falling back, then, he rather held his ground in the faint hope that something would turn up in the form of reinforcements from Spain or even a revolution in the Portuguese capital (if there was one thing that was clear enough, it was that the retreat of the Anglo-Portuguese army had been accompanied by thousands of civilians, civilians who could not but go short of food and might in the end turn to revolt).

Forlorn though these hopes were, Masséna's situation was not quite as desperate as might otherwise have been the case, for many people had refused to leave their homes, while others had tried to conceal quantities of such commodities as corn and salt cod in secret hiding places. By the ruthless application of terror, then, the French were able to get in just enough food to stave off starvation for a considerable time, albeit at terrible cost to the civilian population. The result was a long stalemate that lasted many months, the only developments being the dispatch of a column of troops back to Spain n the hope of obtaining help, a retreat on the part of Masséna to a fortified camp he had built around the town of Santarem and, finally, the arrival of 9,000 French reinforcements under *général de division* Jean-Baptiste Drouet, who had been assigned a new corps improvised from 20 replacement battalions belonging to regiments that were already serving in the Peninsula. Hold on though the French commander might, however, there was a limit to what his increasingly mutinous and disgruntled forces could take and, with losses from sickness rising at an alarming rate, on 5 March 1811 Masséna pulled out and made for the Spanish frontier. Delayed by supply problems, the Anglo-Portuguese forces did not come up with his men for several days and even then were kept at bay by a series of rearguard actions that cost both sides many casualties. To hasten their retreat sill further, the French abandoned most of their baggage and artillery and by 22 March the exhausted survivors were once more in contact with the garrisons of Almeida and Ciudad Rodrigo.

By now, then, the French were little more than a horde of fugitives. Yet, to the consternation of many of his commanders, on 22 March Masséna suddenly issued orders for a march on the Tagus valley in the hope of getting into contact with the French forces in Andalucía and again threatening Lisbon. In the circumstances, no plan could have been more foolhardy. Thus Masséna's desire to salvage some crumb of success from the campaign is understandable enough, but the district into which he was proposing to march was one of the most barren in the entire Peninsula, whilst, deeply demoralised, the troops had little food, ammunition, clothing, footwear or transport, as well as being all but completely bereft of cavalry and artillery, around half the army's horses having either died for want of forage or been slaughtered for food. Absolutely horrified, *maréchal* Michel Ney therefore refused to obey and tried to continue the march, only to be removed from his command and sent to Spain in disgrace. With 'the bravest of the brave' gone, all resistance to the scheme collapsed and the miserable columns therefore dragged themselves southwards into the barren mountains of the Serra da Estrella. For a few days the attempt to reach the Tagus was sustained, but very soon even Masséna had to admit defeat: food could not be found, most of the roads were impassable to wheeled transport, and the troops were in a state of complete disbandment. Finally thwarted by the reality of the situation, on 29 March the French commander

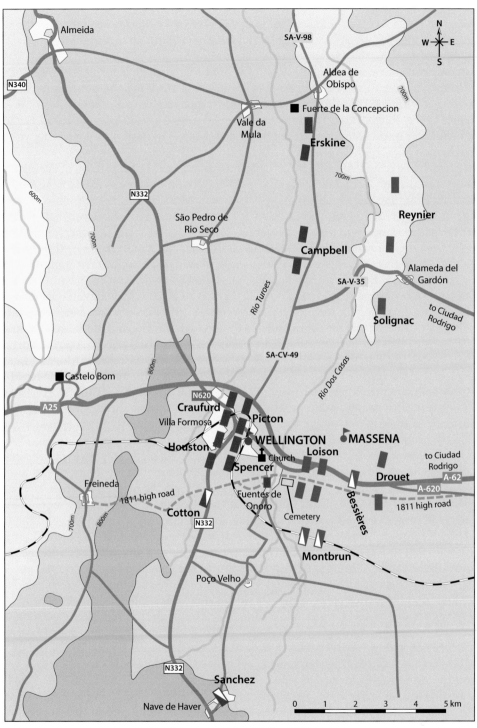

Fuentes de Oñoro, 3 May 1811.

gave up and ordered his men to head for the frontier. Extraordinarily enough, however, with only 40,000 men left in his tattered ranks and the Anglo-Portuguese army closing in fast, he still did not make for the relative safety of Ciudad Rodrigo, but rather lingered in a defensive position strung out along the River Côa in the hope that he might somehow avenge Buçaco. Yet in this, too, he was to be disappointed. Attacked in thick fog and pouring rain on the morning of 3 April 1811 by three of Wellington's divisions at Sabugal, *général de division* Jean Reynier's corps fought extraordinarily well, even launching a series of fierce counterattacks, but by midday it was all over, and the French fled the field in great disorder having lost 600 casualties.

Sabugal being only a few miles from the Spanish border, the third invasion of Portugal was finally over, the only Frenchmen left in arms in the country being the garrison of Almeida. However, being the redoubtable fighter that he was, Masséna was not yet finished. In the wake of Sabugal, Wellington had invested Almeida, and it was all too clear that sooner or later the garrison must succumb to starvation. The Portuguese fortress, though, was the one trophy from the campaign of which Masséna could still boast and he therefore threw himself into the task of saving it, if only for a brief while. Hastily refitting his men from the ample magazines that had been established in such places as Salamanca and Toro, within a month he had got his army ready for action once again, this being a truly remarkable achievement in view of the drubbing his forces had undergone over the past six months. Reinforced by a small cavalry division that the commander of the forces in Navarre and the Basque provinces, *maréchal* Jean-Baptiste Bessières, had led to its assistance, on 26 April the Army of Portugal once more advanced to the attack. Ostensibly the objective was the relief of Almeida, but the French lacked the transport to bring up more than a limited amount of food and could not possibly maintain themselves in the vicinity of the city for any length of time. The real aim, it may be assumed, then, was Wellington's destruction. In theory, such a goal was not unattainable, for, with some of its strength drawn off in an attempt to save Badajoz (currently under attack by the forces of *maréchal* Jean de Dieu Soult) from falling into the hands of the French, the Anglo-Portuguese army could only muster some 37,000 men compared with Masséna's 48,000. The newly-formed 7th Division was largely composed of raw recruits and foreign deserters, and the open nature of the border country made its marked shortage of cavalry particularly worrying. Yet all this only begged the question of whether Wellington would fight. As Masséna knew all too well, his opponent could simply withdraw beyond the Côa and wait for hunger to force the French to retreat, whilst, if he fought at all, it would only be on ground that was immensely strong. That being the case, it is difficult to see why the game was worth the candle, it being extremely unlikely that the French commander could possibly obtain the success of which he dreamed. As it happened, Wellington decided to stand and fight, but from the French point of view the whole affair seems singularly pointless.

Having decided to hold his ground, Wellington certainly chose a very strong position. His army was drawn up on a low ridge between the abandoned and semi-demolished Fuerte de la Concepción and the tightly-packed village of Fuentes de Oñoro, the last settlement on the highway from Ciudad Rodrigo to Almeida before it crossed the frontier into Portugal, while its centre and left were screened by a deep ravine through which ran a stream called the Dos Casas; also helpful, meanwhile, was the fact that the configuration of the ground was such as to allow Wellington to position most of his infantry in dead ground that could not be fired upon by French artillery. Encountering the Anglo-Portuguese array on the morning

Fuentes de Oñoro viewed from the start-line of the French attack on 3 May; the road is the old highway from Ciudad Rodrigo to Almeida. (Author's collection)

Back-alleys in the village of Fuentes de Oñoro; many of them being *culs-de-sac*, such places often became death-traps as the fighting in the village ebbed first one way and then the other. (Author's collection)

of 3 May, Masséna quickly decided that the best means of making progress was to seize the village which, strongly garrisoned, was thrown forward on the slopes that led down to the Dos Casas. Early in the afternoon, then, his leading division charged across the stream and forced its way into the warren of alleys and courtyards that lay beyond, the result being several hours of bitter street-fighting that was much complicated for both sides by the fact that the attackers included the red-coated Légion Hanoverienne. Losses were heavy for both sides, but in the end a gallant bayonet charge by the 71st Foot and several other units sent the French tumbling back across the Dos Casas, the fighting then coming to an end for the day.

For the time being, then, Masséna had been stymied, but he was by no means prepared to give up the fight. On the contrary, having spent the whole of the next day reconnoitring the Anglo-Portuguese position, he at length concluded that the best way to defeat Wellington would be to march around his right flank, this was more than somewhat 'in the air', and leave him the choice of either retreating or improvising a new line running westwards to a further rivulet called the River Turoes that ran parallel to the Dos Casas a mile to the west. Realising that something of the sort was afoot, the British commander sent out the newly-arrived 7th Division to occupy the tiny village of Poço Velho two miles south of the end of his line, but, in doing so, he had badly misjudged the situation, for, weak in terms of both numbers and quality, this force was unlikely to be able to stop a serious attack. Also available, true, was the whole of the Allied cavalry – four regiments of British or Portuguese light-dragoons and the two regiments of lancers that had been brought in by Coronel Julián Sánchez, an officer of the garrison of Ciudad Rodrigo who had escaped with the mounted detachment of the local militia when the French commenced siege operations

The empty plains to the south of Fuentes de Oñoro as viewed from Nave de Haver; initially left unguarded by Wellington, they constituted an obvious invitation to envelop his right flank. (Author's collection)

The house of the parish-priest at Poço Velho; the defenders of the village are believed to have made a stand here for some little time. (Author's collection)

Poço Velho viewed from the main position of the Seventh Division; the fields on either side of the road witnessed fierce clashes between the cavalry of the rival armies. (Author's collection)

against the city and spent the winter of 1810–1811 harassing the local occupying forces and transforming his command into a small brigade of regular cavalry – but, even so, the 7th Division could have been annihilated.

In the end, however, disaster was avoided. No sooner had dawn broken on 5 May than thousands of French troops, infantry, and cavalry alike, began to envelop Poço Velho. Fighting bravely, the British and Portuguese cavalry tried to slow them down (despite being stationed barely two miles away in the village of Nave de Haver, Sánchez's brigade took no part in the fight and appears, indeed, to have taken itself off without firing a shot), but their best efforts were to no avail, and they were forced to retreat. With the French in overwhelming strength, the village's garrison was quickly overwhelmed, while the main body of the 7th Division, which had been drawn up in line a little to the west under its commander, Major General William Houston, was soon forced to follow suit, eventually taking up a fresh position behind the River Turoes. Here the retreat stopped, for the French infantry had all turned northwards in the direction of the right flank of Wellington's main position.

Here, however, the crisis had already been surmounted. Increasingly aware of the danger, Wellington had ordered two of his best infantry divisions and a further Portuguese infantry brigade to form a new line from Fuentes de Oñoro to the Turoes. This was likely to prove a hard nut to crack – aside from anything else, for part of its length the new line was protected by a steep-sided ravine – and, given that his troops were in position well before any French troops were ready to get grips with them, the British general could therefore feel perfectly at ease. All that troubled him, indeed, was the position of the 7th Division which was still dangerously isolated. To avoid the possibility of Masséna securing even the partial success that would have been achieved by its destruction, Wellington therefore sent orders for it to fall back still further, whilst at the same time dispatching the Light Division to secure its retreat.

The hillside on which Wellington ranged his new line; the River Turón is on the far side of the high ground in the distance. (Author's collection)

The ground over which the Light Division advanced to protect the retreat of Houston's troops.
(Author's collection)

The parish church of Fuentes de Oñoro; the French were on at least two occasions able to reach the edge
of the little square in which stands, but, in both cases, they were driven back by the fire of troops blocking
the way. (Author's collection)

There followed the most famous episode of the battle. Marching out along the slopes that
led to Houston's position, Brigadier General Robert Craufurd's men briefly drew up in line.
No sooner was the 7th Division on the move again, however, than they began to file back
again. Having now reformed, the French cavalry immediately tried to ride them down, but
the same cavalry units that had already fought so well now again came to the rescue. What
could have been a situation of extreme danger was therefore avoided, the battalion squares

into which Craufurd had formed the bulk of his men being able to retire in good order. That said, the retreat was not without its moments of crisis, a section of the horse-artillery battery attached to the Light Division only saving itself from being cut off by some French cavalry by charging straight at them at full tilt, whilst on the ridge above the Turoes the French also surprised some skirmishers who had ventured too far from the main line and caused some 100 casualties. These were, however, but minor contretemps, and at this point it should therefore have been clear to Masséna that the battle was lost. Knowing that defeat meant sure disgrace, however, he could not back down. Thus, as soon as his flanking move had begun making progress, he had once more sent large numbers of infantry charging into the village. Since then, a desperate fight had been taking place that saw first one side gain the advantage and then the other, as well as forcing both the contending commanders to feed more and more troops into the struggle. On at least two occasions French troops made it almost to the very last buildings of the village, but the defenders stood firm around the parish church and a rocky knoll across the way, and their assailants found that they could advance no further and at length were driven back by a counter-attack similar to the one launched two days earlier.

Unlike on 3 May the French were not expelled from Fuentes de Oñoro altogether by the end of the day – on the contrary, much of the lower part of the village remained in their hands – but, with the failure of his last assault on the church, even Masséna had to concede defeat. That said, he now had a pretext to do so in that his fellow *maréchal*, Bessières, had refused point-blank to release the single brigade of guard cavalry he had brought with him for a last-ditch attack on Wellington's new line. That being the case, the action was called off, though the French commander did not withdraw from the field, but for the next three days lingered in front of his adversary's positions in the faint hope that he might be attacked and thereby get the chance to win a defensive victory. Ever prudent, however, Wellington refused to move, and the result was that in the end Masséna had no option but to retire to Ciudad Rodrigo from where he soon set off to France in the very disgrace which he had anticipated.

All in all, then, Fuentes de Oñoro had been anything but a triumph for Napoleon's arms. At 2,192 as opposed to 1,452 for the Anglo-Portuguese, French casualties had been much higher than those of their opponents, while the morale of Wellington's army had been much reinforced. To make matters worse, meanwhile, large amounts of precious food and fodder had been used up for no purpose whatsoever. As a small crumb of comfort, the garrison of Almeida was able to make a dramatic break-out from the fortress on the night of 10 May and escape to Ciudad Rodrigo, albeit not without a sharp fight at the bridge of Barba del Puerco, but the fact remained that almost a year of campaigning had in effect gone for nothing.

Fuentes de Oñoro Today

Situated in a poor part of Spain with few amenities, Fuentes de Oñoro is not accessible by public transport (the trains that once ran to the border station from Salamanca ceased to operate many years ago, for example), while, such are the distances involved that to walk the battlefield in its entirety would be gruelling indeed. For these reasons, it is assumed that the visitor will be carborne. That said, there are plenty of places which can be explored on foot

The knoll adjacent to the church that helped check the French advance; there seems little reason to doubt that the scene is all but entirely unchanged since 1811. (Author's collection)

The hermitage of Cristo de las Agonías; situated on the eastern bank of the Dos Casas beside the main road, this was conveniently placed to serve as a hospital for the many French troops wounded in the fighting for the village. (Author's collection)

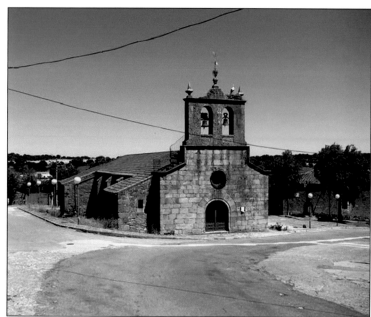

The parish church of Fuentes de Oñoro; although the French several times came within yards of the building, they were never able to take it. (Author's collection)

The clapper bridge across the River Dos Casa at the southern end of the village: the tangle of buildings on the far bank would have provided a plethora of firing positions for the garrison. (Author's collection)

The funerary cross beside the old highway from Ciudad Rodrigo. (Author's collection)

– indeed, one or two, that can only be reached in this fashion – and readers will find that getting out and stretching their legs is in every instance a rewarding experience.

Let us begin with the village itself, this being situated just off the N620 (the main road from Salamanca to Ciudad Rodrigo and the Portuguese border) approximately one mile before the border crossing. Having parked on the Calle del Generalísimo in the centre of the old village near the junction with the Calle de la Iglesia, take the Camino del Cementerio (at the time of the battle the main road from Ciudad Rodrigo), cross the river and ascend the low slope on the other side of the Dos Casas, noting in passing the funerary cross dated 1703 on the left and the hermitage of Cristo de las Agonías on the right; this last would doubtless have provided shelter for many French wounded. Keep going past the cemetery (almost certainly not there in 1811) until the crest just beyond: it may be assumed that it was from here that Masséna first surveyed Wellington's position, here that he placed much of his artillery, and from here, too, that he directed the battle. Returning towards the village, the visitor should take the lane on the left and follow it southwards, making sure to keep right at the y-junction; after a short distance, said lane heads back to the Dos Casas and crosses it by a concrete causeway just beside a mediaeval clapper bridge. Having entered the village, take the first right – the Calle Ribera – and follow this northwards until it reaches the Camino del Cementerio: along the way will be found many houses and alleyways that undoubtedly saw fierce fighting in the course of the battle.

The commanding view enjoyed by the defenders of the knoll beside the parish church.
(Author's collection)

An alleyway in the heart of Fuentes de Oñoro. (Author's collection)

With the tour of the lower part of the village complete, the visitor should now return to the Calle del Generalísimo, cross over to the far side and take the Calle de la Iglesia, this leading directly to the parish church of La Asunción de María: the street, of course, was the site of repeated attacks and counter-attacks. There is a monument to the battle in the square by the church and this marks the furthest point to which the defenders of the village were driven back, while the large stone house on the right must have provided them with a useful strongpoint. Finally, complete the visit to the area round the church by taking the narrow lane between the buildings almost directly opposite: after a very short distance, this leads to a rocky area of open-ground: this is the knoll referred to in many accounts of the battle, and it can easily be perceived how this provided the defenders with a natural redoubt that offered an excellent field of fire.

From the church head straight forwards along the Calle Torre and, just beyond the Avenida de la Estación, cut through the buildings and head downhill along what has now become a narrow country lane (this part of the route can only be undertaken on foot though the going is good and the distances relatively short). After a little distance, take the first right and then turn left at the T-junction: the slopes beyond mark the line which Wellington occupied to foil Masséna's outflanking movement. If the visitor wishes to explore this area further, take the first right and walk westwards in the direction of the Portuguese frontier;

The tangled terrain west of Fuentes de Oñoro in which Wellington formed his new defensive line; the Anglo-Portuguese forces lined the hillside to the right. (Author's collection)

otherwise, head downhill and turn left at the T-junction. Known as the Calle Tesó, the track on which the visitor is now on leads back to the village. That said, at the Y-junction, keep left: although the other fork also gets to Fuentes, the one on the left leads directly to the foot of the Calle de la Iglesia, whilst at the same time providing excellent views of the knoll beside the church.

So much for Fuentes de Oñoro. To reach the rest of the battlefield, it is first necessary to proceed to the Portuguese town of Vilar Formosa. Having crossed the frontier, take the N322 and drive south to Nave de Haver. Just inside the town, turn left on the Avenida Sao Pedro and head north to the junction with the Rua do Carrascal. At the Rua do Carrascal go left and continue out of the town to a junction which offers three possibilities. Of these last take the right-hand-most and proceed northwards to Poço Velho. Before doing so, however, pause to admire the view of the battlefield: this extends all the way to Fuentes de Oñoro and gives a good impression of just how vulnerable Wellington was to being outflanked as well as explaining why the British general posted Sánchez's contingent at Nave de Haver; as an observation post, the place could hardly be bettered.

The short drive to Poço Velho is not without interest: note, for example, how the extensive woods that cloak large areas of the battlefield are far easier to traverse for bodies of troops than their equivalents in other parts of Europe: not only are the trees well-spaced, but there is little in the way of underbrush. At the village, meanwhile, the church and its attendant

The parish church of Poço Velho. (Author's collection)

presbytery are unchanged, while many of the cottages have the appearance of having been around at the time of the battle; as for the countryside around the village, it is possible to follow every step of the fighting – all in all, then, the place is a most atmospheric spot.

To complete the tour, take the road that leads due north out of the village and follow it round to the right past the cemetery, soon after which a pair of right-angled bends mark the line of the frontier. At the first crossroads turn left and continue straight on to a T-junction at which the visitor should turn right and carry straight on, the ground to the left marking the site of the Light Division's rescue mission; having passed under the railway, the road very quickly leads back to Fuentes.

Further Reading

R. Chartrand, *Fuentes de Oñoro, 1811: Wellington's Liberation of Portugal* (Oxford: Osprey, 2002).

15

Albuera

16 May 1811

One of the bloodiest actions of the Peninsular War, the Battle of Albuera was the result of an attempt on the part of the French commander in Andalucía, *maréchal* Jean de Dieu Soult, to relieve Badajoz, this last having just been besieged by Anglo-Portuguese forces under the command of Lieutenant General William Beresford. Outnumbering Soult by almost three to two, Beresford's army, which had been joined by two Spanish armies, the one under the command of *Teniente-General* Joaquín Blake and the other under that of *Teniente-General* Francisco-Javier Castaños, was drawn up in a strong position along the crest of a line of low hills overlooking a shallow river. In the centre of the Allied position, of which the Anglo-Portuguese occupied the left and centre and the Spaniards the right, the village of Albuera provided a natural defensive redoubt, whilst the ridge provided plenty of opportunity for the defenders to take shelter behind the skyline, not that Beresford appears to have made much attempt to do so. Soult, however, was no mean general, and made use of the olive and ilex groves that screened his own position to outflank the Allied right with a large force of infantry and artillery, whilst at the same time distracting Beresford by a demonstration against the bridge that carried the main road from Seville to Badajoz across the river and into the village. That this was not the main attack should have been revealed all too clearly when the large force of cavalry which had ridden forward with the attackers suddenly wheeled to the left and moved rapidly southwards along the valley of the stream (the Río Chicaspiernas) that ran northwards beneath the Allied left wing. In the face of this brilliant piece of grand tactics, the Allied generals were slow to react even when they finally spotted the French flanking column – they seem, indeed, to have been convinced that it was a feint – and their whole army might have been rolled up had a single Spanish brigade of Blake's army, that of *Mariscal de Campo* José de Zayas y Chacón, not checked the French assault by wheeling back across its path and taking up a defensive position overlooking a shallow saddle in the ridge along which Soult was advancing. Given that the troops facing them consisted of two full infantry divisions – those of *généraaux de division* Honoré de Gazan and Jean-Baptiste Girard – and an additional brigade composed of all their grenadier companies, Zayas should by rights have been swept aside, but the men he commanded consisted of some of the best troops in the Spanish army, Blake's forces having remained intact since the middle of 1809 and spent the whole of the previous year in training at Cádiz. On top of this, the French were hampered by the fact that they were arrayed in a very deep formation with their three infantry divisions arrayed one behind the other, matters being compounded by the fact that the leading division halted to fire at Zayas' men rather than pressing on with a frontal assault.

The more recent of the two bridges at Albuera; the battle was fought under skies that were equally threatening. (Author's collection)

The parish church of Albuera: used as a hospital by Beresford, it also witnessed fierce fighting at various points during the day. (Author's collection)

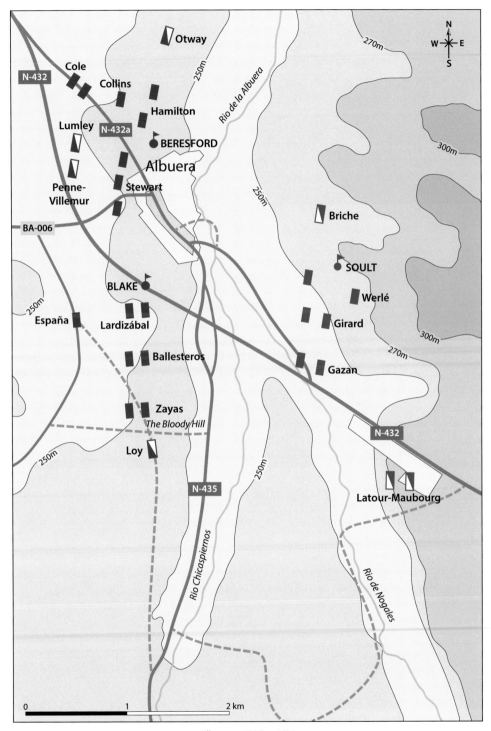

Albuera, 16 May 1811.

Open woodland in the area of the initial position of Soult's army: it was terrain such as this which helped obscure the attempt to outflank Beresford. (Author's collection)

The crest of the knoll seized by the divisions of Gazan and Girard; the Spanish forces that blocked their path occupied the slopes on the horizon on the right-hand side of the photograph. (Author's collection)

The very epicentre of the battlefield of Albuera: to the left is the ground held by Gazan and Girard and, to the right, that defended by, first, Zayas and then Hoghton. (Author's collection)

The ground occupied by Gazan and Girard during their firefight with the brigades of Zayas and, later, Hoghton and Abercromby. (Sarah King)

But for Zayas, all might have been lost. As it was, however, finally waking up to the danger of his situation, Beresford was able to rush most of his British infantry to reinforce the Spaniards, leaving his Portuguese formations, together with some troops from the King's German Legion, to hold Albuera, which for the rest of the day became the scene of fierce of street fighting on account of repeated attempts to enter the village on the part of the French troops who had been left to contain the Allied centre. The first brigade to arrive to help the Spanish, that of Lieutenant Colonel John Colborne, suffered terrible casualties when the commander of the division to which it belonged, Major General William Stewart, launched a premature attack that led to it being charged in the flank by a brigade of light cavalry consisting of the 1er Régiment de Lanciers de la Vistule and 2eme Régiment de Hussards that had burst upon it under the cover of one of the many sudden downpours that marked the day. Of the brigade's four battalions, three – the 1/3rd, 2/48th and 2/66th – were almost completely destroyed and several of their colours taken, while the victorious horsemen swept on to overrun a nearby artillery battery, attack Zayas' men in the rear and even burst in among Beresford's personal staff. By then, however, they were pretty much spent. Under fire from the Spaniards, whose rear rank had coolly faced about to confront the new danger, they were therefore quickly persuaded to retire. That said, amongst the victims of the charge was almost Beresford himself, the latter being at one point reduced to flinging a particularly obstreperous lancer from his horse by main force.

With matters in this state, all that saved the Allies was the fact that, thrown into ever greater confusion, the French flanking column had still not worsted the Spaniards, and that despite the fact that it was supported by two batteries of artillery firing at close range. As a result, the other two brigades of Stewart's division, namely those of Major General Daniel Hoghton and Lieutenant Colonel Alexander Abercromby, had time to relieve the latter and advance against their assailants in line, the Spaniards in the meantime falling back through their ranks and reforming further back. There followed a terrible firefight in which the British lost heavy casualties, including Hoghton, who fell mortally wounded, and the 57th Foot earned the nickname of 'the Die-Hards' – so great was the carnage that the

The scene of the destruction of Colborne's brigade as seen on 16 May 2011: Colborne advanced diagonally from the right, while the French cavalry charged from the extreme left. (Author's collection)

The left flank of the Allied position on the 'fatal hill'. (Sarah King)

swell in the ground on which they and the Spaniards before them took their stand became known in the annals of the battle as 'the fatal hill' – the result being that the contest once again hung in the balance. Seeing this, Beresford should have launched an immediate assault with the considerable forces he now had echeloned facing the left flank of the French flanking column, but exhaustion, indecision and lack of confidence had sapped his will, and he failed to take the necessary action: far from this, indeed, he rather hovered on the brink of ordering a general retreat. Luckily for Beresford, however, an exasperated staff officer, Captain Henry Hardinge, who was later to win much renown in India, rode over to the commander of the 4th Division, Sir Galbraith Lowry-Cole, and urged him to take the offensive. Seeing the oncoming Allied troops, Soult assailed them with infantry, cavalry, and artillery alike, only to see his men repulsed at every turn. Astonishingly enough, indeed, a frontal attack on the Portuguese brigade of Cole's division was turned back by a devastating volley of musketry even though the men concerned were formed in line. Still worse, the French troops on the ridge were now assaulted on their opposite flank by Abercromby's brigade, this last having been sheltered from the worst of the previous firefight. Unable to take any more, the French disintegrated and the battle came to an end with the whole of the French left wing breaking in rout. Thus ended a terrible day. Not counting several hundred prisoners, the Allied armies had lost 5,380 men dead or wounded, over two thirds of them British, amongst whom the casualty rate reached 40 percent, whilst Beresford was so shaken that he appears to have suffered a nervous breakdown: his dispatch, indeed, was so negative in tone that Wellington is reputed to have had it completely rewritten. As for Soult's losses, they were still worse, the *maréchal* having lost at least a quarter and possibly a third of his 24,000 men. The French, true, had been thrown back – burdened by 4,000 wounded, Soult had to retreat – but Beresford's generalship had been very poor, whilst Badajoz was not to fall for another 11 months. Thus, while the siege was resumed, mistaken strategy and a want of heavy guns meant that little progress was made, the operation finally having to be abandoned when Soult and *maréchal* Auguste Viesse de Marmont, the new commander of the French forces in León and Old Castile, managed to unite and advance on Wellington in overwhelming numbers..

Somewhat fraught though it was in many respects, the Battle of Albuera might have been thought likely to remedy some of the tensions that had been affecting the Anglo-Spanish alliance ever since the campaign of Sir John Moore in the winter of 1808–1809. This, however, was not to be. Thus, on the one hand, from Wellington downwards, British observers were inclined to blame the misfortunes of Beresford's army on the shortcomings of the Spaniards

Taken on the bicentenary of the battle, this photograph shows the scene of the attack that won the day for Beresford: the position of Gazan and Girard is marked by the rise in the middle distance. (Author's collection)

The left flank of the position occupied by Gazan and Girard; at the close of the battle this area witnessed desperate fighting between Myer's brigade and the composite grenadier brigade that formed the French reserve. (Sarah King)

The monument to Castaños in Albuera. In so far as can be ascertained, neither the general nor the few troops he brought to the battlefield played any part in the fighting. (Author's collection)

and, in particular, their inability to manoeuvre in the face of the enemy (something in which it has to be said they had a point, the bulk of the Spanish forces present at the battle scarcely having fired a shot), while on the other the Spaniards claimed that Beresford had had to be persuaded to stand and fight by Blake and Castaños; that the British had exaggerated their casualties so as to magnify their part in the victory; and, finally, that the victory had only been gained on account of a last-minute charge on the part of the rallied brigade of Zayas, the troops of Abercromby and Lowry-Cole having supposedly actually been repelled with heavy losses. So entrenched were these claims on the part of the Spaniards that they resurfaced to mar the bicentenary celebrations in 2011. That said, at the level of the grass roots, relations were often much better, a number of British prisoners being able to make their escape from the hands of the French thanks to the help of Spanish civilians in Seville and elsewhere (so many men of officers and men of the 3rd Foot made it back, in fact, that the regiment gained the nickname of 'the Resurrection Men').

Albuera Today

Not having been touched by much in the way of modern development, Albuera is a rewarding battlefield to visit. Now a small town rather than a village, the settlement itself is obviously much bigger than it was in 1811, while, other than the church, there are few buildings that are survivors of the battle, not that this at all surprising, British officers who passed through in the course of the next two years reporting that that every house in the place had been reduced to a roofless shell. As for the battlefield as a whole, this is now in large part under cultivation and is disfigured by a large factory beside the Seville highway on the slopes leading up to Soult's original position, but is otherwise unchanged: passing, as it does, through an area that saw little fighting, even the construction of a modern by-pass has not had nearly the same effect as might have been feared.

Albuera is accessible by bus from Seville and Badajoz alike, while the area that the battle covered is not so big that it cannot be walked in its entirety by foot. In so far as this is concerned, the most convenient route is to start at the monument to Castaños that stands in the Plaza de la Iglesia just to the left of the parish church of Nuestra Señora del Camino and follow the Calle de la Iglesia down the right-hand side of said building, this soon leading to the so-called Parque Wellington with its monument to the 57th Foot and, in addition, the grave of Matthew Latham, an ensign in the 3rd Foot who was horrifically wounded defending the King's Colour of his battalion from being captured by the French cavalry that destroyed Colborne's brigade. The same street also has a small museum. At the far corner of the triangular enclosure carry on across the bridge over the river – the original mediaeval crossing – and turn right along the track that runs along the far side, passing en route an area of open fields that was the scene of part of the demonstration against Beresford's centre which constituted Soult's first move. After perhaps 500 yards, this leads to the more modern bridge constructed in the eighteenth century: this was the epicentre of the first part of the battle. From the bridge continue uphill along what was in 1811 the main highway from Seville. After approximately half a mile turn right at the roundabout, pass under the modern highway (the N432) and follow the service road that parallels the latter. At the far end of the factory complex take the country road that curves around to the left, this marking the

The monument to the 57th Foot that stands in the Parque Wellington. (Author's collection)

approximate position of Soult's initial front line. Said country road is now followed westwards to a small stream (the Río Nogales) where it turns south along the line of the latter for some distance before turning west again and then north. Several hundred yards beyond this last change of direction, another minor road joins the route being followed coming from the south. Shortly beyond this point, take the farm track that will be found leading due westwards. After crossing a second stream (the Río Chicaspiernas), this last reaches a second highway, namely the N435.

Lengthy and circuitous though this route is, it exactly replicates the route taken by the infantry and artillery which Soult dispatched to assail Beresford's right flank, it being abundantly obvious from the ground over which it passes why the British commander was unable to observe the French move, though it undoubtedly helped a great deal that the battle was fought on a day that was at best dull and drizzly (had the weather been dryer, the French flanking column would undoubtedly have signalled its presence by a massive dust-cloud). Assuming that the visitor wishes to press on to the scene of the main part of the battle, cross straight over the N435 and immediately turn left onto a farm track leading uphill to the north. If this track is followed for approximately one mile, it will be found to emerge at a crest overlooking a broad valley to the left and then to descend to a saddle on the other side of which is a prominent knoll crowned by a small farm building. This last is the so-called 'fatal hill' and marks the position at which the brigades of, first, Zayas, and second, Hoghton and Abercromby, confronted the French flank attack. As for the attacks of Colborne's brigade and the 4th Division, these took place on the slopes on the left-hand side of the track.

From the crest follow the same track northwards to the saddle. At the T-junction that will be found there, it is possible to turn left and explore the valley which saw so much drama, one thing that is particularly obvious is the manner in which the outwards swell of the western slopes of the hill seized by the French would have allowed the cavalry that destroyed Colborne's brigade to get very close to its right flank without being observed. However, the main outlines of the field can be viewed perfectly satisfactorily from the T-junction and those visitors who are now weary and foot-sore are probably better advised to turn in the opposite direction and head back to the N435 and thence back to the very welcome cafés and restaurants of Albuera.

So much for a walking tour of the battlefield, something that, while the going is everywhere good and the gradients almost everywhere very gentle, is likely to take a minimum of six hours, the visitor also being advised to take plenty of water and suitable outdoor clothing (on both occasions the author has visited the battlefield, the day was marked by torrential downpours of precisely the sort that assailed the combatants in 1811!). Needless to say, much of the route can be done by car, but it is suggested that those pressed for time proceed to three 'stands' only, namely the eighteenth-century bridge, the high ground beyond the factory complex that marked Soult's centre and, finally, the T-junction between the 'fatal hill' and the final French position, a spot most conveniently reached by ascending the track leading up to it from the N435 (coming from Albuera, this will be found heading up the hillside to the right just across the road from a small farm-complex about a mile south of the junction of the N435 and the N432).

Further Reading

M.S. Thompson, *The Fatal Hill: the Allied Campaign under Beresford in Spain in 1811* (Sunderland: privately published, 2002)

P. Edwards, *Albuera: Wellington's Fourth Peninsular Campaign, 1811* (Marlborough: the Crowood Press, 2008)

G. Dempsey, *Albuera, 1811: the Bloodiest Battle of the Peninsular War* (Barnsley: Pen and Sword, 2008)

16

Arroyomolinos de Montánchez

28 October 1811

The Peninsular War, as is well known, gave the English language the term 'guerrilla' and, since the days of Charles Oman, at least (William Napier was much more sceptical), there has scarcely been a history of conflict that has not laid much stress on the activities of the partisan bands to which the concept of the 'little war' – the literal meaning of *la guerrilla* – is almost universally assumed to refer. As for the protagonists in this quintessentially asymmetrical struggle, they were, it was always alleged, parties of armed civilians motivated by a combination of want, hatred of the French and devotion to God, king and fatherland, who had taken to the hills to wage war against the invaders in the manner that they understood best. Joined in ever increasing numbers by fugitives from Spain's many defeats moved by a fervent desire to continue the struggle in a more effective fashion than that associated with the generals of the old army, not to mention peasants and day labourers whose families had been murdered by the French, eager patriots who had fled towns and cities under enemy occupation and escaped prisoners of war, the *partidas*, as they became known, soon begin to spawn an outstanding group of military commanders of their own, all of them, give or take the occasional monk, friar or parish priest, humble men of the people who had learned the trade of killing the hard way, provided their followers with inspirational leadership and flaunted nicknames in the style of popular bullfighters or, in a later age, football stars (one thinks here of such figures as Borbón, El Mozo, El Empecinado, El Médico, El Fraile and El Pastor). Underpinning all this, meanwhile, was claimed to be a populace burning with a determination to beat the French with every possible means that, on the one hand, would never betray the guerrillas to the French, and, on the other, strain every nerve to provide them with food and shelter and word of enemy movements alike, frequently running the most terrible risks in the process. With the number of bands running into many hundreds and that of their members many thousands, thus was born a style of waging war of a sort that had never yet been witnessed that inflicted crippling losses on Napoleon's forces, gravely undermined the morale of the French soldiery, and, according to some observers at least, proved by far the most important factor in the overthrow of the Bonaparte kingdom of Spain, claiming far more victims than the regular armies of Spain, Britain and Portugal combined.

On almost every level, however, this image can be argued to be so much nonsense. As the current author has shown in such works as *Fighting Napoleon: Guerrillas, Bandits and*

Adventurers in the Peninsular War, 1808-1814 (London: Yale University Press, 2004) and *Outpost of Empire: the Napoleonic Occupation of Andalucía, 1810-1812* (Norman: University of Oklahoma Press, 2012), the reality was very different. Thus, while it is true that in the first few months of the war a number of the many provincial juntas that emerged in the course of the uprising and, latterly, the provisional government known as the Junta Central, tried to encourage the formation of irregular bands of the sort envisaged by the traditional model, such groups as were formed had more than something of the bandit about them and sometimes lost no time into sliding into outright criminality. To take just one example a *partida* that was formed in the Andalusian town of Ayamonte at a time when there was not a French soldier for hundreds of miles appears simply to have acted as enforcers for the local *caciques* (roughly 'big-wigs'). Indeed, one can go still further, the fact being that the vast majority of the bands did not owe their origins to the Patriot authorities at all, but were rather quite literally bandits, men who might slit a Frenchman's throat one day and raid an isolated Spanish village the next. In so far as the popular *guerrilla* was concerned, then, it was in reality rooted in crime of a very traditional and widespread sort – as had been the case since time immemorial, the crushing poverty that was the hall mark of so much of Spain meant that the whole country was swarming with robbers and highwaymen – the only thing that saved it from becoming a mere nuisance of no military value whatsoever being the presence in its ranks of a handful of exceptional men who realised that to survive they needed to aspire to something other than a life on the run that would most likely end on the scaffold. It should be remembered here that, not least because of the difficulty of feeding a large number of men, most of the bands were absolutely tiny, often numbering no more than half-a-dozen. No more altruistic though they were than any of their fellow chieftains, they yet possessed sufficient insight, initiative and powers of leadership to militarise their followers, thereby significantly boosting their military effectiveness and, in the process, opening the gates to numerous advantages and opportunities, ranging from vastly increased recruitment, recognition on the part of the Patriot authorities and treatment as prisoners of war should they fall into the hands of the French to the ability to suppress local rivals as mere bandits. Such men were very few in number – a list might include men we have already mentioned such as Juan Martín Díaz and Francisco Espoz Ilundaín (better known as Francisco Espoz y Mina) as well as lesser known figures such as Francisco Longa, Jerónimo Merino and Tomás Jaureghuí – but their ability to weld their commands into flying columns of regular troops, which were eventually absorbed into the army as properly organised brigades and even divisions, ensured that they had an impact that far out-weighed those of the tiny bandit gangs from whose ranks they had originally emerged.

Yet even when the efforts of figures of the sort described here are considered, the fact is that the damage inflicted by the popular *guerrilla* was minimal. Thus, careful analysis of the detailed list of French officers who were killed in the Napoleonic Wars suggests that just 19 percent of the 2,400 such men who fell in Spain perished in clashes with irregular opponents as opposed to 31 per cent who perished in actions involving British soldiers and 50 per cent who perished in actions involving the regular Spanish army alone. While there was certainly a *guerrilla*, it is therefore necessary to explain it by reference to very different models and, above all, to accept that it was the work of regular soldiers far more than it was the work of armed civilians. If we look at the supposed irregulars, then, we find that in many cases, they were not irregulars at all. Of this, there are many good examples, including *Coronel* Julián

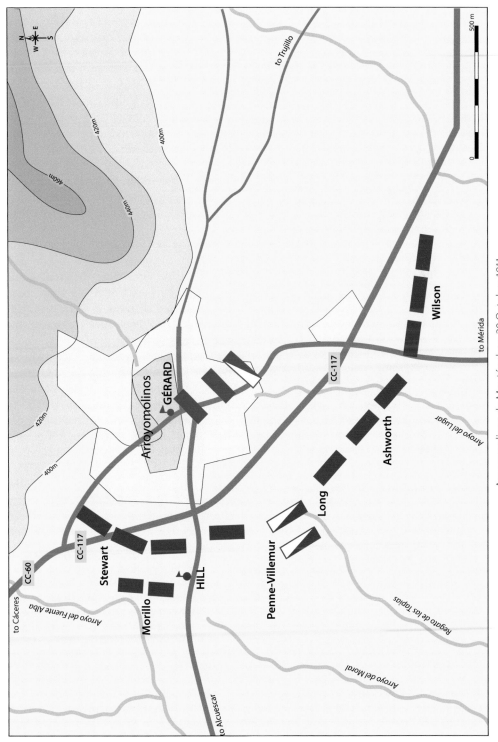

Arroyomolinos de Montánchez, 28 October 1811.

Sánchez García, who was the commander of the cavalry company formed as part of the civic militia formed at Ciudad Rodrigo in 1808; *Coronel* José Durán y Barazabal, a retired officer of the regular army who was appointed to command the volunteer forces raised by the clandestine Junta of Soria; Pedro Villacampa y Maza de Lizano, an officer of the old army who was sent into the hills of southern Aragón at the head of a brigade of regular troops with orders to inflict as much havoc as he could upon the French; Felipe Perena Casayús, a prominent inhabitant of Huesca who was awarded command of one of the volunteer units raised in the town at the start of the war and led it in a series of raids in the Ebro valley until his base was taken by the invaders; and Francisco Ballesteros, who, whilst admittedly a 'new man' (in 1808 he had been no more than a lieutenant in the customs-guard in Asturias), led a division of regular troops in a long series of marches and counter-marches in the wilds of southwestern Andalucía in the period 1811–1812 and in the process fought many minor actions with the French before finally becoming the commander of the Spanish Fourth Army with the rank of *Teniente-General*.

It being in the activities of figures such as these that the real success of the 'little war' lay, it is wrong to see the guerrillas in terms of small bands of cut-throats running around the mountains armed with daggers and blunderbusses. At the same time, the combatants were anything but just Spanish. On the contrary, their ranks were frequently augmented by contributions from Spain's allies. Many of these consisted of raids involving contingents of British sailors and marines of the sort that caused the French such trouble on the Cantabrian coast in the summer of 1812, but on occasion substantial forces of regular troops were involved as well, one such being the action that took place at the isolated Extremaduran village of Arroyomolinos (NOT Arroyo Dos Molinos) de Montánchez on 28 October 1811.

In essence, the story is as follows. In the autumn of 1811, the French forces holding the area of Badajoz – essentially, the V Corps of Maréchal Edouard Mortier – were being watched from across the Portuguese frontier by the *de facto* corps that had been operating in the region for the past six months and fought the French to a standstill at Albuera. Originally led by Beresford, it was now in the much surer hands of Wellington's most trusted subordinate, Lieutenant General Rowland Hill, and consisted of the 2nd and 4th Divisions together with some independent Portuguese formations and a number of cavalry units. Unlike the timorous Beresford, Hill was an active and enterprising field commander, and, hearing that a single French division – that of *général de division* Jean-Baptiste Girard – had been ordered to march northwards from its base at Mérida so as to ransack Cáceres for food and money and also drive away the Spanish Fifth Army, a somewhat ramshackle assembly that had been threatening the crucial road that linked the Tagus and the Guadiana, he resolved on a sudden strike. No sooner had Girard reached Cáceres, then, than Hill set out from his headquarters at Porto Alegre with a force of 10,000 men made up of two of the three British brigades of the 2nd Division (the third followed a day later but did not catch up in time to take part in the battle), two Portuguese brigades, a brigade of British and KGL light cavalry, and a detachment of the Fifth Army. Why Hill included these last troops in his order of battle is by no means clear, but he may have hoped that doing so would both do something to smooth the increasingly fractious nature of Anglo-Spanish relations and give the tatterdaemaelion regiments concerned a taste of victory, while at the same time ridding himself of the need to feed them. Unfortunately, however, in the event Girard spent less time at Cáceres than the British commander had been expecting and started on his return journey

A distant view of Alcuescar viewed from the direction of Arroyomolinos; the shoulder of high-ground on which it stands was undoubtedly of great help in terms of hiding Hill's forces from those of Girard. (Author's collection)

before the Allied column could attack him. Hill, though, was not a man to give up easily, and the result was that his unfortunate troops found themselves committed to a desperate forced march in pouring autumn rains in an effort to catch the French column. For three days the increasingly exhausted Allied troops tramped through the desolate Extremaduran countryside, but, in the evening of 27 October, much helped by the fact that the French retreat was distinctly dilatory, they finally caught up with Girard and his men at the insignificant village of Arroyomolinos de Montánchez and settled down for a cheerless night around the town of Alcuescar a mere three miles to the west (with the men so close to the French, there was no question of them being permitted to light camp-fires and that despite the torrential rain that continued to lash the area).

Extraordinarily enough, meanwhile, despite the fact that he had a brigade of cavalry attached to his division, Girard had no idea whatsoever that there was a substantial Allied force anywhere in the vicinity, and thus it was that, when Hill set his men in motion at four the following morning, with the exception of a single infantry brigade that had gone ahead, the French were still in the process of forming up on the road outside the village. Still worse, their tactical position could not have been more unfavourable, for their most obvious line of retreat if attacked by a force coming from the west was blocked by a range of rocky hills known as the Sierra de Montánchez that rose precipitously from the plain in which Arroyomolinos stood and was crossed by nothing more than goat tracks. As a result, Hill's forces were on the French almost before they knew what was happening. Though most of their comrades were killed or taken prisoner, a few survivors of the picket that had been posted to watch the approaches to the village escaped into the darkness and raised the alarm, they were able to give Girard no more than a few minutes' warning. While the first of the British commander's two infantry brigades charged into the village along the axis of the direct road from Alcuescar with the Spanish infantry in close support, the other circled around the beleaguered French so as to cut the road they had been following in their retreat to Mérida, the Allied pincers being linked by the British and Spanish cavalry.

Not surprisingly, the action that followed was of very short duration. In the village itself, the single battalion still in the place was overwhelmed almost immediately, the only serious resistance coming from a small group of men who retreated to a rocky knoll overlooking the southern exit crowned by a calvary around which they mounted something of a last stand. By an odd coincidence, the men concerned came from the French 34eme Régiment d'Infanterie de Ligne and their assailants from the British 34th Foot,

The western approaches to Arroyomolinos viewed under a lowering sky identical to the one that cloaked the area on the morning of 28 October 1811. (Author's collection)

The track used by Hill' left wing to reach Arroyomolinos. (Author's collection)

The calvary outside the village where a party of the French Thirty-Fourth Regiment of Infantry of the Line made a last stand. (Author's collection)

The site of the cavalry action. (Author's collection)

the drums taken in the course of the fight going on to become one of the latter's most-prized trophies. This gallant little fight having bought Girard a little time, the French commander managed to get the rest of his command moving and duly took the Mérida road with all haste, only to run headlong into Hill's 1,000 cavalry. Hastily turning his infantry about, Girard left his own horsemen to do battle with the new arrivals and made for his last hope of escape, namely a side road that eventually led to Trujillo, but to reach said road the fugitives had first to make it to the very southern tip of the Sierra de Montánchez, for it was only there that it left the scene of the action. Even so, Girard and his men might still have got away, but at the last moment the way was blocked by the column which Hill had dispatched to prevent any French troops from escaping the field. With their discipline now completely broken, the panic-stricken infantry fled for the safety of the hills behind them, only to find themselves faced by precipitous slopes which could not be scaled with any ease. Afforded something of a head start by the fact that they were mounted, Girard and a handful of other officers found a convenient ravine that afforded access to the heights above, while they were eventually joined by perhaps 500 men who either reached the ravine in time or managed to clamber up to the summit by other means, but the vast majority of the infantry and cavalry alike did not have enough time to get away and therefore had no option but to lay down their arms. Barely an hour after it had started, then, the fight was over. For a cost of fewer than 200 casualties, Hill had taken killed, wounded, or taken prisoner around half the 4,000 men with whom Girard had started the day as well as all the latter's baggage, the only bright spot for the French being that the eagles of the two infantry regiments caught at the foot of the *sierra* were somehow saved from capture.

A singularly petty affair in many respects, Arroyomolinos de Montánchez altered the course of the war not a whit, but it nonetheless drove Napoleon into a fury, the unfortunate Girard being recalled to France in disgrace. This, however, was very unfair: while the French commander had made many mistakes, if the over-extended French forces were increasingly vulnerable to sudden attacks of the sort launched by Hill, no-one was more to blame than the emperor. Meanwhile, conducted, though it was, almost entirely by British and Portuguese troops, the action is an excellent example of the real nature of *la guerrilla*, what really mattered as far as this was concerned being, not disorderly irregular bands, but mobile forces of regular or, at least, semi-regular, troops who were capable of taking the war to the enemy.

Finally, there is one footnote that should be added to the story. We come here once more to the figure of John Downie, the commissary whose encounter with the Loyal Lusitanian Legion of Sir Robert Wilson at the time of the action at Alcántara had inspired with the vision of a similarly-organised Loyal Extremaduran Legion. In brief, a series of manoeuvres embracing a mixture of sleight of hand and blatant dishonesty had eventually secured Downie a colonelcy in the Spanish army and, with it, permission to form his legion, and it was precisely at Arroyomolinos that the result of his labours – a single squadron of cavalry – made its debut on the battlefield. To put it mildly, however, the experience was not a success: not only did the unit fail in the face the enemy, but it became the laughing-stock of the entire army, Downie having dressed them in an outfit reminiscent of that of the *tercios* of the sixteenth century in the belief that, so attired, they could not but be inspired by the heroism of their ancestors.

The road to Trujillo (Author's collection)

The area where most of the French infantry surrendered. (Author's collection)

A street in Arroyomolinos. (Author's collection)

Arroyomolinos de Montánchez Today

Isolated in the depths of one of the poorest and most isolated regions of Spain, Arroyomolinos has grown in size relatively little in the course of the past 200 years while many of the buildings seem to have been hardly altered. Meanwhile, other than for the more important routes having been metalled, the road network is all but the same as it was in 1811, the result being that it is possible to follow every detail of the action and, indeed, to explore the rocky tracks that enabled Girard and a few of his men to escape the trap that Hill had sprung on them. Even the countryside – a mixture of scrub, rough pasture and groves of olives and figs crisscrossed by dry-stone walls – retains much of the character of the period. Nor is the action forgotten by the inhabitants, many of whom turn out in full uniform for an annual re-enactment of the events of 1811. All in all, then, Arroyomolinos has the makings of an excellent battlefield visit, the only drawback being the fact that, with the exception of Medellín, it is a long way from any other sites of interest to the student of the Peninsular War.

Further Reading

R. Griffith, *At the Point of the Bayonet: the Peninsular-War Battles of Arroyomolinos and Almaraz, 1811-1812* (Warwick: Helion Books, 2020).

17

Saguntum

September–October 1811

Of all the fortresses fought over in the Peninsular War, Saguntum is by far the most interesting, not least because it was an ancient site of great importance. Situated on a razor-backed ridge that describes a shallow curve above the town of Sagunto – known in 1808 as Murviedro – some 20 miles north of Valencia, it was originally a stronghold of the Celtiberians, but was stormed by Hannibal in 219 BCE at the start of his famous march on Rome and thereafter garrisoned in turn by the Romans, the Visigoths and the Moors, all of whom left their mark on the place, while few sites can be blessed with views that are more dramatic, stretching, as they do, both all the way to Valencia and far out to sea. Another famous figure from history who is associated with Saguntum, meanwhile, is the legendary Cid, who captured it from the Almoravids in 1098 and for three years made it his headquarters. All this makes it a fascinating place to visit it in its own right, in which respect the massive Roman theatre that was constructed just outside the walls on the slopes overlooking the town comes as an added bonus, but for the student of the Peninsular War there is much to see. At the same time, too, discussing events at Saguntum will allow us to say something about the campaigns in eastern Spain that are so often forgotten,

Before going any further, let us begin with a description of the fortress as it existed in 1808. Almost entirely a ruin that had for hundreds of years been plundered as a source of building materials, Saguntum completely covered the summit of the hill on which it was constructed, but was at the same time very narrow, the slopes to the north and south alike being so precipitate that extending the defended area for more than a few yards on either side was very difficult. Meanwhile, the area within the walls was partitioned into a number of different baileys and garnished by two substantial towers. For the first two years of the conflict, military operations had passed it by, but in the autumn of 1810 the then commander of the Spanish forces in Valencia, *Teniente-General* Joaquín Blake y Joyes resolved to make use of it as an outwork, blocking, as it did, the only route the French armies in Aragón and Catalonia could use to invade the region from the north. With the aid of considerable vigour on the part of the inhabitants and soldiery alike, over the next few months much progress was made, whether in terms of the construction of three masonry batteries at various points of the perimeter or the elevation of the existing walls to a more satisfactory height by dint of, sadly enough, demolishing a good part of the Roman theatre which had hitherto been in a state of preservation that was by all accounts quite extraordinary. A year on there was still

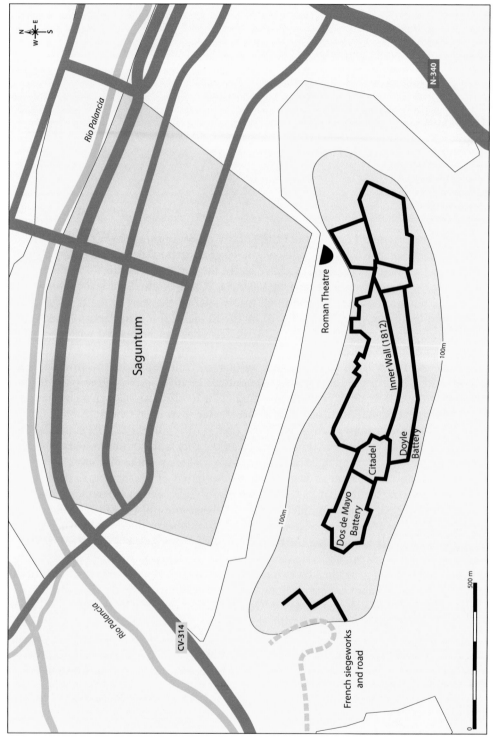

Saguntum, September–October 1811.

much to do, however, including, not least, the construction of bomb-proof shelters for the garrison, who in the meantime, had to make do with nothing better than tents and shanties, and just as importantly, projecting bastions from which flanking fire could directed on any troops who managed to close with the walls. Nor, alas, was there very much to defend the fortress with, the forces concerned consisting of no more than five understrength infantry battalions, of which two were composed entirely of poorly equipped raw recruits, supported by just 17 field pieces of various calibres, many of them very light, the 18 and 24-pounders that were the usual armament of fortresses being entirely absent. In command, meanwhile, was a completely unknown figure, namely a *colonel* who had enlisted in the Bourbon army in 1790 by the name of Luis Andriani.

The northern glacis of the fortress of Saguntum showing the terraces of the Roman theatre and the ugly concrete construction that shelters the remains of the stage. (Author's collection)

The Batería de Doyle, one of three casemated gun positions constructed by the Spaniards prior to the siege; it bears the name of Brigadier General Charles Doyle, a British officer who served as an adviser to the Spanish forces in eastern Spain. (Author's collection)

Whether the preparations that had been made to defend Saguntum were enough was soon to be put to the test. Thus, having taken the Catalan strongholds of Lérida, Tortosa and Tarragona, a feat which saw him elevated to the ranks of the marshalate, the commander of the French forces in Aragón and Catalonia, Louis Suchet, received orders from Napoleon to march on Valencia. That this was so is definitely worthy of comment. By the summer of 1811 it was increasingly obvious that the Emperor was facing war with Russia. This clearly being a challenge of the first order, it followed that the Peninsular War would no longer enjoy first call on France's resources, if indeed it enjoyed any call on them at all. That being the case, logic dictated a switch to the strategic defensive for the only way that the offensive could be maintained in Iberia was keeping the French armies employed there supplied with a constant flow of reinforcements and replacements. What the emperor was demanding, then, was the occupation of still more territory at the very time that his commitment to the struggle was likely to be on the wane, this being a combination that did not bode well for the future. Even as it was, things were difficult enough. Given that he had to leave large numbers of troops behind to defend the territory he had occupied hitherto from the flying columns of individuals like *Mariscal de Campo* Pedro Villacampa y Maza de Lizana, *Coronel* José Durán y Barazábal and *Coronel* Francisco Espoz y Mina, the number of troops that Suchet could devote to the new offensive – some 23,000 men – was far from being especially impressive, but, unlike so many of Andriani's soldiers, the men concerned were all hardened veterans and there seemed no reason to believe that they would not carry all before them when they arrived before the fortress on 23 September 1810.

Certainly, it was in that spirit that Suchet set about the place. Thus, convinced that the morale of the garrison was extremely weak, he resolved on an escalade and, having arranged for the construction of 50 ladders, at midnight on the night of 27–28 September 1811 two columns of 300 men apiece were duly sent to storm the northern walls under cover of a diversion that was mounted against a different sector by a detachment drawn from the division of Italian troops that was among the forces that had marched on Sagunto. However, the arrangement for the attack quickly went awry, for, rather than waiting, as they were supposed to do, for the Italians to mount their demonstration, the troops whose task it was to storm the walls set off before the Italians got into position. Still worse, the defenders did not break, but rather put up a fierce fight and would not give way even when a third column, again of 300 men, that had been held in reserve was thrown into the fray, the result being that Suchet was eventually left with no choice but to order the recall.

With his attempt to escalade the fortress a bloody failure – of the 900 men sent to storm the walls, over a quarter had been killed or wounded – the French commander realised that there was nothing for it but to engage in the lengthy business of regular siege operations and therefore sent orders for the siege train he had brought with him to be moved up forthwith, this having been left in the rear to batter the minor Spanish garrison that had been left to defend the town of Oropesa into surrender some distance to the north. However, while this was all very well, Saguntum occupied so lofty and inaccessible position that finding spots from which a breach could be blown in the walls was extremely difficult. Indeed, there was only one direction from which such an attack could be mounted, namely the somewhat gentler slopes that ran down from the eastern-most point of the defences. To make use even of these the French engineers had first construct a special road up which they could drag the heavy guns they needed, not to mention build the necessary entrenchments, this last proving

The sector of the northern defences that held off Suchet's first assault on the night of 27–28 September 1811. (Author's collection)

The slopes at the western end of the fortress from which Suchet launched his formal siege operations; the track constructed by the French to bring up their siege guns is still clearly visible. (Author's collection)

a very difficult task due to the exceptionally rocky nature of the ground; not until 16 October, indeed, was everything ready. Once the guns opened up, however, the defences overlooking the batteries soon began to crumble away and, with the Spanish guns too few to make an adequate response, after less than two days a small breach was seen to have been blown in the so-called Batería del Dos-de-Mayo, this last being one of the three casemated positions that had been added to the defences in the course of the preceding year. Well aware, as he was, that he had fallen well behind Napoleon's expectations with regard to how long the conquest of Valencia should take, Suchet was eager to end the siege as quickly as possible and therefore immediately ordered an assault, only for this to be beaten off once again with the loss of some 300 men in the face of further prodigies of valour on the part of the Spaniards.

With further attacks of this sort out of the question on account of the impact a third failure would have had on the morale of his forces, the French commander regretfully fell back on regular siege operations, his aim being eventually to bring his siege train right up the foot of the Dos-de-Mayo battery and ensure that it was pounded into rubble. How long matters would have continued had the process carried on is difficult to say, for the garrison was in good heart and continued to maintain a heavy fire on the troops working in the trenches, but fate now took a hand in the person of *Tenente-General* Joaquín Blake. Ensconced with his field army behind a defensive line that was in construction stretching westwards from

The interior of the Batería del Dos-de-Mayo. (Author's collection)

Valencia along the course of the River Guadalaviar, the Spanish commander had hitherto been relying on the operations of commanders such as Espoz y Mina, Villacampa and Durán in the hope that, with so many of Suchet's troops drawn away to take part in the invasion of Valencia, they would cause such havoc in Aragón that the *maréchal* would have to turn back to secure his home-base. In this, however, not least because Napoleon had ordered the transfer of two divisions of fresh troops from Navarre, he was disappointed, the siege continuing unchecked. Conscious that he could not leave Andriani to be overcome by the French without making at least some attempt to help him, on 24 October he therefore marched north at the head of an army of 28,000 men, his plan being to hold Suchet with his right wing in the coastal plain while sending his much stronger left wing to take the French in flank. Given that the opposing French forces numbered a mere 14,000 men, this plan should have had a good chance of success, but Blake had placed excessive faith in the ability of his troops to take on the French in the open field, far too many of them being either raw recruits or men who had a poor record on the battlefields of the previous three years. Rather than driving all before them, then, when battle was joined the next day, the Spanish left therefore collapsed in the face of a series of cavalry charges, thereby leaving Suchet free to crush the rest of Blake's army, albeit not without some fierce fighting. By the end of the day, then, the relief force was streaming away to the shelter of its entrenchments having lost as many as 6,000 casualties.

Much of this having taken place in full view of Andriani's beleaguered garrison, the effect on its morale can only be imagined, and Suchet had no sooner summoned the governor to surrender the next day than he capitulated without demur, Valencia going the same way on 8 January 1812 after the French commander had pierced the line of the Guadalaviar and surrounded the city in a further battle that took place on 26 December. That said, the gallant defence mounted by the garrison of Saguntum had an impact on the history of the

Distant view of the battlefield where Blake was defeated on 25 October 1811 as seen from the southern battlements of Saguntum; the smoke and dust, and, by extension, the general course of events, would have been clearly visible to the defenders. (Author's collection)

Peninsular War that was of the greatest possible importance. In brief, having already destabilised the position of his forces in the Peninsula by having them embark on a fresh offensive, Napoleon responded by, not just authorising Suchet to bring up two divisions from Aragón, but also ordering both King Joseph's Army of the Centre and Marmont's Army of Portugal to send troops to attack the city from the west, Marmont being further ordered to take over many of the positions hitherto held by the forces of the king around Madrid. What this meant, of course, was that the Portuguese frontier was stripped of most of its defenders and the garrison of Ciudad Rodrigo left without support, a fact that troubled the Emperor not at all, it being his fixed assumption that the Anglo-Portuguese army was too weak to take the offensive. As we shall soon see, however, he could not have been more wrong.

Saguntum Today

Situated directly above the town of Sagunto, the fortress of Saguntum is extremely easy to locate, while its remains can be explored without difficulty, the only real difference in the site being a new wall that the French constructed along the northern summit of the ridge in rear of the defences held by Andriani in the face of Suchet's first attack. Meanwhile, the area around the Dos-de-Mayo battery is particularly evocative and all the more so as the slopes below it are in much the same state as they were in 1811, even exhibiting traces of the French siege works. Finally, away from the fortress, it is also possible to visit the site of the battle of 26 October, but this is much cut up by new roads and so cloaked with groves of orange trees that it is very difficult to navigate.

18

Ciudad Rodrigo

7–20 January 1812

In many ways, the year 1811 had been one of great frustration for the Allied cause. Thus, despite the terrible damage inflicted on *maréchal* Masséna in the course of his abortive invasion of Portugal, the arrival of substantial reinforcements and the fact that the dilapidated Portuguese army could now be relied upon to take the field in offensive operations, clearing the enemy from Spain in accordance with the new orders that Wellington had received in the wake of the French retreat from Lisbon had proved impossible. Thus, engaged though the French were in a seemingly never-ending series of campaigns against the Spaniards, whose battered armies had, despite a series of terrible defeats, never given up the struggle against the invaders, they had been able to concentrate overwhelming numbers against the Anglo-Portuguese and force them to retreat every time they crossed the frontier, while, to make matters worse, if they had lost Almeida, the French retained of Ciudad Rodrigo and Badajoz – the major fortresses that controlled the two chief crossings from Portugal into Spain.

By the end of 1811, putting an end to this stalemate had become essential. For all their courage, the Spaniards were under severe pressure: badly defeated in actions at Sagunto and the River Turón, their last major field army had been bottled up behind the inadequate defences of the city of Valencia (which proceeded to fall into the hands of the enemy only eight days into 1812), while the irregular bands and flying columns of regular troops that continued to harass the French in the interior of the country could not be expected to hang on forever without the support of more substantial formations. Wellington, then, was gravely worried, but, reinforced though he now had been by a substantial train of siege artillery, he could do no more than keep his forces closed up just inside the Portuguese frontier and wait for a chance to strike a blow at his initial target of Ciudad Rodrigo, a blow that could only be struck should the French make a serious mistake. Fortunately for him, not to mention for Spain and Portugal, that mistake was not long in coming: indeed, it had already been made.

To understand this, we need to turn for a moment to the situation outside Spain. Discounting a short-lived Austrian revolt against the steady growth of French power in 1809, Britain had since 1807 had no supporters among the great powers of Europe. Still worse, by dint of some clever personal diplomacy, Napoleon had in that year secured a *de facto* alliance with Russia. In this situation, the French ruler beyond doubt had the capacity to win the war, but to do so he needed to retain the support of the tsar, Alexander I. This was by no means an impossible task – Alexander hated Britain and was deeply impressed by Napoleon – but the

Emperor was simply incapable of tempering his behaviour in the fashion that was necessary and alienated the tsar to such an extent that by 1811 all hint of Franco-Russian friendship had been swept away. Determined to impose his will on Alexander, indeed, Napoleon resolved on war, but this had catastrophic effects on the situation in Spain and Portugal. Although the French commanders in the Peninsula were instructed to continue with offensive operations (which in the autumn of 1811 more than anything meant the attack on Valencia), the constant stream of reinforcements and replacements that had sustained their campaigns hitherto was switched off overnight, and some troops even withdrawn to take part on the attack on Russia. What this meant on the ground was quite simple: as Wellington soon found out thanks to his highly efficient intelligence services, the Portuguese frontier was stripped of troops as more and more men were pulled eastwards by the campaign in Valencia. With the French capacity to attain numerical superiority on the frontier in consequence quite wiped out, the way was open for the British commander to take the offensive.

Ciudad Rodrigo viewed from the Tesón Grande. (Author's collection)

The Puerta de Santiago: the eastern exit from Ciudad Rodrigo, this was the target of a feint attack during the assault of 19 January 1812. (Author's collection)

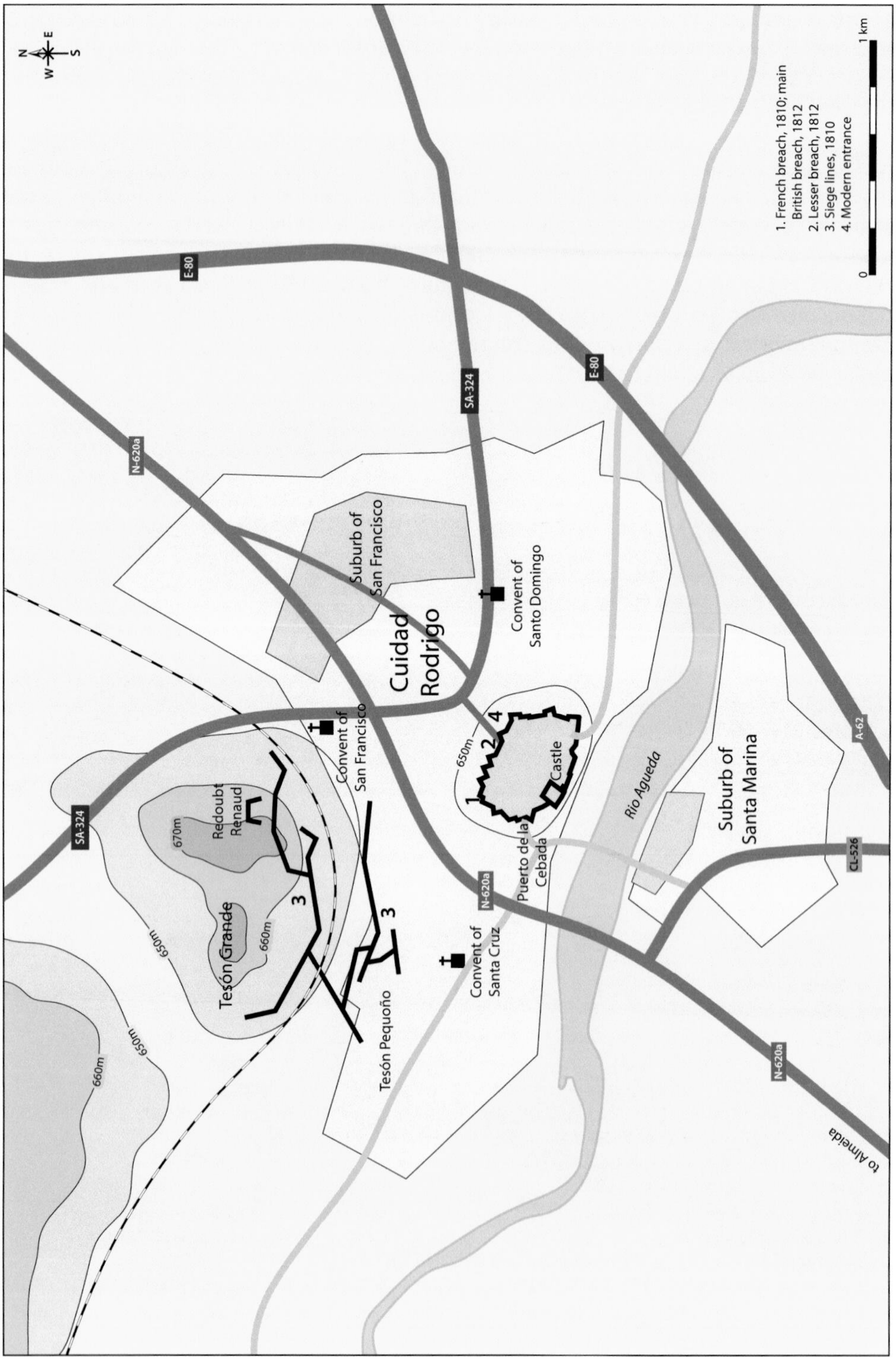

1. French breach, 1810; main
   British breach, 1812
2. Lesser breach, 1812
3. Siege lines, 1810
4. Modern entrance

Ciudad Rodrigo.

The bridge across the River Agueda at Ciudad Rodrigo as viewed from the topmost battlements of the castle. (Author's collection)

Situated on a low rise on the right bank of the River Agueda, Ciudad Rodrigo was easily the more vulnerable of the two border fortresses that remained in French hands at the beginning of 1811. Its defences were imperfect in their design, the mediaeval city walls having been left in place rather than being torn down in favour of modern ramparts, and the bastioned trace, or *fausse-braye*, that had been erected to cover them built too low to protect them from direct fire, just as it was itself left only partially protected by the glacis. There was no Citadel either, its place being taken by a castle positioned on a high bluff directly overlooking the bridge that carried the main road to the Portuguese frontier across the river. As if all this was not enough, meanwhile, the northwestern angle of the defences was overlooked from within easy cannon shot by two ridges known as the Tesón Pequeño and the Tesón Grande, it being precisely from these positions that the French had breached the walls when they took the fortress from the Spaniards in the summer of 1810. In an attempt to dissuade further assailants from doing the same thing, the French had since erected a small redoubt on the Tesón Grande, while, in the low ground some distance to its right, they had transformed the outlying monastery of San Francisco into a makeshift fort by reinforcing the walls with extra masonry and piercing them with loop-holes. Finally, a substantial suburb having grown up outside the eastern walls of the fortress, this had been enclosed by a breastwork, and another monastery outside the western walls – that of Santa Cruz – prepared as a strong-point on the same lines as that of San Francisco. However, equipped, as he now was, with a proper siege train, in the end Wellington had little to fear from the defences, and, for that matter, the garrison, this last consisting of the distinctly insufficient total of just 2,000 men and 153 guns, a figure rendered rather less impressive than it first seems by the fact that there were a mere 167 gunners within the walls. As for the governor, *général de brigade* Jean Barrié, he does not appear to have been a man of much energy, and was certainly not on a par with the commander Wellington was to face at Badajoz later in the year.

The castle viewed from the bridge across the River Agueda showing the battery stormed at the start of the attack by the 2º Caçadores and the light company of the 2/83rd Foot. (Author's collection)

The remains of the convent of San Francisco. (Author's collection)

The badly-exposed north-western angle of the defences showing the ditch and *fausse-braie* and, in the distance, the Tesón Grande. (Author's collection)

The winter of 1811–1812 being particularly bitter, Barrié and his men were taken completely by surprise when Wellington's army suddenly burst forth from its cantonments on 8 January 1812 40,000 strong. The very same night the Light Division stormed the isolated redoubt on the Teson Grande, this being taken at the cost of very heavy casualties, where-upon the troops were immediately put to work digging a first parallel and positions for several batteries of siege guns. Progress, however, was slow as the ground was frozen solid while the men engaged in the work came under heavy fire and suffered great misery from the inclement weather. In the end, however, the work was completed successfully, while the most important French outworks – the monasteries of Santa Cruz and San Francisco – were stormed in successive attacks on the nights of 13 and 14 January, the only response of the defenders to all this being to launch a sortie that was driven off after some fierce fighting in the vicinity of the latter building.

As things turned out, 14 January was a busy day for the attackers and defenders alike as the afternoon saw Wellington's siege artillery – thirty-four 24-pounders and four 18-pounders – open fire on the walls. There followed five days of bombardment, and the defences were soon in a sorry state: not only was a massive breach – the so-called 'greater breach' – blown in the *fausse-braye* and the mediaeval rampart beyond in the same place in which the French had holed the defences in 1810, but a narrow aperture – the 'lesser breach' – was also opened up a few hundred yards to the left. Insufficient damage having been done to the glacis, the work would ideally have continued for some days more, but on 19

The greater breach; note the very crude nature of the repairs: Wellington's correspondence is full of complaints at the indolence and incapacity of the Spanish troops tasked with the job of making good the defences in the wake of the siege. (Author's collection)

The site of the lesser breach; the tower that marked the spot in 1812 was never rebuilt.
(Author's collection)

January Wellington received news that the commander of the Army of Portugal, maréchal Auguste Viesse de Marmont, was showing signs of marching to relieve Barrié. Unwilling to be baulked of his prey in the style of Badajoz, he therefore ordered the breaches to be stormed that same night, the want of damage to the glacis being countered by issuing the troops concerned with large numbers of hay-bags in the hope that this would save them injury jumping from the lip of the counter-scarp.

There followed a night of much drama. The attack went in at 7:00 p.m. and soon achieved success. The first troops in action were a party of Portuguese which launched a diversionary attack on the distant east gate and the second a mixed force consisting of the Portuguese 2° Batalhão de Caçadores and the light company of the 2/83rd Foot which rushed across the bridge over the River Agueda and scrambled up the bluff on the other side to secure a small bastion at the foot of the walls of the castle from which it was possible to enfilade the whole of the western face of the defences. The reason this last task was important was that, in an attempt to keep casualties in the column sent to take the greater breach – the bulk of Lieutenant General Thomas Picton's 3rd Division – to a minimum, two units of infantry – the

The end of the glacis and *fausse-braye* viewed from the battery taken by the storming party that rushed across the bridge at the start of the attack: it was here that the 2/5th and the 94th Foot were expected to mount the outer defences and ensure that none of the defenders could flank the main breach. The gate, meanwhile, is the Puerta de la Collada.. (Author's collection)

2/5th and the 94th Foot – had been deputed to emerge from positions in the monastery of Santa Cruz which they had previously occupied, and attack the *fausse braye* and the ditch which protected it from their exposed southern end and clear them of all defenders as far as the greater breach. We come here to yet another defect of the city's defences in that, rather than being continued all the way to the river, the *fausse braye* came to an abrupt end just short of the castle and had therefore been left with its flank completely 'in the air'.

Just as the Portuguese had done at the castle, the 2/5th and the 94th Foot achieved their objectives easily enough and duly advanced to the lip of the greater breach. Despite their efforts, however, the situation here proved to have become distinctly problematic. Though hit by heavy fire as soon as they advanced onto the glacis, Picton's men reached the ditch and were soon swarming through the two parts of the breach. At what appeared to be the very moment of success, however, a massive blast rocked the area, causing heavy casualties among the attackers, including, not least, Major General Henry Mackinnon, who died instantly along with many of the men around him. The cause of this explosion was a large quantity of powder that had been buried in the rubble and blown up by means of a slow fuse, while, when the survivors arrived at the crest of the mediaeval city wall, they found themselves in a trap, the French having cleared away all the debris from the rear of the breach so as to confront any men who got through with a sheer drop, and sealed off the summit with ditches cut in the ramparts, behind which were stationed a pair of 24-pounder cannon. In the event, a series of desperate acts of courage sufficed to clear the way, but, by then, it scarcely mattered. Thus, rushing forward in a second column, the troops sent to take the lesser breach (Brigadier General Robert Craufurd's Light Division) had quickly secured the summit and then turned left and right along the walls to take any surviving defenders in the rear, albeit not without the loss of significant casualties, amongst them Craufurd, who had been mortally wounded by a musket shot.

With Wellington's men now within the walls, further resistance was pointless, and Barrié in consequence pulled all the men with whom he could still communicate back into the castle, his formal surrender being proffered the next morning. Ecstatic at their victory and carried away by emotion, the troops who had entered the town fell into considerable disorder, many of them looting the houses of the inhabitants or drinking themselves senseless, but the situation never got quite so out of hand as it was to do at Badajoz three months later, all the men being back in camp by the following morning. As for the cost of this most rapid and successful of Wellington's sieges, some 500 officers and men had been killed or wounded in the final assault and another 600 in the preceding 11 days of siege, a price that was extremely cheap. That said, the loss of Craufurd was a bitter blow: for all the waywardness that had given rise to the near disaster of the Côa, it is clear that Wellington valued him enormously – any other man would probably have been court-martialled. As for the French, a quarter of the garrison had become casualties in the fighting and all the rest taken prisoner. A far greater loss, however, was the entire siege-train of the Army of Portugal, this having been left in the fortress for safe-keeping: unless these guns could somehow be replaced, Marmont would have no means of re-taking Ciudad Rodrigo and Almeida alike, and therefore no hope of launching a successful counter-offensive.

The section of the glacis beneath the main breach. (Author's collection)

The ditch beneath the greater breach. (Author's collection)

The interior of the Puerta de la Collada: a gem of mediaeval fortress architecture, in May 1812 it witnessed a triumphal return to the city on the part of Wellington. (Author's collection)

Ciudad Rodrigo Today

Situated in a very remote quarter of Spain that has witnessed comparatively little in the way of economic development, Ciudad Rodrigo is a veritable 'jewel in the crown' of any Peninsular War tour, not least because of the wealth of material on the sieges of 1810 and 1812 available from the city's tourist office. Within the walls the street layout is exactly the same as the one encountered by Wellington's troops when they broke into the city on 19 January 1812, and most of the buildings either existed during the siege or date from the reconstruction that followed the city's liberation. Amongst sites of particular note are the castle (now a luxury hotel where a polite request will secure the visitor admission both to the battlements and the garden: there is no need to repeat the author's one-man re-enactment of the capture of the battery by scaling the cliff on which it sits!); the cathedral, whose façade is still peppered with the impact of British and French cannon balls); the palace that was occupied by successive governors of the city and, ultimately, Lord Wellington; and the main square, the site of the worst of the disorder that took place in the wake of the storm. However, the high point of any visit must be the city's fortifications. These are complete down to the last detail – the only significant change is a gate driven through the wall close to the lesser breach in 1914 – and it is possible to follow every episode of the assault of 19

The much-damaged facade of the cathedral. By the time Ciudad Rodrigo was recaptured, it had in large part been reduced to ruins. (Author's collection)

January. Beyond the walls, although the Tesón Pequeño is now buried beneath modern blocks of flats, the shell of the monastery of San Francisco is a prominent landmark, whilst it is also possible to climb the Tesón Grande so as to explore the redoubt stormed by troops from the Light Division (to reach this last, take the footpath that links the Calle Góngora with the railway line – unfenced and largely disused – cross the tracks, and carry on uphill; the way is, alas, blocked at the crest of the slope by a fence, but this is easily surmounted); the view of the city is marvellous and it is easy to perceive the extent to which the defences were vulnerable to bombardment. Finally, from the redoubt can be seen a similar, albeit much larger, fortification further to the north: this was constructed by the Spanish garrison of the city in the wake of its recapture so as to command the northern approaches to the Tesón Grande which would otherwise remain completely hidden.

In so far as monuments are concerned, Craufurd, who was buried in the ditch at the foot of the lesser breach, is commemorated by a number of British-placed plaques on the inner side of the wall beside the new gate, but otherwise the efforts of the Anglo-Portuguese army are barely commemorated, if at all. A plaque inserted into the wall near the greater breach in 1987 says no more than 'Ciudad Rodrigo renders homage to those who liberated the fortress' while the same area is graced by monuments not to Wellington, but rather, first, Julián Sánchez García, a sometime soldier who rose to command the small cavalry component of the militia formed to defend the city in 1808 and led a daring break-out at the head of his men as the French closed in in 1811, thereafter winning fame as a guerrilla commander under the pseudonym of El Charro, and, second, the Spanish general who defended the city in the siege of 1810, *Mariscal de Campo* Andrés Pérez de Herrastí. However, it is pleasing to report that the bicentenary saw the city council go to great lengths to revert the balance, producing a detailed guide to the siege in folio form that pays full tribute to the Peninsular Army, this being available for free from the tourist information office.

Further Reading

T. Saunders, *The Sieges of Ciudad Rodrigo, 1810 and 1812* (Barnsley: Pen and Sword, 2018)

19

Badajoz
16 March–6 April 1812

The most important Spanish fortress in western Spain, Badajoz was a daunting objective for any army. Standing on the south bank of the wide River Guadiana on the highway from Madrid to Lisbon, it was for most of its circumference ringed by massive Vauban-style ramparts up to 40 feet high and protected by no fewer than four imposing outworks: the Fuerte de Pardaleras to the south, the Fuerte de la Picurina to the south-east, the Luneta de San Roque to the east, and finally, Fuerte de San Cristóbal lay on the heights that commanded the north bank of the river and the bridge that led to the city. Imposing as it was, if only because it sat fair-and-square on the most important border crossing between Spain and Portugal, it could not be ignored by any of the combatants, and was in consequence subjected to no fewer than three separate sieges, two of them in 1811 and one in 1812, whilst it was also menaced by the invaders in 1809, though no attempt was made to besiege it as such, the French eventually being forced to retreat for want of food.

Thanks to Wellington's repeated attempts to take the city, the casual reader will automatically associate Badajoz with French control, but in fact it remained a bastion of Patriot resistance throughout the first three years of the Peninsular War. Though, as noted above, the invaders had advanced on the city early in 1809, they had had no success at that point, and it was not for another two years that the garrison saw any serious action. Even then, it might have been left alone but for events elsewhere, namely *maréchal* André Masséna's invasion of Portugal in August 1810. This having quickly run into difficulty, Napoleon sent orders to *maréchal* Jean-de-Dieu Soult to lead some of the troops he commanded in Andalucía to march to the assistance of Masséna. The necessary prelude to any such action being to move on Badajoz, in January 1811 Soult marched on the city from his headquarters at Seville. Operations began on 26 January, and, despite both heavy rain and repeated sorties by the garrison, by 4 February all was ready for the bombardment of the walls to commence, the sector chosen being the southern face of the fortress. Almost immediately, however, a large relief force appeared on the north bank of the Guadiana opposite the city. Commanded by *Teniente-General* Gabriel de Mendízabal Iraeta, the troops concerned drove aside the French cavalry that had been watching the northern approaches to the city and encamped on the heights stretching northwards from the Fuerte de San Cristóbal, only to settle into a state of complete passivity thereafter. Much relieved by this inaction, Soult continued to batter the southern walls and in addition captured the outlying Fuerte

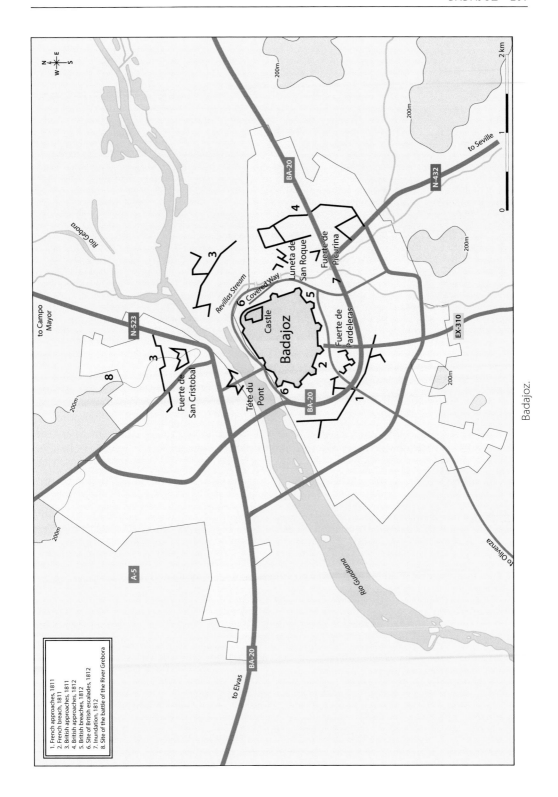

Badajoz.

1. French approaches, 1811
2. French breach, 1811
3. British approaches, 1811
4. British approaches, 1812
5. British breaches, 1812
6. Site of British escalades, 1812
7. Inundation, 1812
8. Site of the battle of the River Grebora

to Campo Mayor

to Elvas

to Seville

to Olivenza

Rio Gebora

Rio Guadiana

Revillas Stream

Fuerte de San Cristobal

Tête du Pont

Castle

Badajoz

Covered Way

Luneta de San Roque

Fuerte de Picurina

Fuerte de Pardeleras

BA-20

N-523

N-432

EX-310

A-5

200m

2 km

Badajoz viewed from the right bank of the River Guadiana, a view that has changed very little in the two centuries that have passed since the Peninsular War. (Author's collection)

de Pardaleras. Not content with this, meanwhile, he also resolved to deal with Mendízabal. Throwing a pontoon bridge across the river, on the night 18 February Soult therefore sent 7,000 troops to attack his camp. Failing to detect the noise of the crossing, the Spaniards were taken completely by surprise. Some 4,000 men either got across the river into Badajoz or managed to escape to the west, but Spanish casualties in this so-called Battle of the River Gébora numbered 8,000 men, whilst gone, too, were all the Spanish commander's guns and baggage. As for the French, they had barely lost 400 men. Nor was this an end to the Spaniards' travails. On 4 March the capable, energetic and courageous governor of the city, *Mariscal de Campo* Rafael de Menacho y Tutlló, was killed on the ramparts. With his place taken by the lacklustre *Mariscal de Campo* José Imaz Altolaguiirre, all heart went out of the defence. Although the breaches were not yet practicable, the storehouses were full of provisions, the garrison in good shape and a large Anglo-Portuguese relief force only a few marches away, within a week Badajoz had surrendered, Spanish losses in all coming to some 20,000 men.

Needless to say, the fall of Badajoz was a major blow to the Allies' cause, but it was not one that the French were ever able to exploit as well as very much a 'poisoned chalice': time and again over the next year Soult and his counterpart north of the River Tagus, *maréchal* Auguste Viesse de Marmont, were forced to strip the garrisons of the regions in their charge in order to fend off threats to the city, the result frequently being to cause them acute embarrassment – indeed, the very day after Menacho was killed saw the troops Soult had left to continue the blockade of Cádiz defeated at Barrosa by Lieutenant General Thomas Graham. Hardly had Soult rushed back to restore order in Andalucía than the garrison he had left behind found itself under threat from the 18,000-strong relief force that had been hastening

The site of the Battle of the River Gebora viewed from the glacis of the Fuerte de San Cristóbal: having crossed the Guadiana further east, the French attacked from the low ground in the middle distance. In 1811, of course, there would have been no buildings. (Author's collection)

towards Badajoz under the command of Lieutenant General William Carr Beresford. Thus, having chased off a division of French troops that had pushed into Portugal, taken the minor fortress of Campo-Maior and retaken Olivenza and Alburquerque, both of which had been pressed into service as outposts, Beresford's three divisions closed in on the city. Very soon, however, things started to go wrong. The only heavy cannon available were those which equipped the nearby Portuguese fortress of Elvas, but, when a consignment of the guns concerned arrived, most were found to be both very old and in appalling condition, while they also varied so much in calibre that it proved very difficult to keep them supplied with ammunition. Meanwhile, the walls of Badajoz had been thoroughly repaired, matters being made still worse by the fact that Beresford settled on a faulty plan of operation. Whereas the best chance of success was to concentrate on the southern walls – the section of the defences which Soult had attacked – it was decided to launch no more than a secondary assault in this sector, most of the attackers' resources rather being deployed on the Fuerte de San Cristóbal. Perched on its lofty bluff across the river, this fort was crucial, for such was its command of the town that the latter could not be held were it to fall into the hands of an enemy. On the other hand, however, it was also immensely strong and built on stony ground that it was hard to work.

When operations began on 8 May, then, progress was very slow: the attackers were hampered by heavy rain; the French artillery outmatched that of the besiegers at every point, something that did not help here being the fact that the Portuguese gunners

Badajoz viewed from the Fuerte de San Cristóbal; commanding the city as it did, the fort was a logical target for any besieging force, but was built on such stony ground that undertaking siege operations against it was very difficult. (Author's collection)

The northern face of the Fuerte de San Cristóbal, this last being the focus of much attention during the second siege of Badajoz. (Author's collection)

The northern ramparts of the Fuerte de San Cristóbal. Though much damaged by bombardment, on 6 and 9 June 1811, these withstood two successive assaults on the part of the 7th Division. (Author's collection)

dispatched to man the guns sent up from Elvas proved to be very poorly trained; two-thirds of Beresford's limited number of engineer officers were killed or wounded in the trenches; the absence of a corps of sappers and miners (something that the British army did not acquire till 1813, meant that all the work of digging the trenches and batteries had to be carried out by ordinary infantrymen who invariably hated the work and were but little disposed to exert themselves; and the governor, *général de division* Armand Philippon, was a most determined opponent, amongst other things launching a sortie that inflicted over 400 casualties on the besiegers.

To put it mildly, this was not a happy story, while after barely a week, it had in any case to be suspended, news having arrived that Soult was marching north from Andalucía with every man that he could spare, Beresford being left with little choice but to abandon the siege in favour of checking the advance of the new arrivals. As we have seen, the result was the Battle of Albuera and, with it, both the defeat of the relief column and the resumption of operations against Badajoz. Yet, notwithstanding the arrival from the northern front of an irate Wellington, events progressed no better than before. Matters were not helped by various geographical accidents, the gallantry and resourcefulness of Philippon and faulty planning that dissipated the British commander's scanty resources and once again pitted them against the immensely strong Fuerte de San Cristóbal, but the key factor was the dubious Allied siege artillery. Still composed entirely of museum pieces that were sometimes as much as 150 years old, this proved incapable of either suppressing the fire of the defenders or opening adequate breaches in the walls. Though some damage was done, the courage and fortitude of the defenders ensured that two assaults on the fort were beaten off with heavy losses. Had the Anglo-Portuguese only been able to hang on, starvation might have been enough to defeat Phillipon, but, by now, large forces were marching to his relief. Without going into the details, begged by Soult for help, the French commander in the Salamanca area, *maréchal* Marmont, who had just replaced Masséna, at the head of the Army of Portugal, had rushed south with every man he could muster and effected a junction with the troops who had been brought up from Andalucía. The result of this manoeuvre being the establishment of an army far bigger than anything Wellington could handle with any certainty of success, on 10 June the British commander raised the siege and fell back to a strong defensive position on the River Caia a few miles inside the Portuguese frontier. This last being too strong to think of forcing, the two *maréchaux* contented themselves with re-supplying Badajoz's magazines and retiring whence they had come.

In theory, then, Badajoz was once more exposed to attack, but in fact Philippon was to be granted a full nine months of respite, Wellington rather electing to strike at Ciudad

The southern face of the Trinidad bastion and, with it, the site of one of the three breaches blown in the walls; it is sobering to realise that the presence of the ditch would have rendered the walls a good 12 feet higher in 1812. (Author's collection)

Rodtrigo before resuming operations in Extremadura. Not until March 1812, then, did the Anglo-Portuguese army reappear before the fortress' walls. Unfortunately for the British commander, however, Phillipon had proved as enterprising in the absence of the enemy as he was in its presence. Thus, in the course of the time that had passed since the second siege, the governor had done everything he could to strengthen the defences, most notably by repairing all the damage to the walls, driving mines under the glacis so as to blow up any trenches that were dug across them; damming a little stream that run northwards to the River Guadiana just below the eastern walls so as to create an extensive inundation, some of the water also being diverted into a the six-foot-deep canal that was dug in the bottom of the ditch protecting the southern face of the fortress; and building new outworks to protect the Fuerte de San Cristóbal. Given the extent of the perimeter, men were not over abundant, the garrison numbering just 5,000 men, but food, cannon and munitions were all plentiful, while the garrison were all seasoned veterans.

If taking Badajoz was always likely to be a costly business, at least Wellington now had the benefit of past experience. In consequence, the mistakes of 1811 were firmly avoided, the attack this time falling, not on San Cristóbal, but on the south-eastern corner of the defences, this being by far the weakest spot in the whole perimeter, being exposed to fire from several different directions, as well as being sited on ground that was much easier to work. Despite heavy rain which flooded the various works and constantly washed away parapets and revetments, progress was rapid, 25 March seeing the storming of the Fuerte de la Picurina with some loss and 30 March the opening of the bombardment. Fire back briskly though the French did, no fewer than three separate breaches having been made in the walls – one in the Trinidad bastion, one in the Santa María bastion and one (by far the largest) in the curtain wall between the two – on 6 April it was decided that all was ready for an assault. This, in fact, was questionable – as at Ciudad Rodrigo, the glacis and counter-scarps had not been broken down – but Soult was on the march once again while it was still unknown whether or not Marmont would join him. Waiting two or three more days would doubtless have made sense, but in the circumstances the best thing seemed to be to go in straight away: better that, certainly, than to be forced to abandon the siege yet again. What followed was a terrible affair. The breaches had been booby-trapped with mines and combustible material, encumbered with a wide range of unpleasant devices designed to injure anyone trying to climb them and crowned with *chevaux de frise,* and the men defending them provided with hand-grenades and large numbers of extra muskets. Unknown to the Anglo-Portuguese, meanwhile, they were also protected by the deep canal that had been dug in the bottom of the ditch in order to let in the water from the inundation. Set to attack these grim defences at 10:00 p.m., the men of the 4th and Light Divisions set to with a will, but they became hopelessly entangled with one another and quickly suffered appalling casualties: many men were drowned in the canal, for example, while others were blown up when the French ignited the bags of gunpowder that had been hidden in the rubble beneath their feet. For two hours the fighting continued, but no lodgement was obtained on the walls and around midnight Wellington ordered the survivors to fall back.

The troops involved having suffered around 2,000 casualties, it looked as though the assault had failed. However, at the last minute Wellington had agreed to the idea of secondary assaults on the castle and the bastion of San Vicente, both of which were points far removed from the breaches, the forces made use of for this purpose being, respectively,

The Santa-María bastion viewed from the vicinity of the central breach; in just two hours this area saw the death or wounding of over 2,000 British soldiers. (Author's collection)

The walls of the castle looking north; Picton's division approached from the direction of the low ground in the middle distance. (Author's collection)

The walls of the castle as seen by Picton's division. (Author's collection)

The bastion of San Vicente showing the ledge that helped the 5th Division scale the ramparts.
(Author's collection)

the 3rd Division of Lieutenant General Thomas Picton and the 5th Division of Lieutenant General James Leith. Breaches, of course, there were none, but the troops concerned were provided with large numbers of ladders. At the castle, in particular, the units sent to storm the walls suffered heavy casualties, including, not least Picton, who was wounded, but eventually the defenders were overcome, by which time the troops were also over the wall at San Vicente, having been greatly helped in this task by the fact that, probably in an effort to avoid the possibility of subsidence caused by the marshy ground on which they were constructed, the lower part of the walls had been buttressed by an extra layer of stonework which culminated in a broad ledge a little below the parapet. Already few in numbers, the defenders were therefore quickly overwhelmed whereupon the triumphant redcoats fanned out into the town. Taken in the rear, the men at the breaches were forced to surrender, while the rest of the garrison fled across the river to take refuge in the Fuerte de San Cristóbal, where Philippon laid down his arms the next morning. For the inhabitants, however, the trauma was far from over. On the contrary, maddened by their losses and convinced that it was their right to sack the town, which many of them believed to be pro-French, the troops ran amok and engaged in violent looting that went on for the next three days, only ceasing when Wellington ordered the erection of a gallows in one of the principal squares.

A typical street in the old city: once the soldiers had penetrated the warren of alleyways which typified the latter, it was impossible to bring them to heel and few officers even tried to do so. (Author's collection)

The Plaza Alta: situated near the castle, this was the site of the gallows which Wellington had erected to put an end to the sack. (Author's collection)

Unpleasant as the sack was – the number of Spanish civilians who died may have been as high as 300 – the storm of Badajoz was a triumph for the Anglo-Portuguese army. At 4,670 killed and wounded, of whom 3,713 had fallen in the storm, losses had been heavier than in most of the army's field battles, but, with both the Spanish border fortresses in the hands of Wellington, the way was open for an advance into the depths of Spain. In short, the rest of 1812 promised to be an exciting few months.

Badajoz Today

Badajoz is scarcely the most attractive of Spain's cities, but it has an enormous amount to offer the student of the Peninsular War. Many of the bastions are still intact, as are the castle, the *tête du pont* that protected the northern end of the bridge across the Guadiana, the Fuerte de Pardeleras, the Fuerte de San Cristóbal and the Luneta de San Roque, though the glacis, large sections of the curtain walls and almost all the redans constructed between the different bastions are long gone, while the fact that the ditch has been everywhere filled in means that, except at the castle, where there was no ditch but rather just a covered way, the defences stand much lower than would have been the case in 1812. At the site of the breaches, a main road has obliterated all trace of the middle of the three, but on either side the bastions whose walls were brought down to form the other two remain extremely imposing. The exact site of the breaches are picked out with the figures '1812' (originally the holes that mark out the individual numbers would have been graced with cannon-balls, but at some point these were removed and taken for scrap). However, so many are the changes to the area that the site is not the most evocative and that despite the addition in 2014 of a new monument to the fallen. In consequence, the visitor is therefore urged to concentrate on the bastion of San Vicente, where the ledge that helped the 5th Division to scale the walls is still very evident; the well-preserved Fuerte de San Cristóbal, whose north-western bastion still exhibits damage from the siege of May–June 1811; and the castle. With regard to this last, the best way to approach it is not via the city but rather a narrow track that leads diagonally up the hillside below its walls (actually the faint trace of a covered way which ran down to the Luneta de San Roque) from the northern end of the so-called 'Parque de la Legión'. Not only does this route give a good impression of the defences as they would have been perceived by Picton's men, but it also gives access to the interior via a small sally-port. Finally, the visitor should also visit the cathedral (the site of appalling atrocities during the sack), the Plaza Alta (the site of Wellington's gallows) and the warren of narrow streets in the heart of the old city, these last making it all too obvious why it proved so difficult to call the troops to order once they had got within the wall.

While the sieges of Badajoz will always be the chief point of interest for those interested in the Peninsular War, the city has one other connection with the period. Thus, in 1767 it became the birthplace of Manuel de Godoy y Alvarez de Faria, a scion of the local nobility who in 1788 travelled to Madrid to take up a position at court as a member of the Guardias de Corps. The story that followed is an extraordinary tale which within five years had seen the young *extremeño* loaded with riches of every sort, given the title Duque de la Alcudía, promoted to the rank of *capitán general* (effectively field-marshal) and appointed to the post of chief minister. As to how all this came about, the reader can find out easily enough

It was not just in 1811–1812 that Badajoz was scarred by war; the damage to this tower was inflicted not by Wellington's guns but rather those of General Franco. (Author's collection)

elsewhere, the important point to note being that by 1808 Godoy had become an object of widespread hatred, hatred that in turn helped fuel the turmoil that led to the fateful over-throw of Charles IV. Rescued from almost certain execution by Napoleon, the erstwhile royal favourite disappeared from the pages of history, but the pages of historiography are another matter. As is often said, history is written by the winners, and, of this, Godoy was a prominent example: for a good century and a half, then, he was lambasted as a womaniser, a wastrel, and an incompetent of no talent whatsoever whose stupidity and self-centredness was in large part responsible for the crisis into which Spain was plunged in 1808. Only in the last few decades has this verdict been challenged by a number of historians, including, not least, the current author, and the revisionist tide eventually became so strong that in 2008 the city council erected a statue in his memory, said statue standing in one of the more modernised sections of the old city at the confluence of Calles Obispo San Juan de Ribera and Juan Carlos I with the Plaza de Minayo.

So much for the sights relating to the Peninsular War, but Badajoz also witnessed a fero-cious battle in the early days of the Spanish Civil War. In brief, on 14 August 1936 the city was attacked by a force of Foreign Legionaries and Moorish auxiliaries drawn from Franco's Army of Africa. Advancing up the Seville highway, the troops were confronted by a substantial force of militiamen, police and soldiers who had remained loyal to the Republic manning the very walls which the 4th and Light Divisions had stormed in 1812. There followed a desperate battle later commemorated by the victorious Nationalists by the grandiose monument that stands just inside the walls, but the Legionaries and Moors quickly broke through along the line of the main road and fanned out into the city beyond, which they proceeded to sack with the same brutality as Wellington's men had shown in 1812. Thus, Republican casualties amounted to over 4,000 men, around half of whom were shot in cold blood after being rounded up and confined in the city's bullring, of which this last still stands just across the road from the bastion of Santa María, other traces of the fighting including bullet holes and the scars caused by exploding shells.

Badajoz, then, has much to offer the visitor in terms of history. That being the case, it is fitting that it should have an excellent historical museum, namely the Museo de la Ciudad 'Luis Morales'. Situated just of the Calle Soto Mancera in the old city, this covers the story of Badajoz from Roman times onwards, but its high point is beyond doubt the so-called Sala de las Batallas, housing, as this does, several dioramas, including four illustrating various stages of the Battle of Albuera, which was, of course, fought just a few miles to the south, and, above all, a massive reconstruction of the final assault on the city by Wellington's forces that does full justice to the terrible scenes witnessed at the three breaches. This last being the case, it is much to be hoped that British visitors will no more complain that Badajoz is an unfriendly place, a comment that is to be found in far too many works that deal with the subject: if it was ever the case in the past, it is certainly not true today.

Further Reading

I. Fletcher, *In Hell before Daylight: the Siege and Storming of Badajoz, 16 March-6 April 1812* (Tunbridge Wells: Spellmount Press, 1984)

20

Salamanca

22 July 1812

Sometimes known as 'Wellington's master-piece' or, alternatively, 'the battle in which Wellington defeated 40,000 men in forty minutes', the Battle of Salamanca took place in blazing heat in the afternoon and evening of 22 July 1812. By the end of the day the French, commanded by *maréchal* Auguste Viesse de Marmont, were utterly broken and fleeing eastwards with all possible speed, thereby leaving the road to Madrid wide open. If it was not a decisive victory, it was nonetheless a shattering blow to French prestige and yet one more confirmation of Napoleon's folly in pursuing the offensive policy in eastern Spain that had opened the way to the recapture of Ciudad Rodrigo and Badajoz and insisting that Wellington was a defensive commander who could be relied upon to miss every opportunity that he was offered and be generally treated with contempt. Nor was *folie de grandeur* restricted to the Emperor, Marmont's defeat having in large part come about because of ambition and over-confidence. All that said, the battle was not just lost by the French but won by the Anglo-Portuguese, the fighting qualities of Wellington's army having been displayed in full and the virtuosity of its commander established beyond a doubt.

Before going on to discuss the battle, we need first to examine the campaign of which it was the culmination, and all the more as the Peninsular-War enthusiast who visits Salamanca can take in not just the battlefield, but also the site of the French citadel whose gallant defence, as we shall see, cost Wellington much time and blood. To proceed, the storm of Badajoz was in the British commander's mind but the prelude to fresh victories. In this respect, there were two alternatives, namely attacking Marmont in León and Old Castile or attacking Soult in Andalucía. Having resolved that the former was the more profitable of the two, towards the end of May Wellington concentrated all his troops save those of Hill in the vicinity of Ciudad Rodrigo. He had decided to attack Marmont on the highly plausible grounds that the liberation of northern and central Spain would infallibly bring with it the evacuation of Andalucía whereas the liberation of Andalucía would in itself make no difference in the north. Given the continued dispersion of the Army of Portugal from Asturias to the Tagus valley, initial success of some sort was certain, but Wellington knew that, with every step that he advanced, the French were more able to fall upon him with overwhelming force. Since every step that he moved into Spain took him further from the safety of Portugal, it followed that as many of the enemy as possible had to be neutralised.

For this purpose, a variety of devices lay readily to hand. Though he had no official authority over the Spanish forces, Wellington now had much prestige in Patriot Spain, the liberation of Ciudad Rodrigo and Badajoz having done much to wipe out the unhappy memories of 1808, 1809 and 1810. Fulsome displays of pro-British feeling therefore began to appear in the press; there were ecstatic demonstrations when the British commander returned to Ciudad Rodrigo on 26 April; and a handful of British officers had even been allowed to establish training depots and model divisions that might in time come to be a basis for the reform of the army that the loss of Sagunto and Valencia had shown to be so desperately needed. In consequence, Wellington had only to suggest a plan for the Council of Regency – a body currently headed by the far from dynamic Duque del Infantado – to agree to its implementation. By this means, then, the commander of the Fourth Army (the Spanish forces in Andalucía), *Teniente-General* Francisco Ballesteros, was directed to strike at Seville from his fastnesses in the extreme south-west of the country; the Sixth Army of *Teniente-General* Francisco-Javier Castaños to besiege Astorga; the Seventh Army – a loose collection of guerrilla formations embracing the commands of such chieftains as *Brigadiers* Juan Dáz Porlier, Francisco Longa and Francisco Espoz y Mina under the overall command of *Teniente-General* Gabriel de Mendízabal Iraeta – to tie down the French Army of the North; and the Second and Third Armies to neutralise Suchet. The great diversion was not just to be left to the Spaniards, however. Thus, Lieutenant General Sir Rowland Hill was instructed to head south should Soult press Ballesteros; the British squadron on the north coast of Spain to raid the French garrisons dotted along the coast; and finally the governor of Sicily, Lieutenant General Lord William Bentinck, to send a division to the coast of Catalonia.

Some minor hiccups aside, this scheme functioned extremely well. In Andalucía the end of May saw Ballesteros strike inland and attack a French division at Bornos. Though he was beaten and forced to retreat, this did not matter, for Hill immediately came forward in Extremadura with the result that Soult had to send many troops to reinforce the forces holding that region. Whilst Hill then entangled the latter in a complex war of manoeuvre, Ballesteros sallied out again, briefly occupied Málaga and then led as many as 10,000 French troops a merry dance through the wilds of Granada before finally heading back to the coast. In the north, the British squadron, which was commanded by the adventurous Rear Admiral Home Popham, sailed up and down the coast, landing naval guns and parties of marines to attack such garrisons as Lequeitio, Guetaria, Castro Urdiales and Santander in company with the forces of Porlier and Longa. Not all these operations succeeded – indeed, Popham and Mendízabal suffered a number of minor defeats – but the Army of the North and its current commander, *général de division* Auguste de Caffarelli, were run ragged trying to keep the situation under control, Bilbao was occupied for a fortnight, and the major port of Santander left in Allied hands for good. With Espoz y Mina, too, extremely active, Caffarelli was therefore, like Soult, out of the fight. In the east, by contrast, things did not go quite so smoothly. Thanks to a combination of foolishness on the part of Bentinck and growing political tension in Sicily, far fewer troops were sent over than had originally been expected, while those that did come arrived much later than planned and eventually did nothing but disembark at Alicante. As for the Third Army, commanded by *Mariscal de Campo* José O'Donnell, it eventually struck north, only to be heavily defeated at Castalla in what was more a gigantic ambush than a battle. Yet, again, the fact that the Sicilian expedition proved a damp squib and O'Donnell particularly maladroit mattered not a jot. Ringed by enemies and unable to borrow any troops from Catalonia, where the commander of

Salamanca, 22 July 1812.

The fort built by the French to defend the southern approaches to the pontoon bridge that spanned the Tagus at Almaraz and was a key link between the French forces in northern and southern Spain. (Rob Griffith)

the Spanish First Army, *Brigadier* Luis de Lacy, was continuing to do his best to cause trouble, Suchet had no chance of sending troops to central Spain and that was all that mattered.

In May, meanwhile, this complicated web of diversion was augmented by an operation of immense strategic consequence. In brief, one place of particular importance to the French was the pontoon bridge that spanned the River Tagus at Almaraz on the frontier of Extremadura in place of the original sixteenth-century structure, this having been blown up by Cuesta in 1809. Although not the only crossing of the river available to the French, this was by far the most convenient for troops marching from Andalucía and Extremadura to join forces with those holding Old Castile and León, the result being that its destruction would cause permanent disruption to the invaders' attempts to defend their dominions. That being the case, Hill was ordered to take one of his two divisions north-east from his current positions around Badajoz and mount a lightning strike on the defenders which were known to amount to fewer than 2,000 men and also to be far out of reach of any significant reinforcement. Not surprisingly given the vital nature of the spot, the French defences were extensive with imposing forts built on high ground at either end of the bridge itself and a line of redoubts high in the hills above overlooking the road from the south, but these troubled Hill but little and on 19 May he duly stormed the French positions and put the garrison to flight, the vital bridge being broken when cannon fire sank one of the pontoons. Once again, then, Anglo-Portuguese troops had intervened in the 'little war' to devastating effect.

That all this greatly favoured Wellington's prospects is not to be denied, but in reality it was scarcely necessary. To have any serious chance of blocking Wellington, the French would have had to give up some of the ground they occupied, but Napoleon was so obsessed by questions of prestige that he could not tolerate a repeat of the evacuation of Galicia in 1809, and had, in fact, forbidden any such move. Of the various French commanders, meanwhile, other than King Joseph and his chief-of-staff, *maréchal* Jean-Baptiste Jourdan, only Marmont – the very general most in need of help – ever thought in wider terms than those of his own province, the rest being inclined to give their fellows minimal assistance, if indeed they gave them any at all. In this there was selfishness and egotism in plenty, but in the circumstances of 1812, it was entirely understandable, for the French were so hard-pressed that reducing one garrison in favour of another was almost certain to lead to disaster of some sort. In the last resort, then, the real issue was not the personal failings of Soult and the rest, but rather want of troops, and, beyond that, Napoleon's belief that he could both have his cake and eat it.

Of this, however, he was soon to be disabused. Thus, on 13 June, Wellington advanced into León with his main army and the tiny force that could be fielded by the Spanish Fifth Army (no more than the single cavalry brigade of *Brigadier* Julián Sánchez), the Sixth Army in the meantime sallying forth from Galicia to blockade Astorga whilst a force of Portuguese militia tackled the more minor post of Zamora. No sooner had the Allies taken the field than Marmont set about concentrating all the men he could, requested help from Caffarelli and Joseph and, in flat defiance of Napoleon, called back a division (that of *général de division* Jean-Pierre Bonet) that he had earlier been compelled to send to distant Asturias. However, whilst he intended to fight, it would be some time before he got enough troops together, and in consequence gave up Salamanca without a fight and fell back eastwards to the village of Fuente Sauco, Wellington in the meantime doing no more than take up a strong blocking position on the heights east of the city, while setting about the siege of three convents – those of San Vicente, San Cayetano and La Merced – situated on steep bluffs situated at the southwestern-most extremity of the city on either side of a deep ravine that ran down to the River Tormes that the French had seized upon as a makeshift citadel.

There now followed one of the several major hiccups which were to mar the campaign. In brief, though blessed with a commanding position, capable of highly effective mutual support, occupied by a substantial garrison, garnished with no fewer than 36 guns and protected by

The site of the convent of San Vicente viewed from the other side of the ravine that split the citadel that the French built to defend Salamanca in two; the ramparts which surrounded it are still clearly visible. (Author's collection)

The gorge of the convent of San Cayetano viewed from the foot of the ravine; exposed, as they were, to the guns of the convent of San Vicente, the troops sent to storm it on 23 June had little chance of success. (Author's collection)

ditches, palisades, extensive ramparts and a wide glacis that had been cleared by tearing down many buildings belonging to the famous university, in the ordinary course of events the convents should have been easy meat, but, not for the last time, Wellington found himself confronting fortifications which might otherwise have been his for the taking with resources that were deeply inadequate to the task in hand. Thus, improvised though the fortifications were, they were impervious to the fire of field artillery and therefore needed the attention of full-scale battering guns. Of these, however, Wellington possessed but four 18-pounders and that despite the availability of numerous heavy cannon at Ciudad Rodrigo and Almeida. Nevertheless, supplemented by six howitzers borrowed from various artillery batteries, on 19 June said 18-pounders opened fire on the convents from the shelter of entrenchments that had been dug for them on the far side of the area that had been razed to the ground to give the defenders a clear field of fire, only for it very soon to become apparent that there was insufficient ammunition for the barrage to be continued long enough to make a real impression on the defences.

As if this was not embarrassing enough, round about the same time as the guns began to run out of shot, it became apparent that one of Wellington's main objectives in besieging the three convents was not going to be realised. In brief, then, the British commander had hoped that Marmont would be tempted to launch a counter-attack in an effort to rescue the garrison, but, although he duly appeared before the heights of San Cristóbal on 19 June, the *maréchal* came to the conclusion that pressing any further forward could not but lead to a major disaster, the result being that the night of 22 June saw him evacuate his encampments and retire on the village of Aldea Rubia some six miles to the east. An interesting question that arises here is why Wellington declined to attack Marmont during the three days that he lingered before his position, this being something that has bever been satisfactorily explained, not least because the Anglo-Portuguese army enjoyed a considerable numerical superiority over its opponents, but, however odd the British commander's failure to move may have been, in the end it was all to the good: persuaded that Wellington was at the very least unwilling to take the offensive, the *maréchal* came to the conclusion that he could run greater risks with him than would have been the case with another commander.

As later events would show, such thinking was in reality dangerous in the extreme, but for the present we need to return to the siege of the convents. With Marmont now out of the picture, Wellington was eager to bring the affair to a conclusion and he therefore resolved on an assault, the target chosen being the convent of San Cayetano, which was not only the most accessible of the three French redoubts, but also the one which had been hardest hit by the bombardment. The troops selected for the task being the rifle and light companies of the two British brigades of the 6th Division, a force of perhaps 400 men, they started off for the convent an hour after sunset at 10:00 p.m. on 23 June. However, brave though the soldiers were, they faced a near impossible task, for, rather than tackling the defences head on, they were rather instructed to attack them in the rear by first running down the ravine that separated San Cayetano and La Merced from the much larger San Vicente and then turning aside to scale the cliff on which the gorge of their goal rested by means of ladders. Quickly discovered by the French, however, the troops were shot down in droves by fire from San Vicente, the many dead including the commander of one of the brigades concerned, Major General Barnard Bowes.

With the failure of this attempt, operations against the French defences slackened off for a little while, but on 26 June a large convoy of ammunition came up from the rear, it therefore proving possible to renew the bombardment. The projectiles used included a large quantity of red-hot shot, and so within 24 hours many of the convent buildings were in flames and wide stretches of the ramparts completely battered down. Even then, the defenders might well have held on, but, threatened by fresh assaults, on 27 June they finally laid down their arms, Marmont's army promptly decamping once again, this time in the direction of the distant River Duero many miles to the north. Though Wellington's army was soon in hot pursuit, there followed a further lull in operations, this being the result of a decision on the part of the British commander to await the arrival of the Sixth Army, which, having blockaded Astorga, was supposed to mover directly to his support. The Spaniards having allowed themselves to be drawn into a full-scale siege of the fortress, however, they failed to appear, the result being that the initiative was temporarily lost to the enemy. Thus, having at last been joined by Bonet, on 15 July, Marmont suddenly sent his troops back across the river. For this decision to take the offensive, he has been bitterly criticised on the grounds that, had he only waited, troops would have reached him from both Burgos and Madrid: having told him earlier that he could spare him no reinforcements, Caffarelli had relented to the extent of sending him a much-needed cavalry brigade, while a deeply alarmed Joseph had decided to march to join him at the head of every soldier he could muster (setting aside a minimal garrison for Madrid, some 14,000 men). In fairness to Marmont, however, it must be said that he not only did not know that these moves were under way, but also had no reason to believe that they would ever come to pass, while, at 44,000 men, his forces were not so very much smaller than those of Wellington. At first, certainly, all went well enough. Having bamboozled Wellington by means of some clever sleight of hand, the *maréchal* managed to get across the Duero unchallenged and over the next few days forced his British opponent to retreat on Salamanca by dint of a series of flanking operations designed to threaten his communications with Portugal. By 22 July, other than the 3rd Division of Wellington's brother-in-law, Major General Edward Pakenham, and some Portuguese cavalry, which were still north of the Tormes, the Anglo-Portuguese army was drawn up just to the south-east of Salamanca along a line of low hills whose southern end was marked by a pronounced butte called the Arapil Chico. Marmont, however, had no intention of trying a frontal assault, and, having first seized the much larger butte known as the Arapil Grande which stood a few hundred yards to the south of the Arapil Chico, he therefore began to march his entire army round Wellington's southern flank. Seeing what was going on, the British commander swung division after division back from their original positions to form a new line running west in a direction roughly parallel to the Tormes, a manoeuvre which he covered by sending the Light Division eastwards to skirmish with the French troops that were still holding the high ground opposite the ridge that culminated in the Arapil Chico, the result of this being a desultory fight that flickered on and off for most of the day around a mediaeval hermitage near the village of Calvarrasa de Abajo. Last but not least, having until now been covering the eastern approaches to Salamanca, the 3rd Division and the cavalry accompanying it were brought across the rear of the army via the Roman bridge that linked

The hermitage of Nuestra Señora de la Peña and, beyond it, the line of heights originally held by the bulk of Wellington's army. (Author's collection)

Wellington's second position as viewed by Marmont from the summit of the Arapil Grande: the undulating nature of the ground made it very difficult for the French commander to interpret what was going on with any degree of accuracy. (Author's collection)

The bare hillside on which the Light Division exchanged fire with the French right wing for much of the day. (Author's collection)

The two Arapiles viewed from the vicinity of Nuestra Señora de la Peña: Marmont marched to outflank Wellington via the dead ground beyond the skyline on the extreme left, while the green area in the middle distance marks the position of the Pelagarcía stream, the only source of water on the battlefield. (Author's collection)

the city with the south bank of the river to a position beyond the right flank of Wellington's new line near the village of Aldea Tejada.

By early afternoon, then, the bulk of the Anglo-Portuguese army was facing south with their backs to the Tormes and the French circling westwards around the two Arapiles. At this point, however, Marmont made a terrible mistake. Having ridden to the summit of the Arapil Grande, he could see much of what was going on in the Allied position, but, such was his conviction that Wellington was a cautious general who was averse to battle, he drew quite the wrong conclusion from what he saw. Thus, not least because a considerable part of the new line which the Anglo-Portuguese was taking up was hidden by a substantial hill called the Cerro de San Román, in his eyes the movements that were in train portended preparations for a retreat to a new position a short distance to the west beyond a minor rivulet called the Zurgüen, preparatory to falling back on the Portuguese frontier, and he in consequence resolved to push on with the same tactics that had carried him south all the way from the River Duero. Very soon, then, the first three infantry divisions to have rounded the Arapil Grande were pounding westwards together with a division of light cavalry commanded by *général de brigade* Jean-Baptiste Curto along a broad plateau known as the Monte de Azán that ran from that eminence for some miles in the same direction in which Wellington appeared to be moving.

In acting in this fashion Marmont was taking a terrible risk, one of the most basic rules of 'horse-and-musket' warfare being never to march across the front of an opponent. Convinced that Wellington would not attack, the French commander was blind to the danger, but in reality, his men were marching straight into a trap. Not only did the French troops on the plateau become more and more strung out, but Wellington had for the past few hours actually been contemplating an attack. Surveying the French through his telescope from his command post atop the Tesón de San Román in between bites at a leg of chicken, the British commander saw his moment. Exclaiming, 'By God, that will do!', he tossed aside his half-eaten luncheon, leaped on his horse and set off at high speed for Pakenham's 3rd Division with its attendant Portuguese cavalry.

The events of the next hour or so were to prove a bitter awakening for the French. Ordered by Wellington to attack immediately, Pakenham led his men to the westernmost extremity

Wellington's view of the Monte de Azán from his command post on the Tesón de San Román; such was the nature of the ground that every detail of the French advance was clearly visible to him. (Author's collection)

The summit of the Pico de Miranda; the village of Miranda de Azán can be glimpsed on the left, while the low hill in the middle distance is the rise that prevented Thomières from spotting Pakenham until the last minute. (Author's collection)

of the plateau along which the French were moving, and then faced left and burst over the crest of the knoll known, from the name of the nearby village of Miranda de Azán, as the Pico de Miranda, to envelop the first French division (that of *général de division* Jean Thomières). Supported only by Curto's light cavalry, who were themselves speedily put to flight by the Portuguese cavalry in the open plain south of the plateau, the astonished Frenchmen were promptly overwhelmed with the loss of more than half their strength including their unfortunate general, who was killed in the mêlée. Thoroughly exhausted by its frantic dash from Aldea Tejada and the fierce struggle which had followed (to their very great credit, Thomières' division had actually managed to check the first onrush of their assailants), the 3rd Division appears to have taken no further part in the battle, but already the torch was being picked up by other units.

The Monte de Azán looking east from the vicinity of the Pico de Miranda (note the Arapil Chico silhouetted on the skyline in the far distance); it was approximately on this spot that Thomières division met its end. (Author's collection)

After setting Pakenham in motion, Wellington had ridden back to his main position and ordered his forces to attack in echelon from the right. First off were the heavy cavalry brigade of Major General John Le Marchant and the 5th Division of Lieutenant General James Leith. Facing these substantial forces was the division of *général de division* Antoine Popon de Maucune, which had halted to cover the march westwards of the rest of the French infantry and, spying Anglo-Portuguese skirmishers in the village of Arapiles, a humble farming community in the centre of the valley that separated the crest which Maucune and his men were lining from the Cerro de San Román, sent down its *chasseur* and *voltigeur* ompanies to do battle with them. In so far as the attack of the 5th Division was concerned, this was pushed forward with the utmost vigour, but, Leith himself having been wounded by a chance shot, it might yet have been thrown back had fresh disasters not overwhelmed the French cause. In brief, stationed just to the right of Leith's men, Le Marchant's heavy dragoons had filed quietly across the valley completely unnoticed by Maucune and ridden up onto the plateau where, hidden by a swell in the ground, they had then formed line. With the red-coated horsemen perfectly positioned to take Maucune's troops in the flank, the result was a massacre. Charging over the knoll which had kept them hidden from sight, Le Marchant's men rode down the French infantry fighting Leith and put large numbers to the sword. Caught up in the rout, meanwhile, was *général de division* Antoine Brenier de Montmorand's division, this last having been marching across the rear of Maucune's position at the moment of Le Marchant's charge, the only sour note being the fact that Le Marchant was shot and killed at the moment of victory.

In only an hour of fighting, then, Wellington had broken the whole of the French left – three divisions of infantry and a division of cavalry – while the confusion in the enemy ranks had been much augmented by the fact that Marmont had been wounded by a British shell. However, the battle was not yet over. Thus, shortly after Leith had advanced against Maucune,

Buildings in the village of Arapiles that have survived from the time of the battle. (Author's collection)

The gentle slopes up which the 5th Division advanced to attack Maucune. (Author's collection)

The left rear of Maucune's position; Le Marchant's brigade formed up behind the rise on the extreme right. (Author's collection)

the 4th Division of Lieutenant General Galbraith Lowry-Cole and the independent Portuguese brigade of *Brigadeiro* Denis Pack had advanced on the empty space between the clump of rocks that had marked the right flank of Maucune's line and the Arapil Grande and, indeed, this last feature itself. At this point, however, things went badly wrong, the 4th Division being ambushed by a large force of French troops – essentially the divisions of Clausel and Bonet and some accompanying cavalry – that had hitherto been concealed in rear of the Arapil Grande and routed with heavy losses, while Pack's men were repulsed by a single volley that was fired into their very faces at the very summit of the precipitous northern slopes of the butte by French infantry that had till the last moment been hidden from their view. As Clausel and Bonet tried to follow up their success by pursuing the shattered 4th Division and trying to break Wellington's centre, the battle hung in the balance for a moment, but Wellington had plenty of reserves and simply moved the fresh 6th Division of Major General Henry Clinton to plug the gap, the French onrush having in any case already been checked by the Portuguese brigade of Leith's division which had wheeled to its left and attacked them in flank. Urging them on, however, Beresford was shot in the chest and forced to quit the field.

The Arapil Grande viewed from the foot of the Arapil Chico. (Author's collection)

The site of the defeat of the 4th Division from the west with, beyond it, the Arapil Grande: note the very steep northern slope – the Portuguese troops sent to take it arrived at the summit badly blown. (Author's collection)

Very soon, then, the French centre had joined the survivors of the left wing in falling back in complete disorder, the Arapil Grande being abandoned in the process. Three infantry divisions which had thus far either seen little combat or been held in reserve – those of *Généraux de Division* Claude Ferey, Jacques Sarrut and Maximilien Foy – were available to covert the retreat and they fought back bravely as the victorious Anglo-Portuguese forces pressed forward to finish the job: ordering up the Light Division, indeed, Wellington had a lucky escape when a bullet struck his saddle holster and bruised his thigh. In most places, however, the French do not seem to have been pushed too hard: most of the Allied troops, after all, were exhausted after hours of marching and fighting in blazing heat. Only Ferey,

The rocky scarp that runs along the northern front of the Arapil Grande just below the summit; forced to sling their muskets to climb it, Pack's men were routed by a French battalion that came forward to the crest of the slope and fired a volley directly into their faces. (Author's collection)

indeed, found he had a real job on his hands, being forced to face a full-scale assault at the hands of the 6th Division. In this final clash, British and Portuguese losses were very heavy, but in the end Ferey, too, gave way, the Army of Portugal only being saved from complete destruction by the onset of darkness.

Truly, Salamanca or, as the Spaniards called it, Arapiles, was a great victory. While Wellington's army had lost some 5,000 killed, wounded and missing, French casualties numbered perhaps 12,000 men, whilst they had also incurred the loss of an eagle and 12 guns. These losses might have been higher still had the pursuit been pressed with any vigour, but in the darkness and confusion Wellington's forces appear to have quite lost their cohesion. Claims that the entire French army would have been destroyed had the Spaniards but kept a garrison in the castle of neighbouring Alba de Tormes are therefore highly disingenuous: the garrison was withdrawn, true, but its presence would have made little difference. Only the next day did the pursuit get under way properly, although there still proved time to inflict yet more damage on the French at the village of García Hernández where the heavy dragoons of the King's German Legion distinguished themselves by the near impossible feat of breaking a battalion of infantry in square. Thereafter, however, the Army of Portugal was allowed to get away unmolested, Wellington following them no further than Valladolid from where he turned south and headed for Madrid. Sadly enough, though, the war was not quite finished with Salamanca. In brief, following the departure of the French from the area, it was decided that the powder left over in the convent magazines should be removed and

The broken terrain extending in the direction of Alba de Tormes which enabled much of the French army to escape at the end of the battle. (Author's collection)

transported to Ciudad Rodrigo for safe keeping. On 5 August, then, said powder was duly loaded into a number of carts and the convoy assembled in the courtyard of an inn near the parish church of San Blas. Out for a morning stroll the next morning, the parish priest stopped to smoke a cheroot with the Spanish soldiers who had been left on guard overnight and the result, alas, was a terrible explosion that caused massive devastation and killed several hundred people, an event which seems to have lingered in the popular memory far longer than that of the battle.

Salamanca Today

Of all Wellington's Peninsular-War battlefields, Salamanca is one of the best preserved, the only thing that really spoils it being the Salamanca-Caceres motorway, the construction of which in the period 2005–2010 effectively cut off the area of Miranda de Azan and made it impossible to walk the full circuit of the field from Aldea Tejada all the way to the Cerro de San Román, an exhilarating experience that the author has never forgotten (that said, dreadful eyesore though it is, the service-station erected just to the east of the carriage-way does make for a useful 'pit-stop', while neither the motorway nor its attendant installations have done any appreciable damage to the battlefield, the former having luckily taken a course through an area which saw little fighting). For those visiting the field today, the best place to start is the museum in the centre of the village of Arapiles, a place which is not much bigger than it was in 1812 and which contains a number of buildings that are almost unchanged from the bloody day when they witnessed fierce fighting between the skirmishers of assorted British and German units and Maucune. From here a number of way-marked trails radiate out across the battlefield taking in such sites as the Tesón de San Román, the two Arapiles and the plateau where Maucune's division was wiped out, these being augmented by a number of helpful and well-designed display panels; if it is open, meanwhile, the museum is also worth spending a few minutes on though it offers little that will be new to those already familiar with the basic outlines of the battle and, indeed, the

Peninsular War. There are, however, several areas which are best viewed from other starting points, namely the slopes west of Calvarrasa de Abajo where the Light Division fought its lone battle with the French right wing, the site of the destruction of Thomières' division and, finally, the area where Ferey's troops caused such heavy losses to the 6th Division at the end of the day, these being best reached as followed.

To begin with the actions of Pakenham and his men, the visitor should drive to the centre of Aldea Tejada (a somewhat complicated business that involves navigating a complex network of highways linked to the motorway and the city's inner ring-road). Having driven into the village on the CL-312 (signposted Tamames), turn left onto the Calle Ancha and, at the town hall, left again into the Calle del Pozo. At the end of the street, turn right onto the Avenida de Extremadura and follow this out of the village until it reaches a crossroads, noting en route the Arroyo de Zurguén, this being the stream which Marmont believed that Wellington was heading for at the start of the battle. At said cross-roads, turn right and head south to Miranda de Azán. Having reached the village, turn left onto the DSA-202 and park at the entrance to the cemetery: the Pico de Miranda will then be found ahead and to the right on the other side of the road. Completely unfenced and still the rough pasture that it was in 1812, the area is worthy of detailed exploration, though be warned: the ascent to the summit is deceptively steep.

To reach Calvarrasa de Arriba and its attendant chapel, return to Salamanca via the DSA-202 and, subsequently, the N-630, and, having reached the roundabout just before the river, turn right onto the N-501 (signposted Madrid). At the next roundabout turn right onto the A-50 motorway (signposted Madrid) and turn off onto the CL-510 at the first exit (signposted Alba de Tormes). Calvarrasa is then a five-minute drive straight ahead. Immediately having entered the village turn sharp right onto the Calle de la Peña (signposted Ermita Nuestra Señora de la Peña). At the end there is ample parking on the edge of steep cliffs overlooking the Pelagarcía stream, in 1812 the only source of water on the battlefield. Situated a little further down the slope, said chapel, a simple rectangular building, was the epicentre of the bickering that took place between the Light Division and the French troops posted on the heights above, while to the west there are spectacular views of the two Arapiles.

There now remains only the site of Ferey's rearguard action. To reach the approximate area in which this took place, return to the CL-510 and drive south until two housing estates are reached facing one another across the road, that on the right being called El Encinar and that on the left Los Cisnes. Just before the buildings begin, turn right onto the Avenida de Castilla-León and, having crossed the roundabout, follow this around the north-western corner of El Encinar until a turning is encountered heading west into an area of scrub. Take this road and follow it to its end, said road more-or-less bisecting Ferey's position.

So much for the battlefield of Salamanca, but we also need to discuss the remains of the forts which cost Wellington so much time and trouble in the weeks before the battle, the area concerned being best reached on foot. Beginning at the Puente Romano – in 1812 the city's river crossing – turn left onto the Paseo de San Gregorio and then almost immediately right onto the Calle San Juan de Alcázar and follow this uphill to the sharp corner at the far end: the convent of La Merced, now entirely demolished, was on the right just before the summit. From the corner carry on along the Calle del Parque: the ravine on the left was the site of the desperate attempt to take the convent of San Cayetano by storm, while the bluff on the far side marks the position of the convent of San Vicente, traces of the ramparts that

The Roman bridge at Salamanca; on the evening of the battle some 5,000 weary French prisoners tramped their way across *en route* for captivity in Britain. (Author's collection)

surrounded it still being clearly visible. Continue to the end of the road – the approximate site of the convent of San Cayetano – to view the broad expanse of exposed foundations that is all that is left of the many university buildings that were torn down to provide said convent with a glacis.

One last place to view in Salamanca, meanwhile, is the Colegio Cardenal Fonseca. Located near the head of the ravine on the Calle Fonseca, in 1812 this was the city's general hospital, but it had previously served as a seminary for the training of Irish priests, the rector of said seminary, Patrick Curtis, famously becoming one of Wellington's most important 'correspondents' in the region, while it was made use of by the British commander as his headquarters. Finally, just nearby in the square of that name is the church of San Blas, it being the latter's parish priest who was the cause of the calamitous explosion of 6 August 1812: having survived the disaster relatively unscathed, it was used as a mortuary in the aftermath of the blast.

Further Reading

R. Muir, *Salamanca, 1812* (London: Yale University Press, 2001)

I. Fletcher, *Salamanca, 1812: Wellington Crushes Marmont* (Oxford: Osprey, 1997)

P. Young and J.P Lawford, *Wellington's Masterpiece: the Battle and Campaign of Salamanca* (London: Routledge, 1972)

P. Edwards, *Salamanca, 1812: Wellington's Year of Victories* (Barnsley: Pen and Sword, 2012)

21

Burgos
19 September–21 October 1812

The summer of 1812 was a time of great triumph for British arms. Having captured the key border fortresses of Ciudad Rodrigo and Badajoz, the Anglo-Portuguese army commanded by Wellington had advanced into León, on 22 July defeating the chief French field army at the Battle of Salamanca. With the French forces in central and northern Spain in complete disarray, the Allied forces then marched on Madrid, entering the capital to a rapturous reception on 12 August. By the late summer of 1812, then, it seemed that Wellington was riding the crest of the wave. Yet all was not as it seemed. With every step that the French were driven back, more and more of their troops were released from the task of holding down their conquests in the face of incessant Spanish resistance. As the invaders had far more men than Wellington, this was a serious issue: by the beginning of September, indeed, the British commander was faced with three impressive masses of French troops, each of which were more-or-less equal to the forces he could muster. With the Spanish field armies ill-equipped, weak in numbers and short of both cavalry and artillery, they were unable to do much to hold back the enemy. The one advantage the British commander enjoyed was that, with one of the enemy concentrations based at Seville, the second in Valencia, and the third in Navarre and the Basque provinces, he occupied the proverbial 'central position' and could therefore strike hard and fast against one opponent before another could arrive to assist it.

Thus was set the scene for the campaign of Burgos. Resolving to move north rather than east, Wellington marched into Old Castile with part of his army, leaving behind several divisions – including, be it said, most of his best units – to hold Madrid. What the British general's precise intentions were is not entirely clear, but it is probable he believed that he would be able to inflict a crushing defeat on some French forces that had rather incautiously moved westwards to relieve various beleaguered garrisons that had been left behind after Salamanca, and then, having thoroughly shaken the enemy, seize the fortress that the French had erected to protect the city of Burgos, thereby blocking any attempt to mount a counter-offensive in the direction of Madrid.

If this was the plan, it depended on winning a quick victory. To ensure that his men could move quickly enough, then, Wellington took only a handful of heavy guns with him, but the question of what should be done if the plan went wrong was never addressed. And went wrong it did: to make up for his lack of numbers, Wellington was relying on linking up with a Spanish army that had been operating on the frontiers of Galicia, but, delayed

Burgos viewed from the castle, showing the Plaza Mayor, the church of San Estebán and the cathedral. So much did the citadel constructed by the French overlook the city that snipers could sometimes pick off men who showed themselves in the streets. (Author's collection)

by logistical problems, the Spaniards were slow to move, and Wellington was unwilling to risk a fight without them. As a result, the French got away, and on 18 September he found himself closing in on the walls of Burgos with neither an adequate siege train nor sufficient ammunition, nor even a tolerable supply of the most basic siege equipment. But here, too, there was a problem: Wellington seems to have believed that Burgos was an easy target that could be taken very quickly, but in fact nothing could have been further from the truth.

What followed was the only significant failure in Wellington's career. To understand how such an end came about, we must first consider the fortress which he had set his men to attack. In brief, this last owed its origins to no less a figure than Napoleon himself. In November 1808 the Emperor had passed through Burgos en route for Madrid. Noting the strategic position of the town, which was otherwise defended only by a mediaeval city wall, he had ordered the construction of a citadel that could serve the garrison as a place of refuge in case of attack. The case of Burgos was not an isolated instance – on the contrary, similar citadels were improvised in many towns and cities – but it was one where the topography particularly favoured the French. Immediately to the north of the cathedral that remains Burgos' crowning glory then, there rises a steep-sided hill – the Cerro del Castillo – that is perhaps 200 feet higher than the banks of the river on which the city stands. Entirely bare of vegetation, it was crowned by a roughly circular mediaeval castle and a large Romanesque basilica, the Santa María la Blanca, while the walls that enclosed the city ran round part of its lower slopes in a great salient that jutted out to the north (though abandoned long

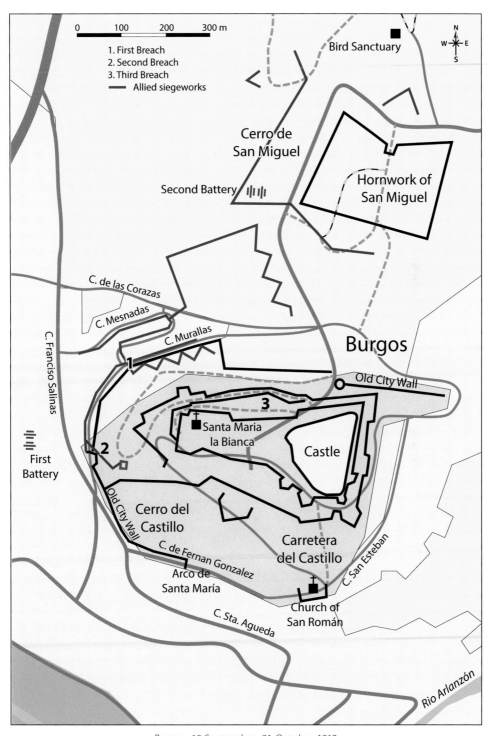

Burgos, 19 September–21 October 1812.

since as a consequence of urban decline, the area – initially, the Jewish quarter – had once been crowded with dwellings). All too obviously, if Burgos was to be as to be defended, it was here, and from January 1809 onwards gangs of Spanish labourers toiled to build the new defences that were deemed to be necessary. To begin with, the keep of the castle was surmounted with a modern gun position entitled the Baterie Napoléon. Next there was the issue of the outer defences. The castle and the basilica stood on an oval plateau that was aligned from north-west to south-east. The south-eastern face, which looked out over the town, was judged to be too steep to assail, and this was therefore covered by only a single rampart, but on its other three sides the castle and the basilica were ringed by two lines of fortifications some 25 feet high, each of which was provided with a number of small bastions and at some points faced with stone. Finally, lower down the northern-most slopes of the hill, there lay the curve of the old mediaeval wall, and, still anything up to 60-feet high, this was provided with stout palisades that served to give its defenders with at least a modicum of cover. Down below, the ground fell away very steeply by as much as 200 feet, while it is also worth noting that the wall was not free-standing: along part of its length the hillside had effectively been scarped in the course of its construction and rose very steeply directly from its top, while, along the rest, centuries of erosion had washed earth down the hillside and filled in the space behind it, this making the task of breaching very difficult.

The modern reconstruction built on the site of the original castle. (Author's collection)

The ditch and north-western bastion of the hornwork of San Miguel: the trees (not there in 1812) give a good idea of the enormous scale of the defences. In the attack of 19 September the troops concerned found that their ladders were not long enough. (Author's collection)

Returning to the defences, immediately to the north-east of the hill on which the castle stood, there rose a second eminence – the Cerro de San Miguel – that rose to roughly the same height, but was separated from it from a deep ravine. Standing well within artillery range of the castle proper, the summit of this hill had also to be held, and it was therefore duly crowned by an imposing outwork known as the Hornwork of San Miguel. Finally, spaced out across the hillside beyond it stood three isolated outworks, these being sited at points where they could overlook areas at which attackers could approach the hornwork in 'dead ground' (at the south-western extremity of the main site, a rather similar role was played by the church of San Román, which, standing, as it did, in an isolated position between the outer-most line of French fortifications and the first houses of the city, had been surrounded by earthworks and palisades and turned into a detached fort).

Such, then, were the defences with which Wellington was confronted. Operations began on the night of 19–20 September with a vigorous assault on the Hornwork of San Miguel, and this was duly carried after fierce fighting (albeit not without some difficulty: the defenders were only overcome when a small force led by Major Charles Cocks of the 79th Foot, a sometime 'exploring officer' with a considerable reputation for dash and courage, that had been sent to distract the attention of the former succeeded in circling its western face and scrambling over the palisade that closed its gorge), but after that fortune turned against the besiegers. Eager to take the fortress quickly, on the night of 22 September a column of 400 volunteers, half of them soldiers of the Guards and half of them soldiers of the King's German Legion, from the First Division commanded by Major Andrew Laurie of the 79th Foot rushed down the hillside from the spot where they had assembled in the lee of the captured hornwork, and made a dash for the city wall. Crossing the sunken lane at the foot of the slope (today the Calle Corrazas), however, they were spotted by the enemy and subjected to heavy fire, whereupon most of the rearward half of the column turned aside and took shelter in the lane. Undaunted, Laurie and the Guards pressed on, and succeeded in gaining the foot of the wall, but they only had five ladders and were beaten back, the many dead including their gallant commander. Having been thwarted in this manner, Wellington next turned to mining. Such operations being facilitated by, first, the very steep slopes leading up to the defences and, second, the very stable nature of the sub-soil, on the night of 29 September Wellington's engineers were able to explode a mine beneath the outer-most wall of the fortress, but the tunnel had been dug slightly too short with the result that only the facing of the wall was dislodged, the attackers in consequence still being faced by an earthen cliff that was difficult to scale and, in any case, so imperceptible in the darkness that the column sent to storm the breach, such as it was, could not even find it. To add insult to injury, meanwhile, a breaching battery for the three 18-pounders that were the only heavy cannon Wellington had with him was subjected to such heavy fire when it opened fire on 1 October that it was silenced in a matter of hours. However, a second tunnel was more successful and on 9 October a massive breach was blown in the wall some 200 yards to the south of the first one, the 2/24th Foot then succeeding in securing a lodgement within the *enceinte*.

Yet success was short-lived, the ground won by the attackers being found to be so overlooked by the second line of defences that it was almost impossible to exploit the foothold that had been obtained, the French also making matters very difficult by launching two

The site of the first breach. Blown by means of a mine, it did not offer much in the way of access to an attacking force in that the gunpowder was placed just short of the wall and therefore did no more than dislodge some of the stone-work, the earthern terrace beyond being left untouched. (Author's collection)

The scarp beneath the outmost of the two lines of ramparts surrounding the castle taken from the vicinity of the first breach, with, to the right, the remains of a cavalier that the French threw up to protect the entrance into the inner defences. Meanwhile, the terrace stretching to the left marked by the goal-posts was in 1812 occupied by enormous mounds of roundshot, the citadel having been pressed into service as a convenient place to store munitions of every sort. (Author's collection)

The yawning gulf in the ramparts that marks the position of the third breach. In the final assault on the fortress, a handful of men from the King's German Legion got onto the terrace to the right, only to be cut down by a column of reinforcements sent down from the next line of ramparts. (Author's collection)

sallies that inflicted heavy casualties on the men in the trenches that were hastily dug in the second breach and atop the walls and undid much of their hard work (nor, meanwhile, did it help that the terrace between the old city wall and the outer line of ramparts had been used to store thousands of cannon-balls, these having been piled up to form enormous mounds that acted as *de facto* ravelins); sadly enough, among the dead was the hero of the storming of the Hornwork of San Miguel, Charles Cocks. Still worse, when Wellington's handful of guns managed to breach a third point in the defences, the assault that followed on 19 October was hopelessly mismanaged, and the attackers driven off, all that was achieved being the capture of the church of San Román by a Spanish infantry battalion, the only such troops employed in the siege (an empty triumph even this, for the French had laid mines under the church and blew it up as soon as the surviving defenders had retired up the hill). This was the end. With the French armies massing for a counter-offensive, on 21 October Wellington raised the siege and embarked on a long and difficult retreat to the Portuguese frontier. Madrid, too, was evacuated, and by late November the Anglo-Portuguese army was back where it had been at the end of January. It was not a good end to the year. The casualties had been heavy – over 2,000 at Burgos alone – and the army's faith in its commander had been severely dented, whilst the impact on Anglo-Spanish relations was significant: in September 1812 Wellington had been appointed to the command of the Spanish army, and the failure of the autumn campaign significantly damaged his credit in the temporary capital of Cádiz; meanwhile, the British blamed all their woes on the shortcomings of the Spaniards.

Burgos Today

Though cloaked in thick forest, the fortress of Burgos is one of most rewarding of Peninsular-War sites. Hardly anywhere else in Europe, indeed, can be seen finer remains either of Napoleonic field fortifications or of a Napoleonic siege. The castle itself was blown up when the French evacuated the city in June 1813, but subsequent reconstruction has restored it to a least a semblance of its state at the time of the siege. Much more interesting, however, are the outer defences, these surviving absolutely intact almost throughout their entire length. In the various other places in Spain graced by such citadels, nothing exists of the earthwork fortifications thrown up by the French but the most fragmentary remains, and this itself is sufficient to lend great interest to the site. But this is not all. For obvious reasons, being extremely vulnerable to such factors as urbanization, it is only very rarely that the various works constructed by the besieging forces survive. In Burgos, however, this is not the case, or, at least, not entirely the case. Though some of the land involved has indeed been lost, much of it remains open, and in several places traces may be found of both approach trenches and batteries. However, the *pièce de résistance* is constituted by the breaches and, in particular, the one blown in the second line of defence at the very end of the siege. Here one gets a particularly strong impression of the horrors which soldiers sent to storm such a feature had to face – only partially repaired, its upper levels remain much as they did in October 1812.

Visitors wishing to explore the site, which is easily accessible from the city centre by drivers and pedestrians alike and enjoys the benefit of good signage, are advised to start on the esplanade in front of the reconstructed castle. From here, way-marked trails can be followed to most parts of the complex. Finally, a folio containing details of the site is available from the tourist information office and the museum inside the walls of the castle.

There are, needless to say, many different ways in which the site may be explored, but it will be assumed here that readers of this book would prefer to do so in the context of the events of the siege. If this is what is desired, the best place to start is the bird sanctuary on the Cerro de San Miguel, the best way of reaching this being to drive up the Carretera del Castillo (in the Peninsular War the only access route to the fortress) from its junction with the Calle San Esteban – the approximate site of the never-rebuilt church of San Román – and then turn left and follow the road down to the bridge that takes it across the ravine between the two hills; beyond the bridge carry on up the hill and take the first left. From the bird sanctuary, a short walk to the north will take the visitor to one of the three small redoubts that the French constructed to keep the approaches to the Cerro de San Miguel under observation, only for them to be overrun with hardly a shot being fired in the early stages of the attack on the hornwork, it being to this subject that we should now turn.

To proceed, then, the bird sanctuary stands at the outer limits of the glacis of the hornwork, the position of this last being marked by the line of trees and underbrush to the right. As such, the ground it occupies was at the heart of the fighting that led to the capture of the position. In so far as the area of the bird sanctuary is concerned, this saw a party drawn from the 42nd Foot (the Black Watch) advance to the lip of the glacis and engage in a prolonged fire-fight with the defenders in an attempt to keep their heads down while other detachments of the same regiment assaulted the projecting bastions of the hornwork to left and right. Positioned out in the open without a shred of cover, the men concerned displayed enormous courage, but they eventually suffered such casualties that they retired in disorder, the fact being that the plan had badly miscarried.

To view what had gone wrong, walk across to the road by which the glacis of the hornwork was reached and take the narrow path that will be found on its right, this leading to the redan that protected said fortification's ramparts from direct fire. As with most of the defences, the area is cloaked with thick vegetation, and it should be remembered that this would not have been present in 1812. Very shortly, the visitor will find themselves dropping down to the road, which at this point runs between the redan and the hornwork along what would have been the latter's ditch. Directly ahead can be seen a sally-port leading to the interior of the fortifications, but, before going through it, the visitor might prefer to head to the right so as to stand beneath the right-hand bastion of the hornwork, this being a spot that witnessed acts of the utmost heroism. Thus, the detachment of the 42nd sent to attack the bastion found that the ladders with which they had been provided were much too short and therefore attempted to climb the walls using bayonets driven into the earth as improvised footrests. For all their efforts, however, they were unable to establish a lodgement on the crest and, like their comrades on the glacis, eventually had no option but to fall back. That said, their efforts are not forgotten, one of the men who was killed, a Sergeant James Foyer, being commemorated in a folksong called *The Ballad of Jamie Foyers* (*sic*) that recounts his death at the foot of the bastion.

From the bastion, head back to the sally-port, taking a moment in the process to admire the massive bastions on either hand, and enter the hornwork, which can then be explored at leisure. Note, however, that it covers a much larger area than it did at the time of the siege, the French having greatly extended its flanking walls. Cock's entrance into the work was therefore in all probability effected in the area of the mobile-phone installation in the centre of the current enclosure, the whole area witnessing fierce fighting as the attackers first struggled to get across the palisade blocking their way and then tried to prevent the garrison from making a dash for the safety of the Cerro del Castillo. It is interesting to note, meanwhile, that one of the soldiers who died in the struggle, a bugler of the 79th Foot's light company named Charles Bogle, is specifically mentioned as being a 'man of colour'.

Having visited the hornwork, take the path that leads downhill from its rear face, this being the remains of a covered way which the French built in the wake of the siege so as to effect a safe communication between the two parts of the fortress. On reaching the road – the Calle de las Corazas – turn right and head under the bridge. Proceed downhill to a turning on the left (the Calle Murallas). After a short distance the mediaeval city wall will be encountered. The visitor is now at the site of the escalade of 22 September. Follow the along until a turning on the right (the Calle Bofordo), noting in passing the projecting turret, known as a *tambor* (literally, 'drum'). This became notorious as a nest of French snipers during the operations that eventually allowed Wellington to breach the outer defences. At the Calle Bofordo, meanwhile, cross the road and descend the flight of stairs plunging straight down the near precipitous slope just far enough to note the steep nature of the declivity, it being precisely this that made mining operations so feasible an operation; meanwhile, it is probable that the entrance to first tunnel lay under modern stairway. Also of interest is the Calle Bofordo, following the line, as it does, of the first parallel and, subsequently, the sap that was dug from there not the foot of the walls: it is probable that, in the decades after the war, the trenches were utilised as a convenient route up the hillside, the path that resulted eventually turning into a full-blown track that in turn became the basis for the modern road.

Moving on, the site of the first breach will be found behind a couple of small trees more or less opposite the Calle Bofordo. Those of a vigorous disposition can experiment with climbing to the top, but, while this can be done, it will quickly be appreciated that to get an assault column to the top would have been a very difficult business. To reach the second breach, carry on along the Calle Murallas until a track is encountered on the left, this marking the site of said breach. Follow the track up the slope and note the fashion in which it suddenly swings sharply to the left beneath a steep earthen bank: herewith a good example of the great problem that dogged all attempts to make further progress in this sector, the breach being completely overlooked by a small enclosed work known as a cavalier that the French had constructed to cover the passage that led from the *terre-plein* above the mediaeval wall to the upper level of the citadel and now served them as a useful base from which to harass the besiegers.

At the top of the track, turn left and continue parallel to the Calle Murallas. Traces of the parapet that topped the old wall are clearly visible and it is probable that said parapet was made use of as a basis for a third parallel (the second ran along the Calle Murallas: just before the line of trees, meanwhile, the area of broken ground on the left conceals the remains of a zigzag sap that was dug in the direction of the main breach. To reach this last, follow the track into the trees until a flight of stairs is seen ascending to the right, this marking the foot of the third breach. Battered down by a new battery situated beside the hornwork this pierced the full depth of the fortress' principal line of defence, which was here thickened by a *fausse braye* – roughly-speaking, a terrace running across the face of the ramparts that provided the defender with an additional firing position. Note, however, that the mediaeval wall was absent in this sector, having been demolished in the course of the eighteenth century. Taking the stairs, climb up to the next level of the defences (the *fausse braye*). Beneath the point at which the visitor now stands, the breach was filled in after the siege and therefore can no longer be seen, but straight ahead it is all too obvious and can be ascended by a curving flight of stairs on its left-hand side. At the top is another *terre plein* backed by the second line of defences: it being this that brought the few members of the storming party who reached the summit of the breach to a halt, the men concerned then being swept away by a column of reserves that charged down from the enclosure surrounding the now much-battered church of Santa María la Blanca by means of the ramp that can be seen a few yards to the right.

Conclude the tour by exploring the final set of ramparts and visiting the castle, though this has little to offer than a small museum and splendid views of the old city, after which it is possible to return to the bird sanctuary via the Carreterra del Castillo.

Further Reading

C. Divall, *Wellington's Worst Scrape: the Burgos Campaign, 1812* (Barnsley: Pen and Sword, 2013)

C.J. Esdaile, *Burgos in the Peninsular War, 1808-1814: Occupation, Siege, Aftermath* (Abingdon: Routledge Keegan Paul, 2014)

22

Vitoria

21 June 1813

British histories of the Peninsular War of 1808–1814 often read as if Wellington's march to Toulouse was one long chapter of victories. As we have seen, however, the year 1812 ended on a sour note for the Allied cause. Thanks to a number of factors, Wellington had been forced to abandon the siege of Burgos, evacuate Madrid, and withdraw to Portugal, leaving the Anglo-Spanish alliance in tatters. Yet all was by no means lost. If the French recovered Madrid, Old Castile and parts of León and New Castile, they never returned to Andalucía, Asturias, Cantabria and Extremadura and were henceforth clearly on the defensive. Meanwhile, the great counter-offensive that had forced Wellington to retreat had only been organised at the cost of allowing such figures as the famous Navarrese guerrilla commander, *Brigadier* Francisco Espoz y Mina to over-run large parts of Navarre and the Basque provinces, while Spanish fury at the retreat had not gone so far as to lead to the withdrawal of a previous offer to give Wellington the command-in-chief of the Spanish army. And, last but not least, the heavy losses suffered in the Burgos campaign were soon made good: not only did improvements in the medical department ensure that large numbers of the sick and wounded returned to duty, but the British government had not lost faith in Wellington and therefore sent him large numbers of fresh troops. With Napoleon all too clearly in desperate trouble thanks to the retreat from Moscow and the only positive development in the French camp being a decision on the part of the Emperor to unite all the imperial forces in Spain under a single commander-in-chief – marred by the fact that said commander-in-chief was none other Joseph Bonaparte, a man of negligible military experience who was openly despised by many of his newfound subordinates – a fresh offensive was unlikely to be long delayed.

   If the auguries for fresh action were very good, organising a new campaign proved far from straightforward. Initially it is clear that Wellington intended to have the Spanish forces advance on Madrid from the south, while he struck eastwards from Portugal, but this idea came to nothing as Patriot Spain was in such disarray that the Cádiz government proved incapable of getting most of its troops ready for action in time to take part in the offensive. Had everything remained equal, this might have been sufficient to postpone the advance, but, in the event, the situation was redeemed by Espoz y Mina and his fellows. Initially, the guerrillas had not been taken much notice of by Wellington, but Napoleon was increasingly concerned at the extent to which they were menacing the French communications in

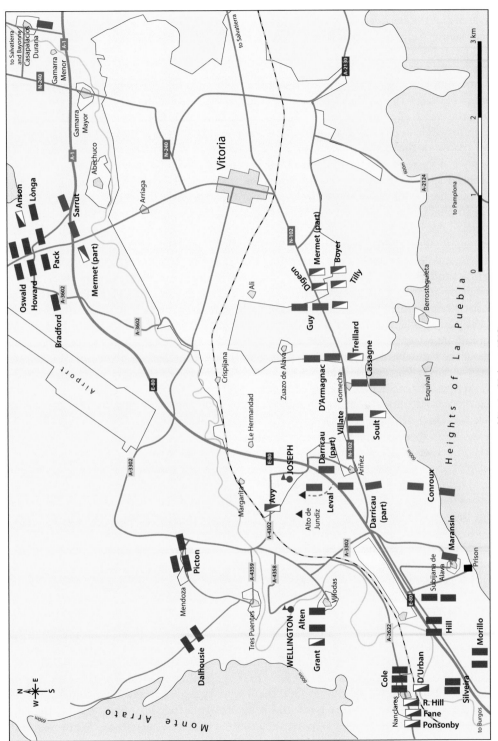

Vitoria, 21 June 1813.

Navarre and the Basque provinces, and in consequence gave orders that a large part of the forces facing Wellington – the so-called Army of Portugal – should abandon their positions and march eastwards to lend their weight to the struggle against the insurgents. Warned by King Joseph and the latter's chief-of-staff, *maréchal* Jean-Baptiste Jourdan, that the consequences of this could be very serious, the Emperor insisted that the Anglo-Portuguese forces were in no state to go on the attack, but in reality nothing could have been further from the truth, the only thing that delayed Wellington from taking the field being the need to wait for the countryside to be clothed in the fresh grass needed by his cavalry and baggage animals.

In the event the advance began on 22 May. Aware that such an eventuality was likely, Joseph and Jourdan had decided that their best bet was to pull back all the French troops in central Spain – the Armies of the South and the Centre – behind the River Duero and hold out there until such time as the troops fighting the guerrillas could join them. In this as in so much else, however, Wellington had outsmarted them. In brief, while he himself advanced on Salamanca with three infantry divisions and the bulk of his cavalry, he sent Lieutenant General Sir Thomas Graham northwards with his other six infantry divisions with the mission of crossing the Duero via a pontoon bridge that had been built well inside Portugal and then swinging eastwards so as to take Joseph and Jourdan in the flank. Taken entirely by surprise, the French commanders fell back in the direction of the French frontier, but their every effort to make a stand was brought to nothing by a further piece of prescience on the part of Wellington. Thus, rather than simply following in the wake of Joseph and Jourdan, he rather struck off to his left, and embarked on a long march through the foothills of the Cantabrian mountains that once again took the French unawares. By 16 June, then, the Anglo-Portuguese army, which had been joined since the start of the campaign by several divisions of Spanish troops, was across the River Ebro, and the French forces falling back on Vitoria, though not before they had blown up the castle that formed the central nucleus of their defences at Burgos.

Having reached Vitoria, Joseph and Jourdan at last turned at bay, their reasons for this decision being manifold. Some of the stray units from the Army of Portugal having now been picked up, they now had some 60,000 men. Retreat any further, meanwhile, and Joseph would have no kingdom left, not to mention no opportunity to pick up three infantry divisions of the Army of Portugal that were still missing and whatever troops might be spared from the regular garrison of Navarre and the Basque provinces. And, last but not least, Vitoria seemed to offer an excellent defensive position, in that the town could only be approached from the west – the direction from which it was presumed that Wellington would attack – by means of a long valley crossed by a series of defensive positions that seemed impossible to outflank (on the French right flowed the River Zadorra, whilst on their left stood a line of rugged hills known as the Altos de Puebla that were largely inaccessible to formed troops).

Much of this thinking was perfectly reasonable, but for one thing. Thus, ignorant of Wellington's precise movements, Joseph and Jourdan had missed the crucial fact that the Allied forces were not just approaching from the west. On the contrary, even as the forces that had been concentrated at Vitoria were making ready for battle, fully half the 90,000 troops that had been brought up to fight them were swinging round their right flank and making for the Zadorra's many fords and bridges. Given the facts, first, that for the past month the whole of Wellington's strategy had centred on a series of outflanking moves, and,

The valley of the River Zadorra viewed from Wellington's command post at Villodas: the twin knolls of the Alto de Jundiz can just be made out in the middle-distance just below the skyline constituted by the Puebla Heights. (Author's collection)

The bridge at Tres Puentes and, beyond it, the knoll that sheltered the Light Division's crossing of the Zadorra from the sight of the French commanders. (Author's collection)

The Puente de Villodas. Situated, like the neighbouring bridge at Tres Puentes at the western end of the battlefield, this was one of no fewer than seven crossings of the River Zadorra that gave access to the open French right flank and had yet been left completely undefended. (Author's collection)

second, that cavalry patrols had discovered that fewer troops lay to the west of them than might have been expected, it seems barely credible that Joseph and Jourdan failed to realise that the same might happen again. What threw them seems to have been the idea that the roads which crossed the mountains that lay immediately to the north of the Zadorra were impassable to large bodies of men. The result of this being that it would take a considerable time for Wellington to get into a position from which he could threaten the French communications, it therefore seemed worthwhile to hold firm for the few days that would be needed for the troops that had been fighting Espoz y Mina in Navarre – at worst only 40 or 50 miles away – to reach Joseph and Jourdan: not only did the French have a chance to fight, then, but they might even snatch a victory from the very jaws of defeat and all the more so as they were convinced that the only way that Wellington could attack them was via the narrow gorge through which the Zadorra made its way into the valley they were defending, something for which they were well prepared, the three separate field armies from which the French array was drawn – *général de division* Honoré Gazan's Army of the South, *général de division* Jean-Baptiste Drouet's Army of the Centre and *général de division* Honoré Reille's Army of Portugal – being drawn up one behind the other across the Madrid highway with their right flank on the River Zadorra and their left at the foot of the Puebla heights.

In reality, however, a French victory was extremely unlikely. Thus, setting aside the fact that Joseph and Jourdain had only 50,000 men with which to resist the 90,000 British, Spaniards and Portuguese troops who were at Wellington's orders, far from attempting to manoeuvre the French into yet another retreat, Wellington was rather planning to attack them at Vitoria. Of all the battle plans that he drew up in the Peninsular War, meanwhile, the one that he hit upon for the coming clash was by far the most ambitious. In brief what was envisaged was a concentric attack for which the Anglo-Portuguese army and the handful of troops from the Spanish Fourth Army which had managed to join it in time for the battle was to be divided into four columns – in reality, *de facto corps d'armée* – of which three were placed under the command of Lieutenant Generals Sir Rowland Hill, the Earl of Dalhousie, and Sir Thomas Graham with the fourth taken by Wellington himself. As to the units which made

Known as the Sierra de Arato, the mountains to the north of the Zadorra valley convinced Joseph and Jourdain that their right flank was safe from attack. (Author's collection)

The western half of the battlefield of Vitoria viewed from the Puebla heights. Today these last are covered with impenetrable scrub, but it is probable that at the time of battle they were far more accessible, if still very rugged. (Author's collection)

up each column, Hill had the cavalry brigades of Brigadier Generals Henry Fane and Victor von Alten, and the infantry of the 2nd Division of Lieutenant General William Stewart, the Portuguese division of *Tenente-General* Francisco Silveira, Conde de Amarante, and the Spanish division of *Mariscal de Campo* Pablo Morillo; Dalhousie his own 7th Division and the 3rd Division of Lieutenant General Thomas Picton; Graham the cavalry brigades of Major Generals George Anson and Eberhardt von Bock, and the infantry of the 1st Division of Major-General Kenneth Howard, the 5th Division of Major General John Oswald, the independent Portuguese brigades of *Marechal de Campo* Thomas Bradford and *Marechal de Campo* Denis Pack, and the Spanish division of *Mariscal de Campo* Francisco Longa; and, finally, Wellington the cavalry brigades of Lieutenant Colonel Sir Robert Hill, Colonel Colquhoun Grant, Major General William Ponsonby and *Brigadeiro* Benjamin d'Urban, and the infantry of Light Division of Major General Karl von Alten and the 4th Division of Lieutenant General Galbraith Lowry Cole. As to what all these forces were supposed to do, in essence Hill and Wellington were to distract the French by launching an attack from the West while Dalrymple and, further east, Graham, burst out of the mountains to the north and attacked them from the flank and rear.

At the last minute the French commanders did realise that all was not what it seemed, but the actions that they took in response – in brief, the dispatch of Reille's forces to hold the northern approaches to the town of Vitoria – were a classic case of 'too little, too late', and so, when battle was joined on 21 June, they found themselves in a difficult predicament. Indeed, if such a thing were possible, the situation now got even worse. Thus, while Wellington's column closed up on the western reaches of the Zadorra, the expected frontal assault failed to materialise, the first Allied troops to attack – the column commanded by Sir Rowland Hill – rather moving against the heights that overlooked the French positions from the south and pushing through the gorge of the River Zadorra. Much perturbed that Wellington might have out-guessed them and be marching round their left flank, Joseph and Jourdan responded by sending large numbers of troops to join the fight for the heights, whilst at the same getting drawn into a desperate battle with Hill around the village of Subijana de Alava, only to find that in doing so they had got themselves into worse difficulties than ever. Thus, not only did a large force of enemy troops suddenly appear out of the mountains to the north and bear down on Vitoria from that direction, but the extreme right of the French front line found itself under attack from still another Allied column.

Initially the Allied troops immediately north of Vitoria under the command of Sir Thomas Graham did not prove much of a foe, for they proved surprisingly slow to attack the French. To the west, however, matters were very different. Having crossed the river by an undefended

The area near the mouth of the Zadorra valley where Hill's forces first came to blows with the troops sent to defend Subijana de Alava. (Author's collection)

Subijana de Alava viewed from the direction of Hill's advance. (Author's collection)

The parish church of Subijana de Alava, the scene of bitter fighting as Hill's troops closed in on the village (Author's collection)

The French front line as viewed by the Light Division after it emerged from the woods that had sheltered its crossing of the river at Tres Puentes. (Author's collection)

The north-eastern slopes of the Alto de Jundíz: driven from their positions by Wellington's forces, the defenders fled from right to left for the safety of the village of Ariñez. (Author's collection)

bridge at Tres Puentes, the famous Light Division pressed forward, and, at some cost, pinned down the few French troops who were left in the sector. Meanwhile, to their left, the 3rd Division poured across a further bridge at Mendoza and made still further inroads into the French position. Centred on two steep knolls that dominated the Madrid highway, the latter was physically very strong, but there were simply too few men in place to hold out against so concentrated an attack, the consequence being that the defenders were soon over-run. Though still fighting bravely here and there, most notably at the village of Ariñez immediately in rear of the old front line, the French were pressed steadily backwards until at length they could take no more and fled eastwards towards Vitoria. In this predicament, one thing, and one thing only, saved the French from complete destruction. Had Sir Thomas Graham, who had been given command of the 20,000 troops sent to advance on Vitoria from the north, shown a modicum of initiative, Joseph would have found himself completely cut off, for Graham had only to seize the roads leading to France from the city – a relatively easy task given his numerical advantage – to trap almost the whole French army. Luckily for the French, however, Graham showed little in the way of either energy or initiative and therefore allowed himself to be checked at the village of Gamarra Mayor, while many of the cavalry sent to exploit the collapse of the French front line elected to pillage the enormous French baggage train rather than pursue the retreating enemy, this last being an event that drove Wellington to absolute fury. In the end, then, by dint of taking a minor road that led eastwards to Salvatierra, a move forced on them by the fact that the division of Spanish troops attached to Graham's command had succeeded in getting across the Zadorra and cutting the main road to France at Durana, Joseph, Jourdan and considerable numbers of their troops got away. That said, at some 8,000 men, their casualties were still enormous while the French also lost almost all their artillery. If not quite the end of the war, it was certainly the end of the Bonaparte Kingdom of Spain.

The Alto de Jundíz viewed from the Puente de Mendoza: urged on by its commander, the 3rd Division advanced across these fields and took the defenders in flank and rear. (Author's collection)

The parish church at Ariñez: like its counterpart at Subijana de Alava, this was the scene of desperate fighting. (Author's collection)

The approaches to Gamarra Mayor viewed from the west: Graham's forces advanced from left to right in the direction of the river. (Author's collection)

A close-up of the imposing monument to the Battle of Vitoria that graces the city centre. As can be seen, this portion of the frieze that surrounds it shows Wellington receiving the acclaim of the local populace, but for many years many locals preferred to believe that the mounted figure was rather Wellington's Spanish aide, prominent local grandee Miguel de Alava. (Author's collection)

Vitoria Today

The city of Vitoria having grown enormously since the battle, much of the battlefield is covered by sprawling industrial estates, while it is also traversed by a major motorway and a railway line. However, the heights scaled by parts of the Allied right wing are worth ascending, if difficult of access and then only on foot, while several of the bridges along the Zadorra are still intact. Also worth visiting are Wellington's headquarters at Villodas, from which a good sense may still be obtained of his perspective on events, that and the village of Gamarra Mayor. Closer to the main French positions, meanwhile, Subijana and the fields to the west and south-west thereof – the area where Hill's troops battled the French as they debouched on to the battlefield – is well worth exploring as are the knolls that marked the French front line (today a nature reserve signposted as the Cerro de Júndiz). Finally, the monument in Vitoria itself is a definite 'must, and all the more so as, somewhat unusually, it is one that does full justice to Wellington's army (that said, a common insistence amongst the locals is that the central figure in the tableau of the Allied forces entering the city is not the British commander, but rather the latter's Spanish liaison officer, Miguel de Alava, a prominent local landowner who is supposed to have rushed post-haste to the city in the hope of saving the populace from pillage at the hands of their liberators).

In so far as directions to the field are concerned, these are probably best divided into four sections, namely Hill's action at Subijana de Alava; the passage of the Zadorra; the French position at Ariñez, and, finally, Gamarra Mayor and Durana, these mirroring the different phases of the battle remarkably well. Let us begin, then, in the same way as the day itself did, with the doings of Sir Rowland Hill. Having bivouacked on the north bank of the Zadorra at La Puebla de Arganzón, a village some miles short of the gorge that led to the French positions, said commander led his forces northwards along the line of the main road from Madrid to the French frontier, pausing only to detach the Spanish troops under his command to ascend the heights of La Puebla by means of a track that branched off to the right just before the gorge and slanted diagonally uphill along the ridge-line. The initial stretch of the route concerned is, alas, now buried under the motorway that runs beside the Madrid highway, but those wishing to explore it can do so by taking the first turning to the right after the roundabout on the very northern edge of La Puebla de Arganzón, turning left at the T-junction on the other side of the motorway and heading along the track to the point at which it swings sharply to the right and turns up-hill; the ascent, however, is extremely steep and should not be tackled on foot by anyone who is not extremely fit. Having passed the gorge, Hill then deployed his remaining troops into line in the area bounded by the junction of the motorway with the A-2622 on the left and the provincial jail (the Centro Penitenciario de Alava) on the right. That done, he then pushed eastwards around the lower slopes of the heights and headed for Subijana, whose garrison can be assumed from the configuration of the ground to have been unaware of his advance to the very last moment. To view the area of the fighting, meanwhile, start at the motorway junction just mentioned, exiting it to the south-east in the direction of the prison. Almost immediately turn sharp left onto the minor road that runs beside the motorway and take the first right (the Subijana de Alava Entitatea). This leads directly to the village, crossing the line of Hill's advance almost at right angles as it does so; note, meanwhile, the isolated knoll to the left of the road: easily accessible on foot, this offers excellent views both of the area of the fighting round Subijana and the twin knolls held by the French at Ariñez.

From Subijana, the visitor will next wish to proceed to the crossings of the Zadorra at Villodas, Tres Puentes and the Puente de Mendoza. To reach this area, take the A-4130 northwards out of the village and, on reaching the motorway services, turn right. At the roundabout carry straight-on, on what has now become the A-3302. Having swung sharply to the left, passed under the motorway and crossed the railway, all under the lee of the French position at Ariñez, this soon reaches the river and for a short distance follows its course. At the fork in the road keep left and the Puente de Villodas will then be found on the left a short distance further on. Having crossed the bridge, take the first right (San Cristóbal Kalea) and head up-hill until the parish church is reached on the right-hand side of the road. Beyond the church and a little further up-hill will be found an area of open ground boasting excellent views of the Zadorra valley: this was the spot from which Wellington commanded the battle for most of the day, while it was also from here that the British commander dispatched the Light Division to seize the bridge at Tres Puentes; to reach the track the latter unit used, carry straight on along San Cristóbal Kalea to the T-junction at the end and turn right: said track will then be found a short distance further on on the right.

The direct route to Tres Puentes now being blocked by a large quarry situated at the very 'elbow' of the river, to reach that village it is necessary to return to the Puente de Villodas and, having recrossed the river, turn immediately left onto the A-4358. Running parallel to the course of the river, this soon brings the traveller to the bridge which the Light Division used to cross the river, after which the turning on the right immediately before the bridge can be used to follow the advance of Alten's men in the direction of the French position at Ariñez (N.B. Though it may be followed on foot without difficulty, this road is not always open to vehicular traffic: if it is closed, drivers will instead have to return to the A-3302 and then reach Tres Puentes by turning left and crossing the Zadorra at the Puente de Mendoza). On reaching the A-3302 once more, turn left and head to the river: the bridge is the Puente de Mendoza, but, unlike its counterparts at Villodas and Tres Puentes, it is not the one that existed in 1813; however, the fields stretching northwards towards the village of the same name have much the same aspect as they did when the 3rd Division surged across them to their commander's shouts of 'Come on, you drunken rascals!', in which respect a mere glance back towards Ariñez is enough to suggest what a shock their appearance must have been to the already embattled defenders.

From the bridge continue northwards along the A-3302 and turn left into the Mendoza itself. On the other side of the small stream that runs through the village will be found the latter's perfectly preserved mediaeval castle, the topmost battlements of which provided Picton with the perfect viewpoint from which to watch the rest of the battle: no wonder, then, that he became so impatient! Finally, observe, too, the ridge immediately to the north-west, it being the presence of this feature that allowed the Welsh general's division to remain out of sight until it at long last went into action.

Having now set the men of both Alten and Picton in motion, it is time to turn our attention to the objective on which they were bearing down, namely the twin knolls overlooking the village of Ariñez. To reach these, return to the bridge and, having crossed it, take the first left. Numbered the A-4302, this soon leads to one of the many huge industrial estates that have swallowed so much of the battlefield. At the roundabout just inside the perimeter take the first exit, and then, at the second, repeat the same manoeuvre. From here head southwards and take the turning to the right immediately before the road passes under the motorway. After a few hundred yards a track will be encountered on the right, this leading to the summit of the higher of the two knolls – the Alto de Jundiz – from which it is possible first to descend into the dip between the two and then to climb up onto the second, this being known as Inglésmendi (literally 'the hill of the English'), a reference to combat that took place there during John of Gaunt's invasion of Spain in 1367. Be warned, however, that the tracks are not suitable for motor-vehicles, and, further, that, particularly in the case of Inglésmendi, the gradient surprisingly taxing. That said, the climb is worth it, it quickly becoming apparent that the French position was very strong, and certainly formidable enough to warrant the complex outflanking movement settled on by Wellington.

Having walked back to the road, return to the fork by which it was reached, turn right, cross the motorway and then turn right again at the T-junction. Ariñez now lies directly ahead, although few buildings remain from the period of the battle other than the parish church. There now remains just the scene of Graham's attack. To reach the area concerned, head back out of the village on the same road as before and continue to a roundabout in the midst of another industrial estate, at which point take the third exit and head due north. Very soon a second roundabout is reached, the third exit of which leads directly to the motorway. Bear right, take the northbound carriage-way (signposted San Sebastián and Irun) and at the third exit head south on the N240 (signposted Vitoria). Gamarra Mayor, the scene of the fiercest fighting, is immediately south of the junction. At the first roundabout, turn right and park in the vicinity of parish church. Take the road to the left of the church (Bastobi Kalea) and turn right beyond the range of buildings into Aspidea Kalea; looking back it will be appreciated that said range of buildings form the background to J.P. Beadle's famous painting of Graham's troops storming the village (it is a pity about the anachronistic 'Belgic' shakos in the picture– an item of dress not introduced until after the close of hostilities in 1814 – but one cannot have everything!). Finally, carry on to the end of the road and turn right into the lane leading back towards the motorway: this marks the general axis of Graham's advance on the village and leads to an area of open fields that, the motorway always excepted, are probably much the same as they were in 1813. By contrast, the village's bridge across the Zadorra has long since disappeared in favour of a more modern structure worthy of the main road that it carries.

To complete the tour of the battlefield, head back up the N240 and take the first exit on the other side of the motorway (the A-3004, signposted Durana). After a mile or so, this leads to the river and, with it, the bridge seized by Longa's division towards the end of the battle after a prolonged struggle with the last remnants of the Spanish army that had been raised by King Joseph. Like its counterparts at Mendoza and Gamarra Mayor, the crossing has been modernised, but in this case the original was left in situ and can still be seen beneath the new roadway. As in 1813, the village is entirely on the further bank, though it has now spread considerably, particularly along the main road, in 1813, of course, the highway to San Sebastián and the French frontier. Finally, to return to Vitoria, take said main road – now the A-3002 – the city centre being but a short drive away.

Further Reading

C. Divall, *Wellington and the Vitoria Campaign: Never a Finer Army* (Barnsley: Pen and Sword, 2021)

I. Fletcher, *Vitoria, 1813: Wellington Sweeps the French from Spain* (Oxford: Osprey, 2000)

23

Maya

25 July 1813

The French army of the Napoleonic Wars was a remarkable institution in terms of its resilience, its endurance and its devotion to its imperial master alike, not to mention the extraordinary dynamism of many of its commanders, the fact that this was the case being shown many times over in the campaigns in Spain and Portugal. Having already observed one example of the astonishing powers of recovery to which this could give rise in the Battle of Fuentes de Oñoro, which saw a thoroughly exhausted and demoralised army that had lost a third of its strength to disease and starvation in its futile blockade of the Lines of Torres Vedras and just been put through the rigours of a difficult retreat turned around by its commander in the space of a single month and launch a dangerous counter-attack, we now come to a second one, namely the series of actions that make up the so-called Battle of the Pyrenees. Thus, 25 July 1813 saw the very same troops that had sustained such a drubbing at Vitoria just four weeks before taking the offensive and in the process giving the Anglo-Portuguese army some very worrying moments. If this was so, it was very much the achievement of *maréchal* Jean de Dieu Soult, the French commander who we last encountered throwing Beresford into such confusion at Albuera. Appointed by Napoleon to restore order on the Pyrenean front in place of the hapless Joseph Bonaparte and his chief of staff, *maréchal* Jean-Baptiste Jourdan, in the wake of Vitoria, Soult threw himself into the task of forging the three separate forces – those of the South, the Centre and Portugal – that had been routed in that action into a single homogeneous army; gathering fresh field-guns and howitzers to replace the 151 pieces taken by Wellington; re-equipping the much-tried soldiery with everything from boots to shakos; and amassing the fodder, food and transport that would be needed if he was to fulfil the orders he had received to relieve the beleaguered fortresses of San Sebastián and Pamplona, of which the former was being subjected to a regular siege by Lieutenant General Sir Thomas Graham and the latter to a close blockade aimed at starving its defenders into submission. To achieve his ends, the French commander had no more than 80,000 men, while he had only been able to supply his troops with four days' rations, but he did possess the advantage of the initiative. Also very helpful, meanwhile, was the fact that Wellington's forces were scattered across a considerable expanse of territory, all of it criss-crossed by rugged hills and mountains and blessed with communication links that were at best tortuous. As if this was not enough, meanwhile, as the normally formidable Anglo-Portuguese intelligence machine had little access to what was going on beyond the

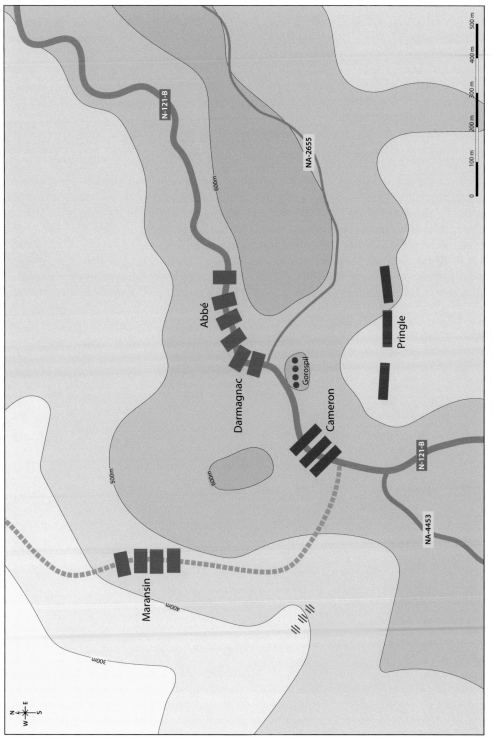

Maya, 25 July 1813.

French frontier, they would almost certainly have the advantage of surprise. Strike hard and fast, or so it seemed, and Soult would have a good chance of achieving a measure of success, and all the more so as he managed to out-guess his opponent in that, whereas Wellington was convinced that any French attack would be directed at San Sebastián and had therefore placed the bulk of his forces close to the coast, the target selected was rather Pamplona. In short, if not quite the proverbial 'near-run thing', the forthcoming campaign was likely to prove a very close encounter.

By choosing to march on Pamplona rather than San Sebastián, Soult immediately ensured that the initial fighting would take place at the passes of Maya and Roncesvalles, these marking the only routes by which substantial forces of all arms could hope to reach said city. In the event both spots saw fierce combats, but it is on Maya that we shall concentrate in this chapter. With regard to Roncesvalles, suffice to say that the French attack was checked for the whole of 25 July, only for the pass to be abandoned in the course of the night when, enveloped in thick fog and uncertain as to what was going on elsewhere, the British commanders on the scene ordered their men to retreat.

Let us begin with the geography of the Maya pass. Commencing at the little village of Espelette, the main road ran up a deep valley that ran more-or-less due south into the mountains before finally ascending to the pass itself. However, this was not the only route that was

Part of the defences of Pamplona. Blockaded by Spanish troops commanded by *Teniente-General* Enrique O'Donnell, the Conde del Abisbal, the garrison of *général de brigade* Louis Cassagne was certain to succumb to starvation unless it could be relieved by Soult's army. (Author's collection)

The tangled countryside to the north of the Puerto de Maya: it is easy to see how the French were able to get so close to the British positions without being observed. (Author's collection)

The summit of the Puerto de Maya viewed under a lowering sky typical of the battles that raged in the Pyrenees in the last week of July 1813; the eminence in the right middle-distance is the knoll held by the pickets of Major General William Pringle's brigade at the start of the battle. (Author's collection)

available to *général de division* Jean-Baptiste Drouet, the French commander whose troops had been assigned to the sector, a rough track known as the Gorospil path ascending the spur of high ground that formed the eastern side of the valley and, having reached the same level as the summit, turned sharply to the right and ran along a narrow ridge crowned by a conical knoll from which the ground fell steeply away on both sides before finally joining the main road. Meanwhile, the approaches to the pass being cloaked in thick woodland, it was at least theoretically possible for even quite large bodies of troops to advance up both roads without being observed by the defenders.

Of its very self, then, the battlefield afforded Drouet various advantages, but these were redoubled by a number of other factors. To begin with, the responsibility for the pass lay in the hands of Lieutenant General William Stewart, the commander of Wellington's 2nd Division, but, if far from the worst, Stewart was not the best of Britain's generals while, he only had two of his four infantry brigades in the vicinity, the third one – the Portuguese brigade of *Brigadiero* Charles Ashworth – being stationed some miles to the east in observation of the minor Puerto de Izpeguí. In all, then, there were just 3,500 men at the Puerto de Maya, a force that seems puny indeed when compared with the 21,000 men who made up the command of Drouet. But, it was not just a question of overall numbers, the reality being even more advantageous to the French. Thus, although the brigade of Lieutenant-Colonel John Cameron was massed on the summit around the point where the latter was crossed by the main road along with four Portuguese field guns, that of Major General William Pringle was represented only by a picket of 80 men posted on the knoll that crowned (and, indeed, almost blocked) the eastern end of the ridge by which the Gorospil path crossed over to the other side of the valley, the rest of the brigade being encamped far below and a good two miles to the rear around the village which gave the pass its name. Astonishingly enough, meanwhile, nether Cameron nor Pringle had thought to place a picket in the border village of Urdax a mile or two to the north or even to send roving patrols into the valley; indeed, even the men above the Gorospil path were next to useless as they had no view whatsoever of the approaches to their position. Finally, as if all this was not enough to undermine the defence, at the moment the French attacked, Stewart was not even present, having ridden

The knoll held by Pringle's pickets at the start of the battle viewed from the high ground to the east of the pass with, below it, the Gorospil path. (Author's collection)

The steep slope that witnessed the unsuccessful attacks mounted by the 2/34th and the 1/39th; losses in both battalions were very heavy. (Author's collection)

off to investigate reports of a French advance – in fact a mere feint carried out by nothing more than a small force of militia – on the village of Les Alduides some miles to the east and that despite the fact that said village fell outside his zone of responsibility, what made this still worse being that command at Maya devolved on Pringle as the senior of the two British brigadiers – a man who had taken up his command just two days before and was therefore a complete stranger to the terrain.

Given all this, it is a wonder that the defenders came out of the fighting of 25 July as well as they did, all they really had on their side being the fact that the six battalions present on the field were all composed of British veterans of the sort who had worsted the French in battle after battle ever since 1808 – that and the fact that the approaches to the pass were so difficult and, above all, narrow, that their assailants could only fight them on a very restricted front and were also unable to make full use of their numerical superiority. At all events, the first shots of the day were fired at around 10:30 a.m. when eight companies of French light infantry suddenly burst out of the woods and attacked the picket holding the knoll overlooking the eastern end of the pass. The men concerned having just been reinforced by four companies in response to a last-minute report that there were French troops in the valley, the resultant contest was not as one-sided as would originally have been the case, but, even with 300 men instead of 80, the picket still had little chance, and very soon all the defenders had been killed, wounded or taken prisoner. Backing up the light infantry, meanwhile, were two of Drouet's three infantry divisions – namely those of *généraux de division* Jean Darmagnac and Louis Abbé – and battalion after battalion was therefore soon filing along the upper stretches of the Gorospil path in an attempt to reach the main road.

In this endeavour, however, the attackers soon found that they were frustrated, the pickets' heroic stand having given Pringle and Cameron just sufficient time to make ready some sort of defence. On the one hand, having been joined by the former commander, the men of

Cameron's brigade stood to arms at the western end of the ridge, while the three battalions of Pringle's force – the 1/28th Foot, 2/34th Foot and 1/39th Foot – hastened up the steep slopes that that led up to the pass from their camps around Maya. However, even with the assistance of a battalion – the 1/50th Foot – that was dispatched along the Gorospil path by their commander, the first arrivals – the 2/34th and the 1/39th – were flung back in great disorder (something that could hardly be otherwise given that the two units not only failed to co-ordinate their movements but were left badly blown by the steep climb). With matters in this state, it seemed that the defenders were on the point of complete collapse, but, to his credit, Pringle managed to restore a measure of order to the situation by mounting a more co-ordinated effort with the 1/28th, which had arrived on the scene rather later than its two fellows, and five companies of another of the units belonging to Cameron's brigade, namely the 1/92nd. Coming to close quarters with the French and engaging them with heavy fire, the troops concerned stood their ground manfully, but they could make no impression on the masses facing them and in the end retired in their turn having suffered terrible losses. Crucially, however, the men of the two units concerned did not stay together, in that the survivors of the 1/92nd fell back on the rest of Cameron's brigade, while those of the 1/28th headed back towards Maya.

With Pringle's brigade completely spent, the defence of the pass was now left in the hands of just three battalions of British infantry, of which two had already suffered heavy losses, and four field guns. Still worse, the French were on the move again in that the troops on the Gorospil path were both pushing steadily westwards along the ridge and beginning to advance downhill towards Maya, while, having remained in reserve thus far, the third division of Drouet's corps – that of Maransin – was now advancing up the main road.

Seemingly completely unaware of this last threat, Pringle once again sought to check the troops on the Gorospil path by sending five companies of the last unit of Cameron's brigade that still remained intact, namely the 1/71st, to block their approach, only for this force to be threatened with envelopment by clouds of skirmishers who pushed around its flanks by scrambling along the slopes on either side of the ridge, the British commander's woes

The ground successively defended by the 1/50th, the 1/92nd and the 1/71st looking west from the position of D'Armagnac's division. (Author's collection)

The position of D'Armagnac's division as viewed from the ground defended by the 1/50th, the 1/92nd and the 1/71st. (Author's collection)

Today no more than a grassy ride, in 1813 this was the main road across the Puerto de Maya, and, by extension, the route by which Maransin's division reached the summit. (Author's collection)

promptly being increased still further by the sudden emergence of *général de division* Jean-Pierra Maransin's division from the woods and dead ground that had thus far sheltered its approach, an event that was quickly followed by the loss of all four of the guns that had been supporting Cameron's brigade. At this, it seemed that the defence could not but collapse forthwith, but, just when all seemed lost, the hitherto-absent William Stewart suddenly re-appeared on the scene and restored a little of the credit he had lost by his foolhardy excursion in the directions of Les Alduides by taking control of the remnants of Cameron's brigade; pulling them back to a safer position that was clear of Maransin's division, while yet still blocking the main road as it started to run downhill from the pass; and, finally, when, having reformed their ranks and got into better order, the French resumed their advance, conducting a skilful fighting retreat that kept the enemy's gains to a minimum, something in which he was much assisted by the timely appearance of a battalion of the neighbouring 7th Division which had marched to the sound of the guns.

For how long Stewart could have slowed down Drouet's advance in this fashion is unclear – his men, after all, were utterly exhausted, had suffered heavy losses and were all but out of ammunition – but, once again, the fortunes of war took a turn that was quite unexpected. Thus Maransin's men were suddenly thrown into complete confusion by the arrival of a fresh force that had no sooner appeared on the field than it launched a fierce attack on their right flank. As to who the new arrivals were, they consisted of the leading elements of the brigade of Major General Edward Barnes, this last commander having been ordered to hasten to Stewart's assistance by the chief of the 7th Division, Lieutenant General the Earl of Dalhousie, but more to the point was the effect they had, first, on the French, several of Armagnac's battalions being put to flight, and, second, the remains of Cameron's brigade, the men of which were sufficiently cheered to launch a spirited counter-attack.

This last affray marked the end of the battle, for Drouet had become convinced that he was facing two full divisions – the 2nd and the 7th – instead of two understrength brigades and therefore made no further effort to press the offensive, while the men of Pringle and Barnes did not have the wherewithal to drive their opponents back over the pass. As a result, the day ended in stalemate. For all that, however, in the end it was the French who could claim most success, for, in the last hours of the day, orders arrived from Stewart and Dalhousie's immediate superior, Lieutenant General Sir Rowland Hill, to retire on his headquarters at the village of Elizondo. Given that fully a quarter – 1,500 men – of the forces who had been engaged at the pass had fallen, this was a bitter blow, but the defenders could yet congratulate themselves on having fought extremely well, cost the French much precious time and inflicted far more casualties than they had suffered, the French casualty list coming to about 2,200. All that said, the affair was deeply resented by Wellington, for the Portuguese guns captured as Maransin's division overran the summit constituted the only artillery pieces he lost in the entire course of the war in the Peninsula and the subsequent campaign in France.

Maya Today

Around 2,000 feet above sea-level, the Puerto de Maya is perhaps the most spectacular of all the battlefields of the Peninsular War. That said, it is also one of the most remote, there being no practical way of getting there other than by car or coach, the road to take in this respect being the N121-B (signposted Amaiur-Maya, this branches off the N121-A – the main highway from Irun to Pamplona – just east of the village of Legasa). Once reached, however, the field is easy to explore, so easy indeed that it is scarcely worth offering directions here, all that needs saying is that the ground is almost completely unchanged from the state it was in 1813, this extending, alas, so far as to include the absence of any monument (the obelisk that can be seen from afar on a knoll above the village of Maya commemorates, not the conflict of the Peninsular War, but the siege of a nearby castle in 1522). Indeed, the only significant difference concerns the roads across the pass in that the Gorospil path has become the main highway, the route that Maransin took to the summit now constituting nothing more than a woodland ride.

24

Sorauren

28 & 30 July 1813

A few miles north of the fortress of Pamplona, the little village of Sorauren witnessed not one but two battles in the Peninsular War, fought though these were but one day apart. That so small and insignificant a place should have become so contested was the fruit of the French breakthrough at the passes of Maya and Roncesvalles on 25 July 1813. As we have seen, the French objective was the relief of Pamplona, and the aftermath of the fighting saw the two columns in which *maréchal* Jean de Dieu Soult had organised his forces press southwards in the hope that they could reach it before the much-discomforted Anglo-Portuguese army could recover its equilibrium and block its way. In this, however, the *maréchal* was unsuccessful, in that, in the nick of time, the commander of Wellington's Fourth Division, Lieutenant General Galbraith Lowry-Cole, succeeded in occupying the a rugged area of high ground – the so-called Heights of Oricaín – a few miles north of the city that occupied the full width of the interval between the twin north-south valleys of the Rivers Ulzama and Arga between the villages of Sorauren and Zabáldica, these being the two routes by which the French forces, much slowed by indecision, poor roads and torrential rain, were striving to reach Pamplona. With Lowry-Cole, meanwhile, were the three infantry brigades of his own division, namely those of Majors General Robert Ross and William Anson, and *Coronel* George Stubbs, and three stray units that had come under his control in the confusion of the past two days, namely Major General John Byng's brigade from the Second Division, *Brigadiero* Archibald Campbell's brigade from the Portuguese division commanded by *Tenente-General* Francisco da Silveira, Conde de Amarante, and, finally, the tiny Spanish infantry division commanded by *Mariscal de Campo* Pablo Morillo. Setting this last formation aside, meanwhile, the men of Ross, Anson and Byng were British and those of Stubbs and Campbell Portuguese. As for deployment, manning the front line were the brigades of Ross, Campbell and Anson, while to the right rear a spur that afforded access to the heights from the valley of the Arga south of Zabáldica was garrisoned by a single unit of British infantry – the 1/40th Foot – and two battalions of Spanish infantry that had previously been sent out from lines before Pamplona to watch for the French approach. Finally, lying back in reserve were the brigades of Byng and Stubbs and, last but not least, the Spaniards.

In retrospect, it has to be said that Lowry-Cole's decision to occupy the massif on which he had chosen to make his stand was open to question, for it was very vulnerable to turning movements down the river valleys on either side that could have led to it being completely

Sorauren, 28 July 1813.

The eastern end of the Heights of Oricain viewed from the foot of the ridge occupied by the French army.
(Author's collection)

The valley between the Heights of Oricaín and the positions of the French army looking east.
(Author's collection)

surrounded, as well as almost totally devoid of practicable lines of retreat. Still worse, just a few miles to the south there was a much safer position that was in the process of being occupied by Lieutenant General Sir Thomas Picton's 3rd Division and a large part of the Spanish forces that had been besieging Pamplona. Why Lowry-Cole chose to do what he did is unclear, but it may be that he felt the sector of the line further south that would have fallen to his charge, namely the heights of San Cristóbal, was too close to Pamplona (something that was certainly arguable, the rearward slopes of said heights actually being within range of the fortress' guns), and, more particularly, perhaps, that he needed to restore his credibility with Wellington, the latter having been much displeased by his entirely unnecessary abandonment of the Puerto de Roncesvalles two days before. With Lowry-Cole badly outnumbered – he had but 11,000 men to Soult's 20,000 – there was a serious risk of disaster, for it was by no means certain that Picton could have come to his aid with any speed, while the nearest alternative – Major General Denis Pack's 6th Division – was as yet some distance from the battlefield. However, in the event such an outcome was avoided, albeit in large part only because the French did not attack straight away, and then, when they finally did so, adopted tactics that were about as unimaginative as it was possible to imagine. Thus, rather than masking Lowry-Cole's division with a small covering force and pushing down the river valleys on either side, when the leading French troops came up on 27 July their commander, *général de division* Bertrand Clausel, had them file onto the high ground that faced the British general's position to the north, thereby effectively committing Soult, who only arrived later in the day, to a frontal attack, a frontal attack, meanwhile, that he felt unable to launch until more of his men had arrived on the battlefield; there would, then, be no general attack until the next day. That said, an attempt was made to evict the troops holding the spur above Zabáldica from their eyrie by a single regiment of infantry, but the Spaniards there – the 40th Foot had not yet reached the position – stood firm, their assailants being driven off without difficulty.

Had Soult attacked straight away, it is just possible that even a head-on attack might have routed Lowry-Cole, the latter's troops being badly outnumbered and also more than somewhat demoralised after the dispiriting retreat of the past few days, as well as entirely lacking

Taupin's position viewed from the foot of the Heights of Oricaín. (Author's collection)

The bridge at Sorauren. (Author's collection)

The track by which Wellington joined Cole. (Author's collection)

in guns and cavalry. As it was, the delay played straight into Wellington's hands, not least because, by dint of a breakneck ride from his headquarters well to the north, it gave him time to reach the battlefield. Around midday on 27 July, then, accompanied only by his military secretary, Lieutenant Colonel Lord Fitzroy Somerset – the one member of his personal entourage who had a good enough horse to keep up with him – he finally reached Sorauren. Dismounting from his horse so as to use the parapet of the bridge that spanned the river in front of the parish church as an improvised desk on which to scribble a note to his trusted subordinate, Lieutenant General Sir Rowland Hill, he was suddenly accosted by a group of the inhabitants with the alarming news that at that very moment a column of French infantry was descending towards the village from the heights above. Having finished his note and handed it to Somerset to carry to safety, the British commander hastily remounted and made off for Cole's position at full speed. To reach the latter, the most direct route was a narrow track that ran diagonally up its forward slope, and so the incident acquired still more dramatic proportions. Thus, delighted to see their chief, whose absence had been much commented on, the waiting Anglo-Portuguese forces burst into loud chants of 'Nosey! Nosey! Nosey!' or 'Douro! Douro! Douro!' as appropriate, an event, of course, that did nothing to encourage their opponents, all of whom were hungry and exhausted. And all the time, of course, as Wellington knew, but Soult and Cole did not, substantial British and Portuguese reinforcements – four whole infantry divisions indeed – were en route to the scene, thereby tipping the balance against the French still further: with the enemy so close, Wellington could not have risked evacuating the position adopted by Cole even had he wanted to, but the truth was that what could have been a death-trap had in a matter of hours become an impregnable stronghold.

Grim though his prospects must increasingly have seemed, Soult had little option but to press on with his offensive, and at about midday on 28 July five of the six divisions he had brought to the field set off to attack Cole's line (the sixth, that of *général de division* Maximilien Foy, had been dispatched to contain Picton's division the previous afternoon). That said, physically getting to grips with the defenders was far from easy. Thus, the massif they occupied was separated from the high ground occupied by the French by a deep valley that inclined upwards from the village of Sorauren in the direction of the River Arga from which it was separated by a cross-ridge that linked the rival positions via a narrow saddle. Beyond said saddle, meanwhile, there was a more or less precipitous drop to the valley beyond, the only place where the going was easier being the spur south of Zabáldica held by the 40th Foot and its two Spanish fellows. Everywhere, meanwhile, the hillsides were not only very steep but also covered in thick scrub and rocky outcrops that would make keeping formation all but impossible. For all that Wellington remained badly outnumbered, then, it was as challenging an assignment as anything the French had previously faced in the Peninsular War.

If Soult's army was defeated in the battle that follows, it should, perhaps, be remembered that it was to its very great credit that it went forward at all. At all events, the French made a fine show. While the division of *général de division* Nicolas Conroux pushed down the

The slope which confronted Taupin's division as it advanced to do battle with Ross' brigade.
(Author's collection)

Ulzama valley in an attempt to get round the Anglo-Portuguese left, those of *généraux de division* Eloi Taupin, Edmé Vandermaesen and Antoine Popon de Maucune struck the defenders head on. Advancing from the valley of the River Arga, meanwhile, the division of *général de division* Thomas Mignot de Lamartinière sought to ascend the spur above Zabáldica supported by four howitzers that had been brought up from the rear (the only artillery pieces the French used in the battle, it having proved quite impossible to get any such weapons into position on the heights), one last division – that of Foy – being dispatched to contain Picton's forces in the position they had taken up around the village of Huarte. However, if all this represented a gallant effort, it was not enough. From the very first moment, indeed, things went wrong for the French. Thus, to his considerable consternation, just minutes before the attack was due to begin, Soult spotted a large force of enemy troops – the first tranche, as it transpired, of the 6th Division – pushing up the valley of the Ulzama from the south, the only possible answer to this threat being to divert the right-hand-most of his divisions – that of Conroux – to block it, the result being a fierce fight which ended with the French troops concerned being driven back into the village. Meanwhile, faced by the steepest of slopes, the divisions of Taupin, Vandermaesen and Maucune reached the defenders completely blown and in a state of great disorder. That said, they yet preformed surprisingly well. Taupin's two brigades, true, were quickly hurled back by Ross' three battalions by means of Wellington's army's standard tactic of a single volley followed by a bayonet charge, but, to their left, Vandermaesen's troops struck the weakest sector of Wellington's line, namely Campbell's Portuguese brigade, and were able, not only to establish themselves on the crest but also to put at least one regiment to flight. Encouraged by this distraction,

The precipitous slopes by which Vandermaesen's division advanced to attack Campbell's Portuguese brigade. (Author's collection)

The eastern end of the valley between the two armies looking towards the saddle where Anson defeated Maucune. (Author's collection)

meanwhile, part of Taupon's division returned to the attack, forcing back the right wing of Ross' brigade to retire and thereby considerably widening the breach in the front line.

With matters in the balance, the fight could have gone either way. Everything, then, depended on events on the French left where Maucune's division, or rather its leading brigade, had been pushing across the saddle to attack Anson and Lamartinière's trying to take the spur above Zabáldica. To deal with the latter episode, first, while the two Spanish battalions were routed, albeit not without a sharp fight, the 40th Foot held the line and eventually managed to drive off its adversaries. Completely out of sight of the main battlefield, however, the 40th's success had little impact on the battle, what mattered a great deal more being the fight on the saddle. By contrast with what happened further to the Anglo-Portuguese left, what took place here was a complete disaster for the French. Thus, come forward in style though they did, Maucune's men was assailed by a storm of fire so intense that they lost almost one third of their men in the space of 10 minutes and were quickly put to flight, whereupon their victorious assailants wheeled to their left and charged Vandermaesen's men in flank. Exhausted from their previous efforts, the latter turned and ran in their turn, the panic then proceeding to spread to Taupin's division as well. Only at Sorauren itself did the French manage to salvage a little honour, an attempt to take the village on the part of the leading elements of the 6th Division being repelled with serious losses.

So ended what, as we shall see, we must call the first battle of Sorauren. It had been a bloody day – Wellington's losses were at least 2,500 men and Soult's perhaps 1,000 more – but there was more carnage to come. In brief, unwilling to concede strategic defeat, the French commander resolved on a manoeuvre that was as foolhardy as it was desperate, the idea being that he would abandon his initial aim of raising the siege of Pamplona and instead strike north-westward in the hope of cutting Wellington off from the troops besieging San Sebastián under

A street in Sorauren: the village was fiercely defended by elements of Conroux's division in the battle of 30 July. (Author's collection)

Sir Thomas Graham, thereby forcing the latter to withdraw post-haste. Launched on 30 July, however, the operation proved even more disastrous than its predecessor. The spearhead of the French offensive – the corps commanded by *général de division* Drouet – achieved a minor tactical success when it struck the forces that had been left to cover the siege of San Sebastián at Lizaso, but the attempt to disengage from Sorauren that was the necessary corollary to the new plan had never been likely to succeed and simply heaped fresh coals on the heads of Soult's unfortunate army. Thus, perceiving what was going on, Wellington ordered his troops to attack the French, the latter for the most part disintegrating in rout, the only substantial resistance coming at Sorauren which was held by a determined rearguard until, seeing that the only alternative was surrender, the troops concerned made a desperate attempt to break out only to be caught and for the most part forced to lay down their arms. Not counting the 800 men lost at Lizaso, by the end of the day Soult's army as many as 14,000 casualties, the only thing that the French commander could now do being to pull the few troops who were left to him back to the French frontier. The Battle of the Pyrenees, then, was definitively over.

Sorauren Today

Although significantly bigger than it was in 1813, Sorauren remains a small village on the main road from Irun to Pamplona (the N121-A) while such modern development as there has been has had little impact on the battlefield (mercifully enough, for example, the by-pass was constructed on the western bank of the Ulzama rather than the eastern one). The bridge over the river on whose parapet Wellington wrote his note to Hill is unchanged as are the parish church and a number of the buildings that surround it. As for the battlefield itself, the French position is largely inaccessible, but some idea of the view presented by the Heights of Oricaín to the oncoming French troops can be obtained by taking the turning beside the church labelled the Calle el Medio and following it through the village, past the cemetery and along the side of the valley that was the epicentre of the battlefield. Having done this, the more ambitious can use the same track to push on up the hillside, but the going is very steep, while, at its higher levels, it runs through thick scrub that obscures the view and makes for frustrating walking. Far better, then, to concentrate on the Anglo-Portuguese position. To reach this, return to the village and take the second turning left walking south from the Calle el Medio (the Calle Larzábal) and follow this out of the village. Having passed the very last house, take the second right and follow this uphill to the next junction. Here the visitor should double back on themselves by taking the hairpin bend to the left, after which a steady climb will bring him or her to the crest of Wellington's position (sadly, there is no sign of the chapel which stood on the western-most summit of the heights of Oricaín at the time of the battle). From here a number of tracks lead to the saddle where Anson defeated Maucune and, beyond it, the spur defended by the 40th Foot against Lamartinière, but this last is best reached by ignoring the turning off at the Calle Larzábal and carrying straight on to a Y-junction. At this take the left fork and, ignoring the track that shortly afterwards heads downhill into the very bottom of the valley, carry straight on to the saddle. From this point the same track leads steeply downhill to the Agar valley passing beneath the 40th's spur as it does so; in general, meanwhile, the terrain in this part of the battlefield is much less changed than it is on the ridges stretching westwards from the saddle, these last being far more forested than would have been the case in 1813.

25

San Marcial

31 August 1813

Practically the last field action fought on Spanish soil in the Revolutionary and Napoleonic Wars, the second battle of San Marcial was the result of a last-minute French attempt to relieve the beleaguered fortress of San Sebastián. The first battle there was fought in August 1794 in the course of Spain's participation in the War of the First Coalition).

In brief, the plan adopted in 1813 by *maréchal* Jean-de-Dieu Soult, who still held the command of all the imperial forces in the western Pyrenees in spite of the failure of the counter-offensive that had been quashed the previous month at Sorauren, was to smash through the Spanish forces that overlooked the main road to San Sebastián from their position atop the towering heights of San Marcial with four divisions, whilst three other divisions crossed the river Bidásoa (which marks the frontier) further inland at Salaín, and broke through the mixed force of British, Portuguese and Spanish infantry that linked the position at San Marcial with that held by the Light Division further south beyond the village of Vera. In theory, this was a good plan, but the morale of Soult's forces was very low in the wake of Sorauren, artillery support all but absent for want of forage with which to feed the gun teams, food so lacking as to be almost non-existent, the French troops too few in numbers and too spread out to deliver a decisive blow at any point, and the terrain very much in favour of the defence. So steep, indeed, are the slopes of the heights occupied by the Spaniards that it is difficult to see how they could have been ascended by formed troops at all, this being all the more the case as they were also covered with thick brushwood; as for the use of cavalry, it was quite unthinkable. Even to reach the defenders, meanwhile, Soult's men had to throw a series of pontoon bridges across the fast-flowing Bidásoa. On top of all this, the Allied forces had copious reserves – behind San Marcial were two full divisions of British infantry – while the Spanish troops in the front line included many of the men who had done well at Vitoria and were commanded by *Teniente-General* Manuel Freyre de Andrade, an officer who was perhaps the most competent Spanish generals of the Peninsular War.

Given all that has been outlined in the previous paragraph, it is scarcely to be wondered at that, although his troops succeeded in getting across the river when they went into action at dawn on 31 August, Soult was unsuccessful. It has to be said, however, that this was not for want of trying on the part of his men. Scrambling up the steep slopes that led to the Spanish positions and driving the defending skirmishers before them, the divisions of *généraux de*

The view north from the summit of the heights of San Marcial: the lofty nature of the Spanish position remains extremely striking. (Author's collection)

Another view of the slopes of San Marcial looking out over the valley of the Bidásoa; note the brushwood that so hampered the French advance. (Author's collection)

The summit of San Marcial; note the potential for making use of a reverse slope though it is unclear whether Freyre ever attempted to take advantage of this feature of the position. (Author's collection)

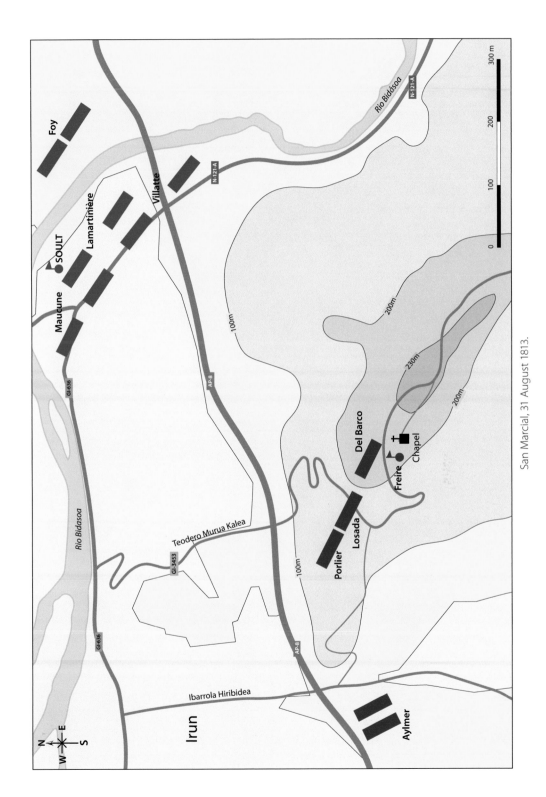

San Marcial, 31 August 1813.

281

The chapel atop the heights of San Marcial from which Freyre directed the battle. (Author's collection)

division Popon de Maucune, Thomas Mignot de Lamartinière and Eugène Villatte managed to get to within musket shot of the summit, only to be driven back to the foot of the heights by a single massive volley followed by a bayonet charge (a tactic seemingly picked up from Wellington's army). This was scarcely a surprise, for the French were so blown and in such disorder when they came to within striking distance of the Spaniards that they were desperately vulnerable to a counter-attack, even when it was one delivered by troops who could be considered inferior to them. Nothing loathe, however, the French infantry tried again, only for their efforts to meet with the same result as before and Lamartinière to be mortally wounded by a musket ball. There followed the crisis of the battle. Unbelievably enough, completely unaided by Soult though they were – far from risking his life in the hope of encouraging his men, the *maréchal* appears to have remained far in the rear throughout – the three French divisional commanders managed to rally the troops for a second time and get them on the move once more at which the Spaniards understandably started to waver. Much alarmed, Freyre responded by sending an officer to beg Wellington for help, but, sensing perhaps that the situation was not nearly so bad as was reported and, further, that, even if the Spaniards did break, the situation was easily repairable, the British general refused to dispatch the troops that had been asked for, instead sending the aide concerned back with a message to the effect that the battle was all but won and that it would therefore be better for the Spaniards to keep the glory for themselves. And so it transpired: with the aid of his divisional commanders, Freyre was able to steady his troops and drive the French back down into the valley in much the same way as before. Beaten for a third time and by now fighting in a torrential downpour that rendered the slopes of San Marcial even muddier and more slippery than before, the latter could take no more and their whole array broke and ran, fleeing back across the now increasingly swollen river into France. Matters having gone equally awry at Salaín, where, having initially pushed back the defenders, the French abandoned their advance when Anglo-Portuguese forces who had been stationed further south began to threaten their left flank and rear. Other than the separate action that took place during the following night at Vera (see Chapter 26), the battle was over.

To put it mildly, there is a certain irony about this day of bloodshed (French losses amounted to nearly 4,000 dead and wounded and their Allied counterparts to some 2,500). Thus, at the very time that the French had been ascending the slopes of San Marcial for the first time, Wellington had launched his final assault on San Sebastián. Fiercely contested though this was, by the early afternoon the assault troops had fought their way over the great breach that had been blown in the walls, whereupon, driven wild by their losses, convinced that a town that was stormed was a town that was theirs for the sacking and, finally, under a strong impression (with some justice: of all the places the French occupied, San Sebastián was for various reasons the one where support for the Napoleonic invasion was at its strongest) that the inhabitants were collaborators who had in some instances actually fought alongside their opponents, they promptly engaged in a round of excesses even worse that seen at Badajoz. Just to add to the horror, meanwhile, in the course of the afternoon, a great conflagration broke out that reduced almost the entire place to ashes, the result being a bitter controversy that continues to dog the memorialisation of the assault to this day.

A country lane ascending the heights from the direction of the French frontier. (Author's collection)

San Marcial Today

Viewed from afar, the heights of San Marcial are easily distinguishable by the small white chapel of that name that crowns their highest point and was presumably commandeered by Freyre as his headquarters. To reach them, assuming that the visitor has arrived in the town by car on the Autopista del Cantábrico (the main highway from San Sebastián, Vitoria and ultimately Madrid), immediately prior to the French frontier, leave the motorway and turn north onto the N121-A, signposted Behobie. At the roundabout, take the third exit (the GI-636) and proceed westwards parallel to the river. After approximately one mile, turn left onto José María Franco Kalea and then take the first right (Teodoro Murua Kalea). Follow this (very winding) road until it reaches a roundabout at which point go straight on, on the GI-3453. After crossing over the Autopista del Cantábrico, this ascends the northern face of the heights by a series of hair-pin bends and eventually brings the visitor out on the summit near the chapel mentioned above; today the ground is heavily forested, but at the time of the battle it would have been cloaked by scrub alone, it in fact being up the slope criss-crossed by the road that the French attacked. At the summit there is ample parking, while a gentle stroll a little further along the country lane into which the GI-3453 now tails out will bring the visitor to an excellent vantage point. The views will be found to be most impressive, while it is difficult not to marvel at the fact that the soldiers of Maucune, Lamartinière and Villatte succeeded getting to grips with the defenders once, let alone three times. Finally, there is a monument to the fallen at the chapel.

Having visited the battlefield of San Marcial, if they have not done so already, many visitors will presumably travel on to see San Sebastián, the easiest way to do this being to head back down the GI-3453, take the turning to the left after the first set of bends and turn right at the T-junction at the foot of the slope onto the Kalea Ibarrola Hiribidea, after which it is a short drive back to the GI-636. On the whole, however, it has to be said that San Sebastián is a disappointing experience for the battlefield tourist. While the city is delightful, most of its Napoleonic heritage has long since vanished. Aside from a fragment of the land wall preserved, incongruously enough, in an underground car-park of a shopping mall miscalled La Bretxa ('The Breach'; this last was rather situated round the south-eastern corner of the defences along the stretch of ramparts facing the river) and the citadel that tops the rocky promontory that overlooks the town known as Monte Urgel, there is little to see of the defences. The mouth of the river – an area that played a crucial part in the assault – has been completely remodelled long-since; and almost nothing remains of the town as it existed in 1813, the only exceptions being the parish church of San Vicente and a narrow thoroughfare that runs beside it known as the Calle 31 de Agosto. More rewarding, then, is the little port of Pasages, situated on the coast mid-way between San Sebastián and Irun, this served Wellington as an important base throughout the autumn and winter of 1813 and will be found to be quite atmospheric.

26

Vera de Bidásoa

31 August–1 September 1813

As we have seen in the previous chapter, on 31 August 1813 *maréchal* Jean-de-Dieu Soult made one last attempt to relieve the doomed fortress of San Sebastián. In this, of course, he did not succeed: not only was the fortress stormed that same day, but the main French column was beaten off with heavy losses by elements of the Spanish 4th Army at the Battle of San Marcial. However, the men who ascended the precipitous slopes on which the Spaniards were arrayed were far from being the only French troops in action that day. Of the seven French divisions engaged in the offensive, only the three that formed the corps of *général de division* Honoré Reille attacked the Spaniards head-on. As for the rest – the corps of *général de division* Bertrand Clausel – other than one division that was held back to act as a flank-guard, these were sent across the river via a number of fords a few miles upstream. One division was held back to guard Clausel's flank from a possible attack on the part of the Light Division, this being stationed on the right bank of the river immediately to the south of Vera.

Pushing up the equally steep hillsides that confronted them, the bulk Clausel's forces endeavoured to fulfil their allotted role of rolling up the Spanish right flank, only very soon to run into Anglo-Portuguese forces which had been marched south to forestall just such a move. Driven back by sheer force of numbers, the leading brigade of these last, that of Major General William Inglis, retired on its supports, but Clausel elected to suspend his advance until such time as he received word that Reille's attack had succeeded. By late afternoon, however, it was clear that the Spaniards had held firm with the result he ordered the three divisions that had crossed the river – those of Edmé Vandermaesen, Eloi Taupin and Jean Darmagnac – to retire whence they had come. This, however, proved easier said than done. In the course of the day, the heavens had opened and unleashed a downpour so extreme that the Bidásoa was soon transformed into a raging torrent. Getting to the riverbank just in time, the leading brigades of Taupin and Darmagnac managed to struggle across to the right bank, but the remainder of the column was left with no option but to head further south and get across the river by means of the narrow bridge that spanned it at Vera. Thus was set the scene for an action as fierce, and, indeed, heroic, as any in the history of the Peninsular War.

Situated in an area of water meadows on the right bank of the Bidásoa, the straggling village of Vera was a key point in Wellington's line. Unfortunately, however, it was not in safe hands. Thus, if the sector was held by the famous Light Division, the latter was under the temporary command of Major General John Skerret, an officer who had for various

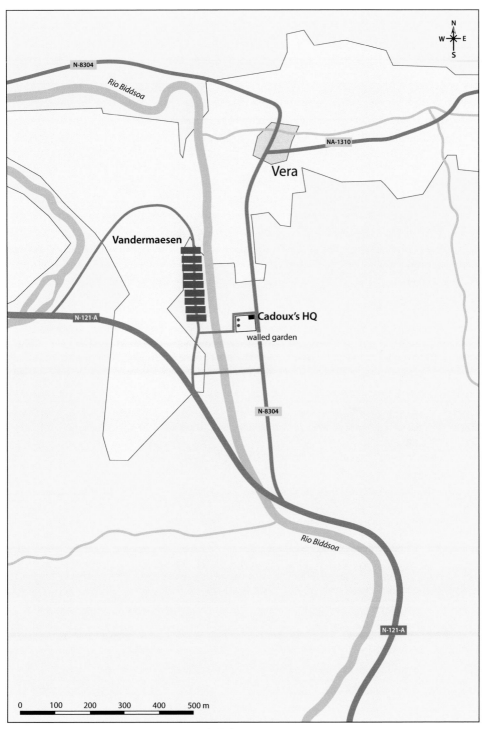

Vera de Bidásoa, 31 August.

reasons thus far seen little action in the Peninsular War and was by all accounts but little competent. Preferring, then, to keep his men in a strong defensive position on the heights of Sant Bárbara some little distance further to the south, the only troops Skerrett positioned in Vera itself was a single company of the 2/95th Regiment under a Captain Daniel Cadoux, a force composed of just 60 men and four officers that was now menaced by around 5,000 veteran soldiers desperate to escape encirclement and make their way back to France.

An interesting character, Cadoux was of French descent and came from the Buckinghamshire town of Aylesbury, while he had previously seen service at Barrosa and in the campaign of Vitoria. Greatly fearing for his isolated men, he had therefore kept the latter grouped around a substantial stone house at the eastern end of the bridge which offered an excellent field of fire as far as the water-meadows were concerned, the idea presumably being that, if the French were to launch a sudden attack on the area, he and his command could make their escape across the river and hold the crossing from the opposite bank, to which end the bridge had been barricaded at its further end. Now, however, Cadoux was facing an attack from completely the opposite direction to the one that he expected, his troubles being augmented still further by the fact that, sheltered by the darkness and the pouring rain, the first elements of the retreating French column were able to storm the barricade that blocked their way and bayonet the two unfortunate sentries posted there before the riflemen woke up to their danger. That said, things were not quite as bad as they appeared, Thus, the bridge was so narrow that it was passable by units in column of route no more than three or four men wide. As if this was not bad enough, once even company-sized units had got

The bridge at Vera viewed from the south; the French were attempting to cross the river from left to right. In the distance, meanwhile, can be seen the hills over which they fought earlier in the day. (Author's collection)

The house used by Cadoux as his headquarters; the lane leading to the bridge is just to its right.
(Author's collection)

The east bank of the Bidásoa viewed from the bridge blocked by Cadoux. To reach safety the French
column had to defile along the bank and then turn right, all the time, of course, under heavy fire.
(Author's collection)

across, there was no room for them to deploy, for, no sooner had the road reached the far bank than it made a right-angled turn to the left and, still extremely narrow, running along the very edge of the riverbank for perhaps 100 yards before taking an equally sharp turn to the right and ran up to the level of the village, though the main part of this was in fact grouped around a road junction a few hundred yards downstream. For the whole distance from the bridge to the water-meadows, meanwhile, the bridge was lined by the high stone wall of the property garrisoned by Cadoux, this being impossible to cross without scaling ladders. Finally, as for the house itself, three storeys high, this stood at the very spot that the road emerged at the edge of the meadows. In short, Cadoux enjoyed as good a position as he could possibly hope for, and all the more so as the rest of the Light Division was no more than two miles away to the south-east.

Not surprisingly, then, the French had no sooner sought to exploit their initial success than they ran into serious trouble. Packed together on the bridge, even in the dark their assault troops offered an easy target for the skilled riflemen of the 95th. In consequence, the bridge was soon clogged with dead and wounded Frenchmen, the ranks of these unfortunates soon being joined by Vandermaesen, who had taken command of the stranded column and was now shot dead as he forced his way into the mêlée in a desperate attempt to speed up the pace of the attack.

By all right, the combat should have ended in a significant British victory, for Skerrett had only to march to the sound of the anything-but-distant guns to block the French escape route altogether, something that a message dispatched to his headquarters by Cadoux the moment the alarm was raised in fact begged him to do forthwith. Yet Skerrett moved not an inch, and, not just that, but sent the unfortunate captain a message ordering him to retire. Realising that to do so would be to guarantee the death or capture of much of his small command, Cadoux ignored Skerrett's order and held the position until daylight. With the coming of dawn, however, the balance swung dramatically in favour of the French who were now able to swamp the British position with musket fire from across the river and even to bring up a pair of mule-borne artillery pieces. Confronted by a second message from Skerrett to withdraw, Cadoux therefore realised that he had no option but to comply, only for this manoeuvre to produce precisely the result he feared, many of his men being cut down as they made their way to safety and Cadoux himself shot dead as he mounted his horse preparatory to getting away. No-one appears to have been with him when he fell, but his last moments cannot have been happy ones, for, just as his men began to pull back, an additional company of riflemen appeared on the meadows together with a second one of Portuguese *caçadores*, the commander of the Light Division having belatedly woken up to his responsibilities. Had the men concerned been sent down to help defend the bridge rather than just to cover the retreat of the defenders, things might have been very different, but, as it was, the French got clear away, brushing aside Skerret's feeble gesture and rapidly disappearing in the direction of the frontier.

Thus ended the combat of Vera. If this can be adjudged a French victory, it was costly in the extreme. Including Vandermaesen, 231 Frenchmen had been killed or wounded for the loss of Cadoux and 16 rank and file dead and three other officers and 39 men wounded, two other men being reported as missing, a loss rate of almost 100 per cent (there were also an appreciable number of casualties – some 34 – in the two companies sent to cover the retreat. That said, the French troops who might so easily have been

The lane leading to the village of Vera from the riverbank; Cadoux's house is on the right.
(Author's collection)

trapped on the banks of the Bidásoa were able to make their way back across the frontier without further let or hindrance, going on to oppose Wellington in such battles as the Nivelle, the Nive, Orthez and Toulouse. A good day for the Peninsular army it most certainly was not.

Vera Today

A pleasant town situated in the foothills of the Pyrenees, Vera (strictly-speaking Vera de Bidásoa) lies just off the N121-a, this being the main highway from Irun to Pamplona. To reach Cadoux's bridge, turn off the highway onto the NA-8304 (signposted Vera) and follow this through the village. On the far side head south until a roundabout is reached in the centre of a modern industrial estate. At said roundabout, turn right and cross the river via the modern bridge. From here it is a short walk to the original crossing where the general layout of the terrain will be found to be exactly the same as it was in 1813. As for the house which Cadoux used as his headquarters, this is situated at the end of the lane leading up from the river bank. Finally, on the bridge itself is a small monument to Cadoux, until the bicentenary of 1808-1814 one of but a tiny handful of monuments specifically commemorating the sacrifice made by the soldiers of the British army, at least 40,000 of whom were killed or died of wounds or disease in Spain, Portugal and southern France between 1808 and 1814.

27

The Nive

9–13 December 1813

Many British historians have always insisted on interpreting the Peninsular War as a seamless struggle that raged continuously from May 1808 till April 1814. As William Napier explicitly recognised when he gave his great narrative the title of *A History of the War in the Peninsula and the South of France,* however, this view is has always been open to question. Thus, while desultory fighting did continue in Spain until the fall of Napoleon, so far as Wellington's army is concerned the conflict really came to an end in October 1813 when it crossed the River Bidásoa and entered France. This is not, of course, to say that the Anglo-Portuguese saw no fighting thereafter – on the contrary, there were four major battles, a siege and many minor actions still to come – but the campaigns concerned took place in a strategic and geographical context that was very different, the author therefore preferring to see them as part and parcel of the bitter struggle that led to the abdication of the Emperor on 6 April 1814. If only because many readers would expect a work on battles and battlefields of the Peninsular War to reach into the green fields of France rather than halting at the Pyrenees, at least some gesture will be made in this direction, in which respect we will begin with the Battle of the River Nive. That said, however, the concession is made with gritted teeth: along with the battles at the River Nivelle, Orthez and Toulouse, the Nive was really part of a new war.

Setting all this aside, to understand what happened in what was certainly a very bloody battle that caused Wellington some moments of real concern, we must return to the situation that pertained in the wake of the fall of San Sebastián on 31 August 1813. Much as had been the case when the Russian army reached the Polish border in December 1812, the great question of the moment was whether the British commander should halt or push on into France. At least initially, his preference was very much the former – not only was Cassagne still holding out in Pamplona (he did not, in fact, surrender until 31 October), but, bedevilled by disputes with regard to the extent of Wellington's authority as commander-in-chief of the Spanish army and growing British dissatisfaction with the constitution promulgated at Cadiz in 1812, relations with the Spaniards were at a low ebb – but in the end diplomatic considerations outweighed these concerns, and on 7 October thousands of British, Portuguese and Spanish troops forded the estuary of the Bidásoa and established themselves in a substantial bridgehead. Wellington being unwilling to advance any further until such time as he could be certain that Napoleon could not turn on him with the full might

Part of the original ramparts of Bayonne; though not unimpressive, the defences were overlooked by higher ground and bereft of any outworks, Soult making good these deficiencies by constructing extensive field fortifications in the countryside beyond the walls. (Author's collection)

of the *grande armée,* there followed another pause in operations, but at length news arrived of the Emperor's cataclysmic defeat at Leipzig. Much reassured, the British commander promptly resumed his advance, the result being that on 10 November his army launched a general attack on the defensive line that *maréchal* Jean-de-Dieu Soult had been building just inside the frontier behind the River Nivelle. Strong though the French position was, there was no stopping the Anglo-Portuguese army and by the end of the day their defeated opponents were streaming away in the direction of Bayonne, the great fortress that guarded the main road that led to Bordeaux and, at length, Paris and which had since Vitoria been strengthened by the construction of massive entrenched camps that covered the whole of the southern approaches with a belt of impenetrable fortifications.

In the wake of the French defeat at the Nivelle, on 9 December Wellington pushed forward once more, his objective this time being to close up on the defences of Bayonne and, with them, the line of River Adour. In itself, there was nothing wrong with this plan, but it did mean that the Anglo-Portuguese army would necessarily be split in two, for the River Adour was joined at Bayonne by a fast-flowing tributary known as the River Nive that rose in the Pyrenees and could only be crossed by a number of fords, Soult having taken care to demolish all the bridges except the three within the walls of the city itself. That this opened the way to a situation that was potentially very difficult was clear enough, for in theory there would be nothing preventing him from massing his entire force against one wing or the other of Wellington's army and thereby achieving a crushing local superiority, but provision was made for this eventuality by throwing a ponton bridge across the Nive close to Bayonne and repairing one of the crossings that had been blown up by Soult some miles upstream at the little town of Ustaritz, it being assumed, meanwhile, that, Portuguese and British alike, Wellington's troops were good enough to stand firm against heavy odds for long enough for

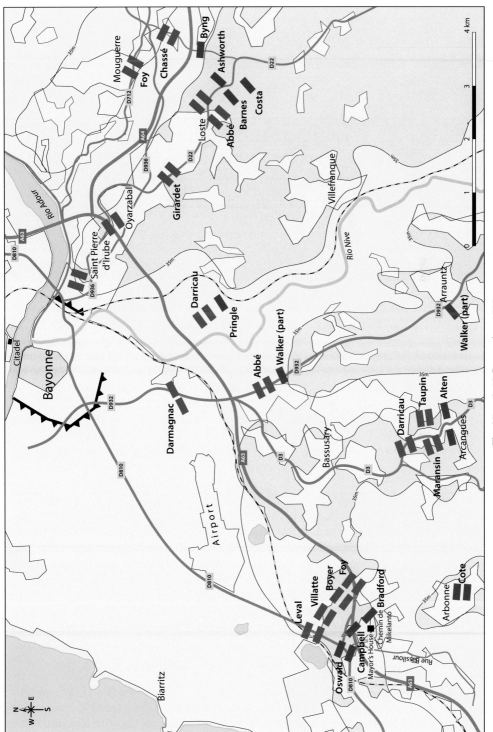

The Nive, 9–13 December 1813.

The River Nive near its confluence with the River Adour at Bayonne; it was by means of bridges such as the one shown that Soult was able to switch his forces between the two battlefields with such ease. (Author's collection)

help to reach them from elsewhere. All then seemed well, then, and all the more so as the French had made no attempt to contest the passage of the Nive and fallen back on Bayonne without a fight whilst at the same time having generally put up a rather uninspiring show at the Nivelle.

Yet all was not well. As we have seen, Soult was a master of the sudden counterattack and, in fact, had merely been biding his time. On the morning of 10 December, much aided by the fact that it had been a night of pouring rain, a large force of French troops sallied forth from the fortifications and crashed into the leading elements of the Anglo-Portuguese forces who had occupied the territory on the left bank of the Nive. As if being taken completely by surprise was not bad enough, meanwhile, the troops concerned were anything but at full strength, for their commander, the newly arrived Lieutenant General Sir John Hope, an officer who had distinguished himself in the battle of La Coruña in 1808, but had seen no action since, had been so certain that Soult would remain on the defensive that at the close of the previous day he had ordered half his force – to be precise, the 1st and 5th Divisions and the independent British infantry brigade of Major General Matthew Whitworth-Aylmer, Lord Aylmer – to fall back to their starting points at the little port of Saint-Jean-de-Luz and the village of Guétary so that least some of his men could take shelter from the dreadful weather. Indeed, it has to be said that Hope's dispositions were in general very poor indeed, the only troops in immediate support of the pickets posted to watch the fortress – two brigades of Portuguese infantry and, behind them, the Light and 7th Divisions – being far too far to the rear, the only factor in favour of the defenders being that the ground between the Adour and the Nive was a tangle of lakes, woods and ravines which was only crossed by two highways, one of them the main road to Saint-Jean-de-Luz and the Spanish frontier and the other a less important thoroughfare to Ustaritz and, ultimately,

The church at Arcangues. (Author's collection)

Saint-Jean-Pied-du-Port, that roughly paralleled the course of the Nive and was in the first instance the main axis of the French advance, Soult's aim being, of course to separate Hope's command from the troops on the other side of the Nive (and, indeed, Wellington, the latter having elected to move up with the right wing of his forces) and then to defeat it in detail.

As we shall see, the difficult terrain over which the battle was fought was eventually to prove decisive, but in the short term there was nothing that could put the situation to rights. Heavily outnumbered, the Allied troops in the path of the French onslaught were driven back in great disorder with the loss of many prisoners; it is not going too far, indeed, to admit that that there was much panic, large numbers of the men concerned simply taking to their heels as fast as their feet could carry them. What saved Hope from complete disaster, however, was the facts, first, that the extremely congested terrain and narrow lines of approach meant that comparatively few of the enormous forces available to Soult – eight infantry divisions together with a division of cavalry – could be got into action at any given time, and, second, that the road to Saint-Jean-de-Luz was blocked at the village of Urdains by a brigade of the 7th Division that was stationed in such a manner that its position could not possibly be forced. Thus, thwarted, at the cost of much precious time, Soult got some of the many troops waiting in the rear to ascend the low hills that separated the two highways in the hope that they could force a way through by means of a country lane that forked off the Saint-Jean-de Luz road and ran more-or-less due south in the direction of the village of Arcangues. Yet this, too, proved equally hopeless for the high ground on which said village stood was held in strength by the Light Division, the main position of which ran along a hedged lane flanked at one end by the village church and, at the other, by a substantial chateau. An initial attack on the part of a single battalion having been shot to pieces, the commander of the French assault, *général de division* Bertrand Clausel, brought up two batteries of artillery to soften up the defenders only for the gun crews to be shot down in droves by the defenders of the village church, these last being not only each and every one of

The interior of the parish church at Arcangues; note the galleries lining the walls that allowed the garrison to pour such exceptionally heavy fire on their assailants. (Author's collection)

The position reached by the French at Arcangues viewed from the vicinity of the parish church. (Author's collection)

them armed with rifles rather than muskets – all of them were members of the famous '95th Rifles' – but, the church being built at right angles to the French line of advance, also gifted with a firing position that allowed three ranks of men to fire on the enemy simultaneously (in brief, one line of men could operate from the shelter of the churchyard wall, a second from the windows of the body of the church and the third from those of the clerestory above). Not surprisingly, then, as at Urdains, the fighting here soon degenerated into a mere fusillade that did little harm to either side.

All this might have been it for the day had it not been for events on the French right flank. Thus, while it was intended that the main effort should be made against Hope's right, Soult had also dispatched two divisions to push along the line of the highway to the Spanish frontier in the hope that this would prevent Hope from reinforcing the troops holding the ground closer to the Nive. Possessed of rather more room to manoeuvre than their comrades further east, the attackers made rather better progress, but in the end they, too were brought to a halt at the hamlet of Barrouillet, where a substantial house belonging to the mayor was had been hastily pressed into service as a strong-point by Hope. Very soon a fierce battle raging round the buildings, Soult's response to this being to reinforce the units who had led the attack with more and more men from his reserves. For a while, the situation was touch-and-go – indeed, at one point, Hope himself was nearly captured – but by this time the men the British commander had sent to the rear the night before were hastening on to the field, the result being that the combat eventually died down, the French having no option but to fall back in the direction of Bayonne.

The mayor's house at Barrouillet: defended with great courage by Portuguese troops, it withstood repeated French assaults. (Author's collection)

A typical view of the scrub that cloaked much of Mantaxurri. (Author's collection)

Thus ended a bloody day which redounded a great deal to the credit of the divisional, brigade and company commanders of the units engaged therein, and not at all to that of Hope who, for all the courage that he displayed on the field, had been shown up as being, at best, imprudent, if not downright incompetent. That said, the important thing was that Soult's grand design had been frustrated, while the same evening produced an added benefit in the form of the desertion of three battalions of troops drawn from various states of the Confederation of the Rhine which had joined the Allies in the wake of the Battle of Leipzig, an event that led in turn to the disarmament of a further 3,000 German troops. Yet the *maréchal* was not finished yet. On the contrary, after two days of inconclusive skirmishing, notable chiefly for the further proofs they gave of Hope's incapacity, on the night of 12 December he pulled the bulk of his men back into Bayonne and sent them back across the River Nive to attack Wellington's right flank.

Once again disaster threatened and all the more so as the same night saw torrential rain that so swelled the Nive that the pontoon bridge that had been erected to link together the two halves of the Anglo-Portuguese army was swept away. There followed a furious battle in which the French initially made much progress, and all the more so given that, unlike on 10 December, the ground was such that it allowed Soult to deploy a 'grand battery' of some 24 field pieces that proceeded to mount a heavy bombardment of the Anglo-Portuguese lines, but the commander facing them on this occasion was not the brave but mediocre Hope, but rather the solid and reliable Sir Rowland Hill, the result being that the troops who faced the French offensive were neither taken by surprise nor caught spread out over an area of ground as much as three miles wide and 10 miles deep. Nor was their only advantage the fact that they were drawn up in battle-array: on the contrary, also important was the fact that they occupied excellent hill-top positions that could only be attacked head-on, and

The summit of the Mantaxurri. (Author's collection)

The road that formed the axis of Soult's attack on 13 December looking south towards the summit of Mantaxurri. (Author's collection)

even then only on a narrow front, on account of the fact that the valleys between them were blocked by extensive millponds. Hill, true enough, had only two divisions – some 14,000 men – to six on the side of Soult, but, exactly as had been the case on 9 December, there were enormous difficulties in getting most of the men concerned into positions from which they could engage the Anglo-Portuguese: as we shall see, indeed, in the end it was this that brought the French to grief.

This, however, is to anticipate the course of events. Let us first, then, look at the course of the battle in a little more detail. To summarise, Hill's forces were deployed athwart the main road from Bayonne to Saint-Jean-Pied-du-Port which made its way up on to the rolling hills that separated the Nive from the Adour by means of a spur that was then known as Haut Saint-Pierre but is now rather called Mantaxurri. On either side of this feature and cut off from it by deep valleys that had, as we have seen been dammed to serve as millponds, meanwhile, were two other ridges, both of which were ascended from the north by cart tracks, the one on the left being marked by a chateau and the one on the right by the village of Mouguerre. No sooner had firing begun than the French set off to climb all three spurs, with a full division – that of the tough and experienced Jean Abbé – tackling the one in the middle, and the ones on either side being assigned single brigades only. Of the three thrusts, the most important was obviously the one in the centre and the men concerned pushed forward with some vigour, making use of dense clouds of skirmishers rather than close-order columns of attack. In the face of this attack, the defenders concerned – initially the Portuguese brigade of *Brigadiero* Charles Ashworth – for some time held firm but at length the pressure of numbers began to tell while the arrant cowardice displayed by the commander of an infantry battalion sent to reinforce the line led to a widespread retrograde movement that allowed the French virtually to gain the summit. Nor was this the limit to the French success, the troops on the left having succeeded in taking the village of Vieux Mougerre (on the other flank, by contrast, the attack on the spur crowned by the chateau had quickly petered out).

By now the reinforcements that had immediately been sent to Hill by Wellington (who had as chance would have it, once again been caught on the wrong side of the Nive) were getting close to the scene of the fighting, but a convulsive effort on the part of Soult might yet have gained him at least a partial victory. However, such was the congestion in the French rear that the necessary reinforcements could not be brought forward quickly enough, while there is, too, some suggestion that Soult lost his nerve at the crucial moment. With the French troops in the front line increasingly exhausted, they were wide open to a counterattack that, Hill being the highly proficient commander that he was, was not long in coming. Behind the lines, then, he had had ready and waiting an entire division of Portuguese infantry throughout, and these troops now surged forward in style, the disordered French promptly giving way and fleeing for the safety of Bayonne. As for the breaking of the pontoon bridge, meanwhile, it turned out to have had no effect whatsoever: delayed though the reinforcements sent to Hill most certainly were, in the event the French were driven off before any of the men concerned could get to grips with the enemy.

With the repulse of this second attack, Soult's bolt was well and truly shot, for his men were as exhausted as they were demoralised and clearly incapable of further offensive action, their losses in killed, wounded and prisoners coming to nearly 6,000 men, to which must be added the 4,500 German troops who had either crossed the lines or been disarmed and sent

The northwestern extremity of the ridge that anchored the British right flank. Cleared by the French without difficulty when the commander of the 3rd Foot panicked and evacuated the lower ground in the middle distance, it witnessed fierce fighting in the closing moments of the battle. (Author's collection)

to the rear. At a little over 5,000 men, Wellington's casualties had been far from insignificant, but the prize had been very great, for there was now no chance of any further French counter-offensives, all that Soult could hope to do being to conserve Bayonne and hold the line of the Pyrenees and even that not for very long.

The Nive Today

Heavily encroached on though they are by the growth of Bayonne and the construction of new motorways, the two battlefields associated with the fighting of 9–13 December 1813 are certainly worth a visit, but they are far from easy to navigate as well as for the most part set in terrain which is, to put it mildly, very cluttered by comparison with the vast open spaces of, say, Medina de Río Seco or Salamanca. Nor does it help that a number of the villages that dot them have either changed their names or been swallowed up by more modern developments. To begin with the assault on Hope, the key sites are clearly Arcangues and Barrouillet. Of these, the former does not present too many problems for the visitor, for all that is required is to drive south from the outskirts of Bayonne on the D932 (signposted Ustaritz); fork right on the D3 (signposted Bassussary) at the junction just south of the motorway; and finally, at the roundabout where the D755 bifurcates from the D3, take the first right (the Chemin de Jaureguiborda). The church will then be found a few hundred yards along on the left. There is a small monument to the fallen in the churchyard, but the most interesting thing by far about the church is the galleries which line the walls, a number of the balustrades being deeply scarred by marks which are attributed to riflemen chopping meat or vegetables on them with their sword bayonets. To reach the mayor's house at Barrouillet (a name that has now disappeared from the map), meanwhile, take the D810

The monument to the French army on the ridge near Vieux Mouguerre. (Author's collection)

southwest from Bayonne (signposted Saint-Jean-de-Luz) and, having passed the motorway junction, turn left on the Rue Bassilour; at the roundabout just beyond said motorway, take the second exit and then the first left (the Chemin de Mikelanto), after which the mayor's house will be found after approximately half a mile at the end of the first turning to the left: please be advised, however, that the grounds are private and should not be entered without the permission of the owners. Within them, however, are the carefully tended grave of three officers of the Guards who died in the course of the struggle.

Lamentably, the battlefield of 13 December is not much easier to explore. As a starting point, the visitor should take the D712 from the eastern outskirts of Bayonne and, after passing through the suburban village of Basladia, this ascends the ridge that marked the Anglo-Portuguese right flank, crowned though it is by the monument erected to *maréchal*

The graves of Captain and Lieutenant Colonel Samuel Martin and Lieutenants and Captains Charles Thomson and Henry Watson in the grounds of the mayor's house at Barrouillet. Note the roundshot which, according to the owners, was dug up in the course of the construction of the tennis court visible in the background. (Author's collection)

Soult and his army, a spot which offers extensive views of the Mantaxurri ridge across the valley to the south-west. What is more problematic is finding the area where Hill checked Abbé's attack as much of it is now covered by up-market housing estates. That said, there are a few places where sufficient open country remains to be able to gain some idea of what the field was like. To reach the scene, take the D635 from the southern outskirts of Bayonne to the roundabout where it ends in the suburb of Oyarzabal and from here continue south on the D22 to the locality of Mendixta, the main part of the fighting having taken place between this place and the district slightly further along the road known as Loste.

Finally, there is the city of Bayonne itself. A pleasant place, the most tangible reminder of its past are its ramparts, considerable parts of which have survived as the central feature of a beautiful public park. However, more emotive still is the story that pertains to the suburb of La Negresse. For obvious reasons, the name has in recent years become the subject of bitter public controversy, but in many ways this is a great pity, for 'la negresse' was seemingly a real person, a black woman from Haiti who married a French soldier in the course of Napoleon's doomed attempt to regain the colony of Sante Domingue, came back to France with him as a *vivandière* and, probably in the wake of the Battle of Vitoria, established a wayside tavern at a spot on the road to the Spanish frontier a mile or two outside Bayonne.

Further Reading

I. Robertson, *Wellington Invades France: the Final Phase of the Peninsular War, 1813-1814* (London: Greenhill Books, 2003)

N. Lipscombe, *Bayonne and Toulouse, 1813-1814: Napoleon Invades France* (Oxford: Osprey, 2014)

28

Bayonne

14 April 1814

There are few battles sadder than those fought after the wars of which they form a part have been ended by a peace settlement, something that was, alas, quite common in the days when news could usually travel no fast than a ship could sail or a horse could gallop. However, if there is one type of battle that is sadder still, it is one that is embarked upon by a commander who knows that hostilities have come to a close, this being, alas, exactly what transpired at Bayonne on 14 April 1814. In brief, by far the most important fortress in south-west France, the city had to be taken or at least neutralised before Wellington could advance any further into France than he had done in the wake of his having breached the line of the Pyrenees by means of his victory at the Battle of the Nivelle in November of the previous year. In consequence, the British commander resolved on besieging it at the outset of the offensive he was intending to launch in conjunction with the invasion of France by the forces of Austria, Prussia and Russia that had been in train since the end of December and was currently producing a series of desperate battles in Champagne. To do this, however, he had first to drive away the field army of *maréchal* Jean-de-Dieu Soult which still numbered some 36,000 men in spite of having the *maréchal* having had to send substantial reinforcements to the increasingly beleaguered Napoleon; otherwise the French might seek to attack his line of communications and to cut him off from his current base at Saint-Jean-de-Luz. Due to heavy rain, operations were delayed much later than the Allied commanders in the north would have liked, and it was therefore not until 14 February that the Anglo-Portuguese army sallied forth from its cantonments and took the field once more. Badly outnumbered, Soult could do nothing to stop the advance of his opponents and therefore fell back to the line of the River Gave d'Oloron, a position far enough to the east to ensure that Wellington could operate against Bayonne without any fear of his French opponent creating difficulties.

By the beginning of the last week of February, then, all was ready to set about the siege of Bayonne. Protected by formidable defences, as we have seen, this sat on the left bank of the River Adour at the spot where it was joined by the latter's tributary, the River Nive. Across the river, meanwhile, a suburb – that of Saint Espirit – had spread up the steep hill by which, having crossed the Adour by means of an impressive stone bridge, the highway to Bordeaux and, ultimately, Paris, climbed the bluffs that overlooked the river, the summit of said bluffs being occupied by a massive citadel whose guns completely commanded the city together with, but a few hundred yards to the east of the latter's walls, the suburban village of Saint

The heights on the right bank of the Adour which mark the site of the citadel of Bayonne; cloaked by thick woodland, entrance is strictly *interdit*. (Author's collection)

Pierre. In short, the situation of Bayonne was not unlike that of Badajoz, and Wellington decided that it therefore made sense to revert to his original plan for the capture of the latter on the premise that, if the city should fall, the citadel would be able to continue to hold out, whereas, should it rather be the citadel that was taken first, its substantial firepower would render the city untenable. So far, so good, but this in turn meant that the Anglo-Portuguese army would somehow have to get across to the right bank of the Adour. Wellington's answer to this problem was daring in the extreme. In brief, his solution was to build a pontoon bridge across the very mouth of the river, to which end he had requisitioned a large number of the barges that in normal times carried the coastal trade of Saint-Jean-de-Luz whilst at the same time constructing a powerful battery that could cover the crossing from any interference on the part of the French which last were in the meantime to be bluffed into thinking that the main effort would be made against the city rather than the citadel.

Having briefly returned to the Anglo-Portuguese camps before Bayonne to ensure that everything was in place for the planned operation, the British commander rode east once more to rejoin the troops he intended to lead against Soult. Left in charge of the siege operations was Lieutenant General Sir John Hope, an officer who had distinguished himself at La Coruña in 1808, but had then not returned to the Peninsula until November 1813. It was not, perhaps, Wellington's most inspired choice for so important a command, but the Anglo-Portuguese commander was nothing if not an aristocrat – after all, if the common soldiers called him 'Nosey', his nickname among the officers was rather 'the peer' – and Hope the son of a Scottish earl, and it seems likely that, not for the first time, he allowed his prejudices to get the better of him. That said, Bayonne did not seem the most testing of assignments. Major fortress and, what is more, one provided with a very strong garrison of almost 14,000 men, though it certainly was, there was little or no chance of an army of relief arriving on the scene, while Hope had almost 30,000 troops with which to achieve his objectives, at least half of them good-quality British regulars. At first, indeed, all went well enough: notwithstanding some delays due to the weather, the bridge was successfully

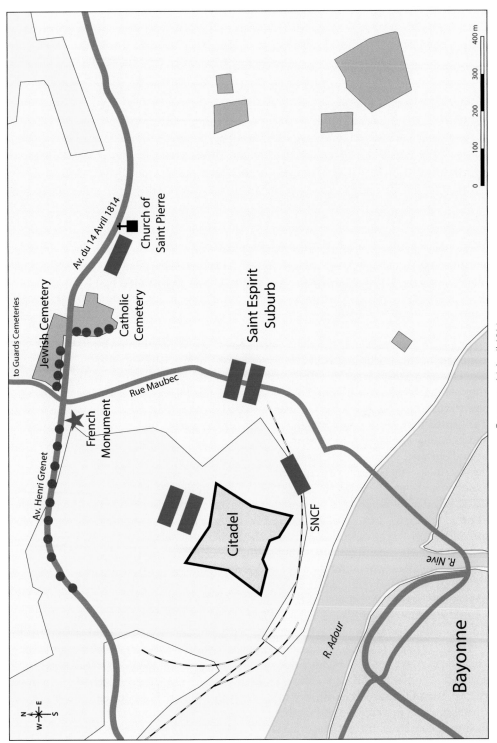

Bayonne, 14 April 1814.

thrown across the river and the French completely taken by surprise. Yet, having ensured that the fortress was shut off from the outside world, Hope did not press his advantage and, instead of opening a formal siege, merely maintained a loose blockade in the belief that the garrison was short of food and could therefore simply be starved into surrender, the result being that no field works were constructed. As the defenders remained fairly quiescent, meanwhile, the troops holding the front-line posts – a small chateau a few hundred yards to the north of the citadel; a sunken lane at the foot of the glacis; the city's Jewish cemetery; and, finally, the parish church of Sant Etienne – became ever more relaxed, a lot of fraternisation taking place across the lines: in brief, the war seemed all but over and life a matter of live and let live.

However, this state of affairs did not last. On 12 April, two days after Wellington decisively defeated Soult at the Battle of Toulouse, news arrived that Napoleon had been deposed. Apprised of this almost as soon as Hope – something of which there is not the slightest doubt – the governor, *général de division* Pierre Thouvenot, a grizzled veteran who had served as an artillery officer in the army of the Bourbons and had seen little in the way of glory under the Republic and Napoleon, appears to have decided to take advantage of the situation to make his name. On the evening of 14 April, then, Thouvenot massed around half his forces in the Saint Espirit suburb and sent the men concerned storming up the hill to attack the Anglo-Portuguese outposts, while still more troops sallied forth from the citadel, whose guns in the meantime opened fire in all directions. Taken at least in part by surprise, many of the foremost pickets were cut down or taken prisoner, a fate that also befell Hope himself, the British commander having rashly galloped to the scene of the action with no more escort than two of his *aides-de-camp,* only for the little party to run head-long into a group of French soldiers as they ascended the sunken lane that ran along the foot of the glacis. However, thereafter things started to go badly wrong. Unclear as to exactly what they were supposed to achieve and confused both by the darkness and the fire of the citadel's guns, the attackers lost all cohesion, while determined groups of defenders managed to secure cemetery and church alike and open fire on the milling crowds of enemy troops. Losses on both sides were heavy, while the Anglo-Portuguese losses included Major General Andrew Hay, the commander of one of the two brigades unlucky enough to have men in the line when the French attacked, who was killed while attempting to organise the defence of the church, but there could be but one end to the affair. Thus, fresh British and Portuguese troops quickly moved in from both flanks and within a very short space of time, the French were in full flight, whether back into the citadel or down the hill back to Saint Espirit.

So ended an affair which did its progenitor's reputation no good whatsoever: if they did not quite go so far as Wellington, who described Thouvenot as a 'blackguard', even some French commentators found it hard to stomach what they regarded as a breach of the laws of war. Meanwhile, it had been a bloody night, British casualties having amounted to 838 killed, wounded, and taken prisoner, and those of their opponents some 910 all told. As for the fortress, its fate was altered not a whit, though Thouvenot did not surrender for another fortnight and even then only because he was positively ordered to do so by *maréchal* Soult, still French commander in the southwest despite the setbacks he had suffered at the River Nive and, later, Orthez. All in all, it was a very sour note on which to end a conflict that had hitherto been marked by great civility in so far as relations between the British and the French were concerned (in fact, Bayonne was not the scene of the very last action of the war

The Rue 14 Avril with, to the right, the wall of what in 1813 was the Jewish cemetery; though taken by surprise, the men of Hay's brigade mounted a gallant defence against repeated French attacks. (Author's collection)

The parish church at Saint Pierre; heavily damaged in the course of the fighting, it had to be given a completely new façade. (Author's collection)

The west wall of the graveyard of the church of Saint Pierre; ensconced in its shelter, men of Hay's brigade inflicted heavy losses on the French. (Author's collection)

precipitated by Napoleon's intervention in Spain, this rather occurring at Barcelona where the French garrison attempted a similar sortie two days later only to be repelled with heavy losses; in contrast to Bayonne, however, it had not yet received news of the downfall of the Emperor).

Bayonne Today

Although Bayonne has expanded enormously since 1813, it is possible to explore the area where the fighting took place with relative ease. The bridge across the Adour, of course, is still there, while the old high road – now the Rue Maubec – is lined at its lower levels with buildings that may well have witnessed the fighting. From the traffic intersection at the top, a short walk to the right along the Rue 14 Avril will take the visitor to the cemetery held by Hay's troops (now much extended) and, a little further along on the other side of the road, the church of Saint Pierre. In the other direction, meanwhile, the Avenue Henri Grenet follows the course of the sunken lane where Hope was taken prisoner, the angle that it forms with the Rue Maubec being filled by the citadel, which is fully intact, but heavily shrouded by trees and off-limits even to photography, being the headquarters of 1er régiment de

Witnesses to slaughter: old houses in the Rue Maubec. (Author's collection)

parachutistes d'infanterie de marine – the French equivalent of the SAS. However, just near the junction with the Rue Maubec, there is a memorial to the troops who fought Hope in 1814 featuring the so-called 'wounded eagle' (a common symbol of the downfall of Napoleon that can also be seen at Waterloo). A little further away, meanwhile, may be found two of the saddest relics of the. entire war in the Peninsula and the south of France, namely the Cimetière des Coldstream Guards and the Cimetière des 3rd Guards, these marking the

Some corner of a foreign field that is forever England: the Cimetière des Third Guards at Bayonne.
(Author's collection)

graves of a number of officers of Stopford's brigade of the First Division who, having been killed in what truly was a most needless episode of bloodshed, were interred on the fringe of the camping-grounds occupied by their respective regiments. As the author knows from bitter experience, while they are marked on maps of the area (both paper and virtual) and provided with local signage, the two sites are very hard to locate, but they are nonetheless well worth the effort to visit, as well, of course, as a very appropriate note on which to end this guide to the struggle of which the men who lie there were some of the very last casualties. Of the two, the Cimetière des Third Guards is by far the easiest to find, situated as it is, just off the end of the Avenue des Coumeres.

Further Reading

I. Robertson, *Wellington Invades France: the Final Phase of the Peninsular War, 1813-1814* (London: Greenhill Books,2003)

N. Lipscombe, *Bayonne and Toulouse, 1813-1814: Wellington Invades France* (Oxford: Osprey, 2014)

Bibliographical Note

For a general history of the Peninsular War, see C.J. Esdaile, *The Peninsular War: a New History* (London: Penguin Books, 2002). That said, those seeking a more human face to the war might wish to consult C.J. Esdaile, *Peninsular Eyewitnesses: the Human Experience of War in Spain and Portugal, 1808–1814* (Barnsley: Pen and Sword, 2008) while D. Gates, *The Spanish Ulcer: a History of the Peninsular* (London: Allen and Unwin, 1986) is a digest of the military campaigns.

Having reviewed the 'top-down' historiography of the Peninsular War, it is now time to consider some of the more specialised reading. Given that each chapter has a list of works that may be consulted in respect of the individual action which it details, the aim in the remaining pages of this essay will rather be devoted to thematic works covering such issues as the commanders, the armies, the guerrilla war, and the diplomatic background; for the sake of brevity, meanwhile, coverage will be restricted to works in the English language alone. Let us begin, however, with the issue of the mechanics of combat, the most obvious works to consult here being B. Nosworthy, *With Musket, Cannon and Sword: Battle Tactics of Napoleon and his Enemies* (New York: Da Capo Press, 1996) and, more particularly (because many of its examples are drawn from the Peninsular War), R. Muir, *Tactics and the Experience of Battle in the Age of Napoleon* (London: Yale University Press, 1998). Next, we have the commanders. In so far as the British are concerned, Wellington, of course, has had numerous biographers, but by far the best, and, indeed, the most recent, is the incomparable R. Muir, *Wellington: the Path to Victory, 1769-1814* (London: Yale University Press, 2013), while Sir John Moore and Sir Rowland Hill are covered by C. Oman, *Sir John Moore* (London: Hodder and Stoughton, 1953) and G. Teffeteller, *The Surpriser: the Life of Sir Rowland Hill* (Brunswick, New Jersey: University of Delaware Press, 1983). The French are less well served but two of the most important commanders in the Peninsular War are discussed in J. Marshall-Cornwell, *Marshal Massena* (Oxford: Oxford University Press, 1965) and P. Hayman, *Soult: Napoleon's Maligned Marshal* (London: Weidenfeld and Nicholson, 1990), while there is also a biography of Joseph Bonaparte in the form of M. Ross, *The Reluctant King: Joseph Bonaparte, King of the Two Sicilies and Spain* (London: Sidgwick and Jackson, 1976). With regard to the armies, there is much on the British army, good examples being P. Haythornthwaite, *The Armies of Wellington* (London: Weidenfeld and Nicholson, 1994), P. Haythornthwaite, *Redcoats: the British Soldiers of the Napoleonic Wars* (Barnsley: Pen and Sword, 2012), E. Coss *All for the King's Shilling: the British Soldier under Wellington, 1808-1814* (Norman, Oklahoma: University of Oklahoma Press, 2010), and A. Bamford, *Sickness, Suffering and the Sword: the British Regiment on Campaign, 1808-1815* (Norman, Oklahoma: University of Oklahoma Press, 2013); meanwhile, for the Spaniards, see C.J. Esdaile, *The*

Spanish Army in the Peninsular War (new edition; Nottingham: Partisan Press, 2012), for the Portuguese, R. Chartrand, *The Portuguese Army of the Napoleonic Wars* (three volumes; Oxford: Osprey 2000), and, for the French, the highly idiosyncratic but nonetheless useful J.R. Elting, *Swords Around a Throne: Napoleon's Grande Armée* (London: Weidenfeld and Nicholson, 1989). On the *guerrilla*, C.J. Esdaile, *Fighting Napoleon: Guerrillas, Bandits and Adventurers in Spain, 1808-1814* (London: Yale University Press, 2004) has no competition in terms of general texts, but can be supplemented by three regional surveys, namely C.J. Esdaile, *Outpost of Empire: the Napoleonic Occupation of Andalucia, 1810-1812* (Norman, Oklahoma: University of Oklahoma Press, 2012), D.W. Alexander, *Rod of Iron: French Counterinsurgency policy in Aragon during the Peninsular War* (Wilmington, Delaware: Scholarly Resources, Inc., 1985) and J.L. Tone, *The Fatal Knot: the Guerrilla War in Navarre and the Defeat of Napoleon in Spain* (Chapel Hill, North Carolina: University of North Carolina Press, 1994). And, finally, there is the diplomatic background, for which see R. Muir, *Britain and the Defeat of Napoleon, 1807-1815* (London: Yale University Press, 1996).